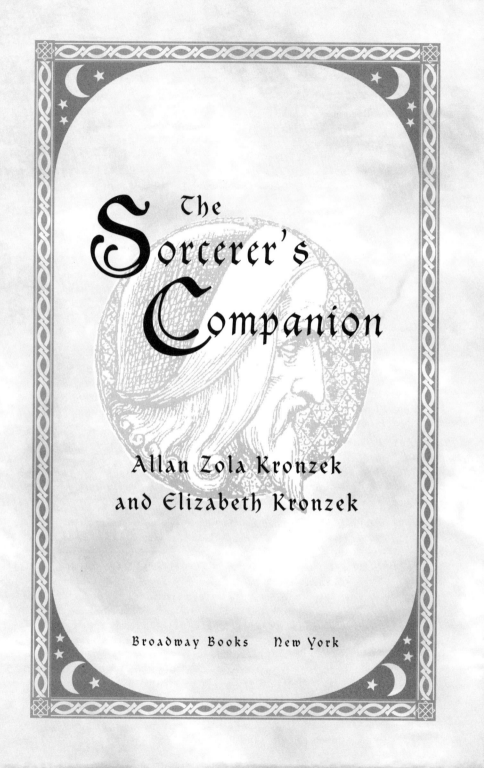

The Sorcerer's Companion

Allan Zola Kronzek
and Elizabeth Kronzek

Broadway Books   New York

BROADWAY

Broadway Books titles may be purchased for business or promotional use or for special sales. For information, please write to: Special Markets Department, Random House, Inc., 1540 Broadway, New York, NY 10036.

BROADWAY BOOKS and its logo, a letter B bisected on the diagonal, are trademarks of Broadway Books, a division of Random House, Inc.

Visit our website at www.broadwaybooks.com

First edition published October 2001

Designed by Ellen Cipriano

Library of Congress Cataloging-in-Publication Data
Kronzek, Allan Zola.
The sorcerer's companion: a guide to the magical world of Harry Potter/
Allan Zola Kronzek & Elizabeth Kronzek.—1st ed.
p.   cm
Includes bibliographical references.
Summary: Explores the true history, folklore, and mythology behind the magical practices, creatures and personalities that appear in J. K. Rowling's Harry Potter books.
1. Rowling, J. K.—Characters—Harry Potter—Handbooks, manuals, etc.
2. Potter, Harry (Fictitious character)—Handbooks, manuals, etc.   3. Children's stories, English—Handbooks, manuals, etc.   4. Fantasy fiction, English—Handbooks, manuals, etc.   5. Wizards in literature—Handbooks, manuals, etc.
6. Magic in literature—Handbooks, manuals, etc. [1. Rowling, J. K.—Characters—Harry Potter—Handbooks, manuals, etc.   2. Potter, Harry (Fictitious character)—Handbooks, manuals, etc.   3. Fantasy—Handbooks, manuals, etc.
4. Wizards—Handbooks, manuals, etc.   5. Magic—Handbooks, manuals, etc.]
I. Kronzek, Elizabeth, 1969–   II. Title.

PR6068.093 Z75 2001
823'.914—dc21   2001035659

ISBN 0-7679-0847-3

15 17 19 20 18 16 14

To Ruby, with love.
——A.Z.K.

�֎

To my mother, who's always there.
——E.K.

Contents

x

Introduction

If you're like most Harry Potter fans, you probably know that Harry's prized possession is his broomstick, Hermione's favorite subject is arithmancy, and a magnificent creature called a hippogriff helped Sirius Black evade capture. But did you know that wizards were once thought to fly on pitchforks, arithmancy is an ancient form of fortune-telling, and the hippogriff was first mounted by the legendary knights of Charlemagne? Or that Professor Dumbledore's friend Nicholas Flamel, creator of the Sorcerer's Stone, was a real person?

So quickly do the astonishing adventures of Harry and his friends fly by that we rarely have a moment to consider the wealth of real mythology, folklore, and history that shimmers just beneath the surface. One of the great pleasures of reading the Harry Potter books comes from the extraordinary richness of the magical universe they contain—fashioned partly from J. K. Rowling's seemingly boundless imagination and partly from the vast collective lore of magic from around the world. Potions and charms, giants and dragons, cauldrons and crystal balls—all have intriguing and often surprising histories going back hundreds and sometimes thousands of years. Magic wands like those sold in Diagon Alley were once fashioned by Druid sorcerers out of the sacred yew tree. Love potions are traceable to ancient Greece and Rome. And books of spells and curses—required reading at Hogwarts School of Witchcraft and Wizardry—were highly popular (and much frowned upon) during the Middle Ages.

The Sorcerer's Companion allows the curious reader to look up anything "magical" from any of the first four Harry Potter books and discover a wealth of fascinating and unexpected information. How did the Sorcerer's Stone get its power? What were the first magic words? Did J. K. Rowling dream up the terrifying basilisk, the seductive veela, or the vicious grindylow? And if she didn't, who did? *The Sorcerer's Companion* has the answers.

The history of magical beliefs is vast, and in writing this book we have had to leave out far more than we put in. Barely mentioned are the rich traditions of magic and mythology of China, Africa, India, Japan, Australia, and South America. Rather we have limited our focus to those aspects of lore directly related to Harry's world. Nearly all of the magical practices taught at Hogwarts are rooted in the Western magical tradition, which emerged from the ancient empires of the Middle East, Greece, and Rome. Imaginary creatures like the centaur, the manticore, and the unicorn come from the same rich tradition. Many other magical beings, such as elves, gnomes, goblins, hinkypunks, and trolls, have their roots in the folklore of northern Europe and the British Isles.

When we first began writing *The Sorcerer's Companion* we asked Harry Potter fans what subjects interested them the most. Some wanted to know more about spells, charms, and curses. Others were eager to learn about boggarts, red caps, or the difference between witches and hags. We expect you, too, will have your own particular interests and will follow them as you choose. This book is not intended to be read straight through in alphabetical order, although it certainly can be. You might want to start with the **Magic** entry for an introduction to this fascinating subject. But actually, you can start anywhere—and chances are, you'll end up everywhere.

In each entry, we've tried to provide an overview of the subject and its roots in mythology, folklore, and history. Whenever a word appears in bold, that means it has its own entry. Following most entries, you'll

find this symbol  and an abbreviation indicating one place in the Harry Potter books where the subject appears. "SS 5/71," for example, refers you to *Harry Potter and the Sorcerer's Stone*, chapter 5, page 71. CS refers to *Harry Potter and the Chamber of Secrets*, PA refers to *Harry Potter and the Prisoner of Azkaban*, and GF refers to *Harry Potter and the Goblet of Fire*. All references are to the American editions.

In researching *The Sorcerer's Companion* we learned many curious things we never expected to know, like how to read tea leaves, get rid of goblins, safely harvest mandrake root, and use arithmancy to choose a breakfast cereal. We feel more secure knowing how to recognize a demon and what to do if attacked by a ghoul (never, ever hit him twice). We hope all of this information is as interesting to you as it is to us. You never know when you might need it.

Amulet

𝔄re you unusually susceptible to colds and infections? Do you have a tendency to attract the wrong kind of attention? Are you plagued by bad luck? If the answer to any of these questions is yes, an amulet might be just what the doctor ordered. In fact, centuries ago, an amulet often *was* what the doctor ordered—to ward off disease, avoid misfortune, or chase away evil spirits.

An amulet (from the Latin word *amuletum,* meaning "a method of defense") is an object thought to magically protect its owner from harm. Amulets can come in any size, shape, or material. Indeed, when Hogwarts is struck by a mysterious epidemic of **petrification,** Neville Longbottom tries to protect himself with an amulet made from a smelly green onion! Amulets range from small pendants, rings, and pouches of herbs (worn around the neck to prevent disease) to sizable statues and wall hangings intended to protect an entire household, building, or village. The ancient Babylonians liked to wear tiny, jewel-encrusted clay cylinders to ward off evil spirits. The Romans collected sculptures of Priapus, the god of luck and fertility, and many Americans still hang lucky horseshoes over their doors to guard against misfortune and unwelcome visitors.

Amulets have been present in virtually every society since the beginning of recorded history. The earliest amulets were probably just chunks of stone or metal whose bright colors or unusual shapes suggested they might have magical properties. (In India and Thailand, pieces of pink coral are still used to ward off the evil eye.) Over time, however, it became customary to make amulets in the shape of animals, god and goddess figures, and magic symbols. Images of horns and hands (symbolizing fertility and life) and drawings or carvings of the human eye (suggesting eternal watchfulness) appear on amulets throughout the world. Many amulets also have **magic words,** short **spells,** or the names of gods written on them.

Although their appeal is nearly universal, amulets are most closely associated with the ancient Egyptians, who wore them everywhere—even to the grave. It was customary for **mummies** to be buried with dozens of beetle-shaped amulets called scarabs. These small stone figurines, named after a real type of Egyptian beetle, were supposed to prevent the deceased person's soul from being eaten by Ammit the Devourer—a dreadful part-lion, part-hippo, part-crocodile who guarded the scales of justice in the Egyptian afterworld. Apparently, the more important a person was, the more scarabs he took to the afterworld. When King Tutankhamen's body was unearthed some eighty years ago, over 140 amulets were found tucked away in the wrappings of his mummy! Other common Egyptian amulets like the *ankh* (an Egyptian hieroglyph symbolizing life) and the *wadjet* (commonly known as the Eye of Horus) served more practical purposes: protecting living Egyptians from death, disease, and the evil eye.

Unfortunately, amulets do have their limitations. For instance, they can only protect you from the specific dangers for which they are designed. A scarab may scare Ammit the Devourer, but it's useless against **vampires, hinkypunks,** and treasure-hungry archaeologists. And if you're going to do battle with the forces of evil, it's im-

The ankh *symbolized eternal life and was worn to protect against disease.*

The Evil Eye

The frightening notion that a look can kill has existed in almost every civilization throughout history, inspiring the creation of amulets and many other defenses against supernatural malice. The evil eye—a hostile glance believed to cause misfortune, illness, or even death—is mentioned in both the Old and New Testaments of the Bible, as well as in the texts of ancient Sumeria, Babylonia, and Assyria. In the Middle Ages, witches were said to use the evil eye against anyone who crossed them, causing the victim to take ill, lose the love of a spouse, or experience financial ruin.

Small children and animals are said to be especially vulnerable to the evil eye. In many places where evil eye superstitions are still strong, it is considered unwise to call attention to the beauty of one's children for fear that someone with the evil eye may cast a jealous gaze upon them.

The primary defense against the evil eye is an amulet—often in the shape of a frog, a horn, or, in the case of the ancient Egyptians, an eye known as the Eye of Horus. If no amulet is available, a quick response in the form of a symbolic hand gesture (holding up the index and little fingers to form "horns") is recommended if an evil glance comes your way. Other defenses include **hex** signs, shamrocks (in Ireland), garlic (in Greece), and barley (in India). Bells or red ribbons tied to livestock or children's clothing are also thought to divert the attention of the evil eye.

Believed to protect the wearer against evil and injury,
the Eye of Horus was one of the most popular amulets in ancient Egypt.

portant not to confuse amulets with their close cousins, **talismans.** Unlike enchanted swords, **invisibility cloaks,** and other classic talismans, amulets do not endow their owners with magical abilities. An amulet cannot be used as a weapon, only as a shield. So if you're planning some epic adventure—like slaying a **dragon**—you should probably swap your lucky rabbit's foot for the sword of Sir Godric Gryffindor. But if you prefer to stay home where it's nice and cozy, nothing beats an amulet for keeping hostile forces at bay.

CS 11/185

Arithmancy

Hermione, who scoffs at **tea-leaf reading** and **crystal-ball** gazing, seems an unlikely fan of arithmancy—a method of fortune-telling based on names and numbers. Yet this ancient form of **divination** is one of her favorite subjects. Perhaps that's because, unlike other methods of predicting the future, arithmancy isn't based on interpreting fuzzy images or attributing meaning to random shapes and squiggles but on hard-and-fast rules and mathematical calculations—just the kind of brainwork Hermione seems to enjoy.

Arithmancy (from the Greek *arithmo,* meaning "number," and *mancy,* meaning "prophecy") has been used by **magicians** and **wizards** for more than two thousand years to help people analyze and

develop their strengths and talents, overcome obstacles, and chart their future paths. Also known as "numerology," arithmancy is based on two very old ideas. The first is that a person's name contains important clues to their character and destiny. The second, advanced more than 2,500 years ago by the Greek sage Pythagoras, is that each of the numbers between I and 9 has a unique meaning that can contribute to the understanding of all things. Arithmancers combined these two ideas and, over the centuries, developed many complex systems for converting names into numbers and analyzing the results. One of the most widely used systems involves extracting three key numbers from a person's name—the *Character Number*, the *Heart Number*, and the *Social Number*—and interpreting the outcome according to a set of established meanings. This system, which we suspect is the one taught at Hogwarts, was widely known by the Middle Ages and is still used today. All it requires is a pencil, paper, and the ability to add and spell.

The first step in analyzing a name is to convert it to a set of numbers. Each letter of the alphabet is assigned a numerical value between I and 9, according to the following chart:

```
I 2 3 4 5 6 7 8 9
A B C D E F G H I
J K L M N O P Q R
S T U V W X Y Z
```

As should be clear, the letters A, J, and S have the value of "I," B, K, and T have the value of "2," and so forth. To analyze any name, write it down, and beneath each letter enter the corresponding numerical value. As an example, we'll analyze the name **Nicholas Flamel,** the medieval alchemist who was reputed to have created the **Sorcerer's Stone:**

```
N I C H O L A S   F L A M E L
5 9 3 8 6 3 I I   6 3 I 4 5 3
```

When you have all the numbers written down, add them up. In this case, the result is 58. According to the procedures of arithmancy, when a total exceeds 9—which it usually does—it must be "reduced" to a single digit by adding the component numbers together, more than once, if necessary. Thus, 58 reduces to 13 (5 + 8 = 13), which reduces to 4 (1 + 3 = 4). The final result—the reduced number of *all* the values in the name—is known as the *Character Number.* This number indicates the general personality type of the individual, according to a system of interpretations to be presented shortly.

The next number to be derived is the *Heart Number,* which refers to the individual's inner life and is said to indicate desires and fears hidden from others. The Heart Number is the total of all the vowels in the name, reduced to a single digit.

$$\begin{array}{ccccc} \text{N I C H O L A S} & & \text{F L A M E L} \\ 9 \quad\quad 6 \quad 1 & & 1 \quad\quad 5 \end{array}$$

These numbers equal 22, which reduces to 4 (2 + 2 = 4). In this instance, the Heart Number and the Character Number are identical, but this will not always be the case.

The third number to be derived is the *Social Number,* which refers to the outer personality, the face an individual shows to the outside world. The social number is determined by adding up the value of the consonants in the name.

$$\begin{array}{ccccccc} \text{N I C H O L A S} & & \text{F L A M E L} \\ 5 \quad 3 \, 8 \quad 3 \quad 1 \, 6 \, 3 & & 4 \quad\quad 3 \end{array}$$

In this case the total is 36, which reduces to 9 (3 + 6 = 9).

With the Character, Heart, and Social numbers in mind (4, 4, 9) it is now possible to sketch out a portrait of the subject using a set of positive and negative personality traits traditionally associated with each number. These traits are based partly on the ideas of Pythagoras, but were also influenced by many others.

The Meaning of the Numbers

ONE: This is the number of the individual. Ones are independent, focused, single-minded, and determined. They set a goal and stick to it. They are leaders and inventors. Ones find it difficult to work with others and don't like to take orders. They can be self-centered, egotistical, and domineering. They are often loners.

TWO: Two represents interaction, two-way communication, cooperation, and balance. Twos are imaginative, creative, and sweet natured. Peace, harmony, commitment, loyalty, and fairness are characteristic. But two also introduces the idea of conflict, opposing forces, and the contrasting sides of things: night and day, good and evil. Twos can be withdrawn, moody, self-conscious, and indecisive.

THREE: Three represents the idea of completeness or wholeness, as in the trios "past-present-future" and "mind-body-spirit." The Pythagoreans considered three to be the first "complete" number because, like three pebbles laid out in a row, it has a beginning, a middle, and an end. Three indicates talent, energy, an artistic nature, humor, and social ease. Threes are often lucky, easygoing, rich, and highly successful, but they can also be unfocused, easily offended, and superficial.

FOUR: Like a table that rests solidly on four legs, four indicates stability and firmness. Fours enjoy hard work. They are practical, reliable, and down to earth; they prefer logic and reason to flights of fancy. They are good at organization and getting things done. Like the cycle of the four seasons, they are also predictable. They can be stubborn, suspicious, overly practical, and prone to angry outbursts. The conflicts possible with "two" are doubled in four.

FIVE: Five is the number of instability and imbalance, indicating change and uncertainty. Fives are drawn to many things at once but commit to none. They are adventurous, energetic, and willing to take risks. They enjoy travel and meeting new people but may not stay in one place very long. Fives can be conceited, irresponsible, quick-tempered, and impatient.

SIX: Six represents harmony, friendship, and family life. Sixes are loyal, reliable, and loving. They adapt easily. They do well in teaching and the arts, but are often unsuccessful in business. They are sometimes prone to gossip and complacency. The Pythagoreans regarded six as the perfect number because it was divisible by both two and three, and was the sum as well as the product of the first three digits ($1 + 2 + 3 = 6$, $1 \times 2 \times 3 = 6$).

SEVEN: Perceptive, understanding, and bright, sevens enjoy hard work and challenges. They are often serious, scholarly, and interested in all things mysterious. Originality and imagination are more important than money and material possessions. Sevens can also be pessimistic, sarcastic, and insecure. Seven is sometimes considered a mystical or magical number because of its associations with the biblical seven days of creation, and the seven heavenly bodies of ancient astronomy (Sun, Moon, Mercury, Venus, Mars, Saturn, and Jupiter).

EIGHT: Eight indicates the possibility of great success in business, finance, and politics. Eights are practical, ambitious, committed, and hardworking. They can also be jealous, greedy, domineering, and power hungry. Eight is said to be the most unpredictable of numbers and can indicate the pinnacle of success or the depths of failure; the potential to go either way is present from the beginning.

NINE: Represents completion and achievement to the fullest degree, as it is the "complete" number, three, expressed three times ($3 \times 3 = 9$). Nines dedicate themselves to the service of others, often as teachers, scientists, and humanitarians. Strongly determined, they work tirelessly and are an inspiration to others. However, they can also be arrogant and conceited when things don't go their way.

According to these interpretations, we can now say that Nicholas Flamel (4, 4, 9) is a hardworking, down-to-earth person. He takes a practical approach to solving problems. He is emotionally stable, but may have some inner anger and suspicions; however, the face he shows to the world is that of a kind and generous humanitarian. Finally, we can add a few finishing touches to this portrait by returning to the original array of numbers, to see if any digits occur more frequently than others. In this case the numbers 3 and 1 occur most often, indicating that, in addition to what we already know, Flamel is someone who seeks perfection, has the ability to make money easily, and goes about things with single-minded focus. Most of this, amazingly, seems to be true of the famous alchemist (see **Nicholas Flamel** for details about his life and personality). As with most systems of divination, however, the more you know about the subject beforehand, the easier it is to pick the best of many possible interpretations. The real challenge is to create a portrait of an individual without benefit of hindsight.

Like **astrology,** arithmancy also claims to be a system for determining lucky and unlucky days. As a general rule, favorable days are those that correspond to an individual's character number. An "eight" personality, for example, would be advised to schedule important events like starting a business or getting married so that they occur on the 8th, 17th, or 26th of the month (each of which reduces to 8). Since any name or word can be converted to a number, arithmancy is also used to reveal "hidden kinships" among people, places, and things—the theory being that words and names that share the same numerical value are related and naturally go together. Thus a six will be best off driving a brand of car that reduces to 6, such as a Honda or a Toyota, whereas a seven would be happier driving a Ford. A two will be most romantically compatible with another two. Fives should consider living in a city that reduces to 5 (such as Tokyo or Pittsburgh), and so forth. Although we don't recommend it, virtually all of life's decisions can be made "according to the numbers," from the friends one associates with to the foods on the breakfast table (eggs = 2, toast = 3, corn flakes = 4).

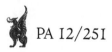

Astrology

When the **centaurs** of the **Forbidden Forest** comment on the brightness of the planet Mars, they're doing more than making a casual comment about the beauty of the evening sky. Their words are a veiled prediction of something ominous to come, involving anger, violence, and perhaps bloodshed and revenge. These centaurs practice astrology and can read the future in the stars.

Astrology should not be confused with astronomy, although both share the same Greek root, *astron*, which means "star." Astronomy is the scientific study of the heavenly bodies, such as stars, planets, moons, comets, and meteors; astrology is a more fanciful pursuit that seeks to explain and interpret the influence of the heavenly bodies on earthly life. Both disciplines emerged in ancient Babylonia (modern-day Iraq) more than 7,000 years ago when sky watchers first began to keep accurate records of the movements of the sun, moon, and stars. One of their earliest observations was that although most of the stars remained in the same positions relative to one another, a handful did not. Along with the sun and the moon, these so-called "wandering stars," which the ancients thought to be the homes of gods, traveled across a narrow band of sky known as the zodiac. Today we know that these wanderers are not actually stars but planets ("planet" means "wanderer" in Greek).

In time, the Babylonians assigned meanings and resident deities to the planets based on their appearance. For example, Mars, which has a distinct reddish glow, was considered fiery and bloody and became identified with the god of war (Nergal for the Babylonians, Ares for the Greeks, and Mars to the Romans); Venus, which outshines every star in the sky but can disappear for six weeks at a time, was the bringer of

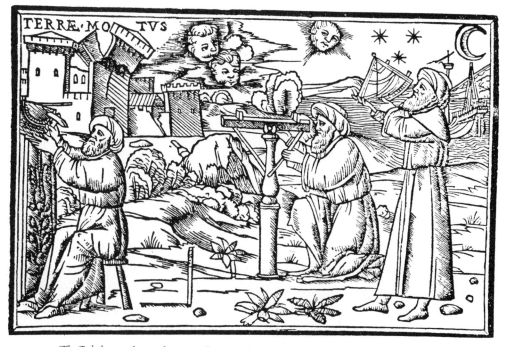

The Babylonian sky watchers were the first to keep good records of all of the celestial events they observed. They drew the first star maps around 1800 B.C.

love, faithful or fickle; and Saturn, which appears to roll across the sky more slowly than the other visible planets because it is the most distant, was associated with evil, old age, despondency, and death. Only the five planets visible to the naked eye (Mercury, Venus, Mars, Jupiter, Saturn) were known, and all were thought, along with the sun and moon, to revolve around the Earth, which was then believed to be the center of the universe.

In addition to observing the shifting patterns of the cosmos, Babylonian sky watchers tried to correlate what they saw with events on Earth, such as earthquakes, floods, and other natural disasters. Their reasoning was simple: They believed that everything in the universe was interconnected and that events in heaven must therefore reflect, or even foretell, events on Earth. For instance, the appearance of a comet, the most unpredictable of all celestial events, might forebode a major occurrence, such as the death of a king. More common events—such as full moons, eclipses, the appearance of a halo around the moon, or the convergence of two or more planets—were less ominous but could still herald news of a famine, storm, flood, epidemic, or other disaster.

Thus astrology, even in its most basic form, was an important tool of **divination**. Its practitioners searched the sky for omens and recurring patterns and made predictions. But unlike astrologers today, who work for many individual clients, ancient astrologers restricted their attention to the king and the society as a whole.

This changed in the fifth century B.C., when the concept of the zodiac as a set of twelve constellations became fixed and astrologers began to cast personal **horoscopes** for individuals. The Greeks and Egyptians became interested in astrology in the third century B.C. and added many new and complex procedures to the field, linking it to medicine and **magic**. Not only were the positions of the stars and planets thought to forecast events, but it was widely believed that the stars affected the physical nature of everyone and everything on Earth. Each sign of the zodiac was said to influence a different part of the human body, and every flower, herb, and medicinal plant was said to be ruled by a different planet. Even minerals and gems absorbed influences from the stars. A physician, therefore, needed to understand the principles of astrology in order to diagnose and treat his patients. Similarly, **magicians** who wished to conduct experiments, cast spells, or make **talismans** needed to understand astrology to determine the planetary influences and discover the most favorable time to carry out their activities. A love **spell**, for example, would best be timed to coincide with the influence of Venus rather than Saturn.

From Greece and Egypt, astrology spread to Rome, where it was widely accepted as a wonderful new addition to the many systems of divination already in use. A number of influential thinkers railed against astrology as a worthless superstition, and practitioners were repeatedly banished from the city, but public demand kept bringing them back. After the fall of the Roman Empire in the fourth century, astrology ceased to be an important factor in European life until the twelfth century, when knowledge of the subject was reintroduced from Arabic sources.

During the Middle Ages, universities in England, France, and Italy taught astrology, and most European kings and queens employed court

European royalty often consulted astrologers before making important decisions.
This is said to be a portrait of the great French astrologer Nostradamus.

astrologers to cast their horoscopes and advise them on the best days for taking action. In Renaissance England, Queen Elizabeth I chose the mathematician and astrologer John Dee to select the date for her coronation according to the planetary influences. In France, the famed astrologer Nostradamus performed similar functions for Queen Catherine de Medici. And although the Church was generally hostile to astrology, Pope Urban VIII hired an astrologer in 1629 to perform magic rituals to counter the anticipated ill effects of a series of eclipses.

At the same time, however, the scientific revolution was under way. In 1542, Copernicus stated that the sun, not the Earth, was the center of the solar system. This seemed to threaten the very basis of astrology, since the planets supposedly radiating their influence down on Earth were, in

Disaster and Disease:
Blame It on the Stars

Got the flu? The word "flu" is short for "influenza," but when someone in the Middle Ages said they were sick from "influenza," they certainly weren't talking about a virus. The word originally meant "influence," and referred strictly to the astrological influence of the stars and planets. People believed it was this influence, not germs, that made them sick. The word "disaster" likewise comes from astrological beliefs and is a combination of *dis,* meaning a "negative quality," and *astron,* meaning "star." When a calamity happened, the cause was often attributed to *dis-astron,* or a bad star.

fact, not circling the Earth at all. In the seventeenth century, other scientific discoveries followed, and serious-minded people for the most part turned away from astrology. Yet even as astrology lost prestige, astrological almanacs became immensely popular and people began to keep track of their own good and bad days without the aid of a professional. Indeed, the monthly and daily predictions found in magazines and newspapers today are part of a tradition that began with those almanacs centuries ago.

Astrology today occupies a peculiar position. Although it retains none of the intellectual respectability it once had, its popularity is vast, and many people take astrological advice as profound truth. Still, skeptics abound. In fact, several of the most skeptical people we can think of happen to be students at a certain school of witchcraft and wizardry.

The Zodiac

Thousands of years ago, ancient sky watchers observed that as the sun and planets moved across the sky each year, they always traveled along the same narrow path around the Earth. This pathway, which the Greeks named the zodiac, was divided by astrologers into twelve equal sections called "signs," each associated with a constellation—Aries, Taurus, Gemini, Cancer, Leo, Virgo, Libra, Scorpio, Sagittarius, Capricorn, Aquarius, or Pisces—and a time of year. Astrologers use the position of the sun and planets within the zodiac to make predictions and to determine the personalities of people born under different signs. The characteristics associated with each sign were developed thousands of years ago but have been elaborated over the centuries. Here are some of the basics:

ARIES THE RAM (March 21 to April 19): People born under the sign of Aries are characterized as energetic, enthusiastic, direct, independent, creative, and impatient. Because rams "ram" their way forward, Aries are also said to be aggressive, determined, and quick-tempered.

TAURUS THE BULL (April 20 to May 20): As might be expected from a bull, those born under the sign of Taurus have reserves of strength and stamina and can be stubborn, too. But they are also thought to be reliable, warm, patient, artistic, and dependable.

GEMINI THE TWINS (May 21 to June 20): Geminis are held to be versatile, lively, curious, clever, and articulate, but often superficial. Like Castor and Pollux, the mythological twin brothers for whom the constellation is named, Geminis are said to be devoted to their families.

CANCER THE CRAB (June 21 to July 22): Cancers are considered to be intuitive, sympathetic, moody, tenacious, family-minded, imaginative, and domestic. Like the crab, they may be hard on the outside but soft on the inside.

LEO THE LION (July 23 to August 22): Leos are described as confident, dramatic, self-reliant, generous, outgoing, and proud. Like the king of the jungle, they can be dominating, brave, and demanding of attention.

VIRGO THE VIRGIN (August 23 to September 22): Virgos are considered analytical, attentive to details, diligent, shrewd, and critical, and have a tendency to be perfectionists. Associated with the image of a maiden, Virgos can also be modest and prudent.

LIBRA THE SCALES (September 23 to October 22): Libras are said to be stylish, good-natured, idealistic, romantic, and intelligent, but often indecisive. The constellation of Libra is visualized as a scale, and Libras are said to be balanced in their thoughts and emotions and to weigh things carefully.

SCORPIO THE SCORPION (October 23 to November 22): Scorpios are considered passionate, intense, secretive, magnetic, powerful, and vindictive. Like their spider namesakes, Scorpios can be quick and bold and strike when the time is right.

SAGITTARIUS THE ARCHER (November 23 to December 21): The constellation Sagittarius is depicted as a **centaur** pulling a bow, and Sagittarians are said to love the outdoors, sports, and animals. Honest and philosophical, they are also thought to be restless, adventurous, and high-spirited.

CAPRICORN THE GOAT (December 22 to January 19): Like goats, Capricorns are said to be stable, dependable characters who can nonetheless leap over dangers and butt away things in their path. They are also described as ambitious, well organized, disciplined, practical, and materialistic.

AQUARIUS THE WATER-BEARER (January 20 to February 18): Aquarians are described as original, visionary, friendly, and idealistic, but also detached and obstinate. Traditionally pictured as a figure holding a water jug, the image is said to symbolize helpfulness and altruism.

PISCES THE FISH (February 19 to March 20): As befits the sign of the fish, Pisces are said to love water and swimming. Sensitive, receptive, emotional, imaginative, and empathetic, they are also reputed to be disorganized and impractical.

The Meaning of the Planets

Astrologers believe that the sun, the moon, Mercury, Venus, Mars, Jupiter, Saturn, Uranus, Neptune, and Pluto each represent a unique aspect of personality or character. These are their traditional meanings:

THE SUN, the brightest, largest body in our solar system, represents a person's essential personality, their core traits and general approach to life.

THE MOON represents emotional reactions, instincts, and unconscious needs.

MERCURY, named for the Roman messenger god, represents communication. The swiftest of the planets, it also stands for intelligence and change.

VENUS, the brightest planet in the sky, is named for the Roman goddess of love. It symbolizes romance, relationships, love, and beauty.

MARS, named for the Roman god of war and recognized by its reddish color, symbolizes aggression, physical energy, and the ability to take initiative.

JUPITER, the largest planet in the solar system, represents good fortune, opportunity, and the ability to broaden one's horizons. Jupiter was the supreme god of the Roman pantheon, the equivalent of the Greek god Zeus.

SATURN, the slowest moving of the visible planets, represents obstructions, fears, and challenges. Saturn was a Roman god of the harvest.

URANUS, named for the Greek sky god Ouranous, represents a person's eccentric and rebellious side. It indicates sudden change, upheaval, and impatience.

NEPTUNE represents imagination, creativity, dreams, and the ability to distinguish between reality and illusion. Named for the Roman god of the sea, Neptune represents things that are deep.

PLUTO, the farthest planet from the sun, represents obsession, the unconscious mind, and the ability to transform one's life. Pluto was the Roman equivalent of Hades, Greek god of the underworld.

Banshee

Seeing a banshee is the scariest thing Harry's classmate Seamus Finnigan can imagine. And for good reason: When one of these mournful apparitions appears before an Irishman, it means a member of his family will soon die.

A fixture of Irish folklore since the eighth century, banshees are not evil creatures, but their haunting cries can make them quite terrifying. Their most distinctive physical features are their eyes, turned fiery red from centuries of weeping for those they loved and mourn. Most often described as a tall, gaunt woman with streaming white hair, the banshee usually wears a green dress covered by a gray, hooded cloak. Occasionally, however, she may appear as a small old woman or a beautiful golden-haired girl dressed in red.

Each banshee is said to be devoted to just one extended Irish family, serving them for centuries, but appearing only when a family member is about to die. The most famous banshee of ancient times was named Aibhill, and she haunted the royal family of O'Brien. According to legend, the aged king Brian Boru went off to the battle of Clontarf in 1014 knowing he would never survive, for Aibhill had appeared to him the night before, washing the clothes of soldiers until the water ran red with blood.

In later years banshees were known to herald a death by wailing or keening under the window of the dying, sometimes floating up several stories to do so. In a famous account from the seventeenth century, a guest at an Irish estate described her fright upon hearing a voice in the middle of the night: "I drew the curtain, and in the casement of the window, I saw by the light of the moon a woman leaning into the window, with red hair and pale and ghastly complexion. She spoke loud, and in a tone I had

never heard, and then, with a sigh more like a wind than breath, she vanished." As it turned out, someone had died in the house during the night.

A banshee may also remain at a distance, a solitary figure who signals a death by pacing the hills around the family home (the word "banshee" comes from the Irish *bean si*, meaning "woman of the hills") or sitting on a stone wall. Sometimes she is not visible at all, but her piercing wails leave no doubt about her presence. On the rare occasions when several banshees appear together, it forebodes the death of someone very great or revered.

Only the oldest families, who can trace their lineage to the legendary Irish heroes of the early Middle Ages, are said to have banshees. Originally, this included only families whose last names began with "O'" or "Mac," but after centuries of intermarriage hundreds of others can now make this claim. Attuned as banshees are to bloodlines, they will follow their families wherever they may go. Thus, the banshee's wails are said to be heard in England, America, and anywhere the Irish have settled.

Basilisk

The basilisk is one of our favorite monsters. Depending on who tells the tale, it is a venom-spitting serpent, a ferocious lizard, a towering **dragon,** or a full-fledged chimera sporting the head and wings of a rooster attached to the body of a **snake.** Like the enormous green serpent that Harry encounters in the Chamber of Secrets, the basilisk is always frightening and often deadly, having the power to kill its victims by its stare alone.

We first hear of this charming reptile from Pliny the Elder, the first-century Latin writer whose book *Natural History* reflects much of what ancient Romans believed about the natural world. According to Pliny, the basilisk is a small but lethal snake, no more than twelve inches long, and native to North Africa. Known as "king of the serpents" because of the crownlike markings on its head (*basiliskos* means "little king" in Greek) the basilisk advanced upon its prey with its body held upright, rather than wriggling across the ground like other snakes, and could set fire to bushes and break stones apart simply by breathing on them. The basilisk lived in the desert, not necessarily because it chose to, but because no matter where it lived, the land was eventually reduced to desert by the beast's scorching breath. Its venom was so powerful, Pliny reported, that if a rider on horseback killed a basilisk with a spear, the venom would rise up through the spear, kill the rider, and then kill the horse as well.

If a snake can have an Achilles' heel, the basilisk had two: It could not tolerate the scent of a weasel or the sound of a rooster crowing. To slay a basilisk by weasel it was necessary to first lure the serpent into a weasel's den and then block the entrances and exits, whereupon the serpent would succumb to the weasely fumes. Death by rooster was far easier as, according to the Roman writer Claudius Aelian, the mere sound of a cock crowing would cause the basilisk to go into convulsions and die (it was to protect the basilisk in the Chamber of Secrets from just such a fate that Tom Riddle arranged the demise of several roosters at Hogwarts). But perhaps the best defense of all was to hold a mirror up to the basilisk, turning its own fatal gaze against it and causing it to die of fright.

Like many an imaginary creature, the basilisk was probably based on a real animal—in this case the Egyptian cobra, which has a lethal venom, moves with its head held upright, and has markings on its head resembling a crown. As was common in antiquity, however, writers who described the customs and creatures of foreign lands often did so without ever having left home. Rather, they based their reports on the secondhand accounts of foreign travelers who no doubt embellished their tales to make them more interesting. As reports were told and retold, the lore of the basilisk grew.

By the Middle Ages popular books of mythical beasts had begun to describe the basilisk as a bizarre monster having the body of a snake (it was *all* snake in Greek and Roman traditions) and the head, wings, and sometimes feet of a rooster. This version of the creature, which legend had it could now be found in England as well as in Africa, was known as a cockatrice as well as a basilisk. The unlikely combination of snake and chicken apparently arose from stories concerning its birth, which told of the basilisk hatching from a rooster's egg that had been laid in a hillside and incubated by a **toad**. It is this image of the basilisk that was widely known and depicted in medieval art and heraldry, sometimes with a body covered in feathers, sometimes in scales.

The basilisk of the Chamber of Secrets, however, is clearly of the older type, strictly a serpent and a huge one, too, as befits the heir of Slytherin.

 CS 16/290

The Basilisk Today

The modern namesake of the mythical basilisk is an amazing tropical lizard found in the rainforests of Central and South America. A member of the iguana family, it lives in trees and among rocks and is able to sprint across the surface of water, standing on its hind legs, holding its body almost upright. It is an excellent swimmer and climber and dines on insects, spiders, and other small animals. Because it can apparently walk on water, it is sometimes called the Jesus lizard.

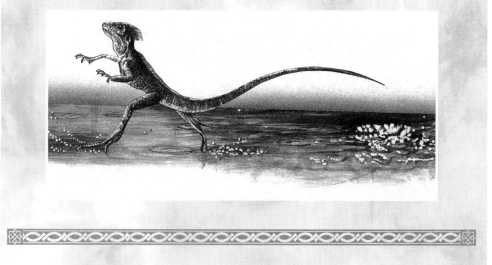

Boggart

The boggart is well known in Northern English folklore as a shape-shifting spirit that, while normally invisible, can materialize as a human, an animal, a skeleton, or even a **demon.** Most boggarts, like the one Professor Lupin keeps in a closet at Hogwarts, delight in frightening people. Some are merely mischievous, resembling the **poltergeist** in their efforts to create chaos in an orderly household. According to tradition, you know one of these meddlesome creatures is around when doors slam for no reason, candles suddenly go out, tools disappear, and mysterious noises echo through the house. Other boggarts of a more vicious nature lurk on dark roadsides and frighten lonely travelers, sometimes causing injury or death.

The boggart is a relative, some might say the evil twin, of the far-more-friendly brownie. Brownies appear in English folktales as household helpers who take great personal responsibility for the homes in which they live and bring good luck to the homeowner. They clean up messes, complete unfinished chores, make bread, harvest grain, herd sheep, and mend broken tools and clothes. In return for their labors, they are entitled each evening to a bowl of milk or cream and a piece of cake. An offer of any greater reward is taken as an insult, and brownies are easily offended and angered. When offense occurs, a boggart may appear to take the brownie's place.

Household boggarts are said to be dark, hairy, and ugly, with overlarge hands and feet. To complete the look, they dress in rags. In centuries past, when a house was thought to be infested with a boggart the owner usually made great efforts to get rid of it. But boggarts were stubborn, and sometimes a family might be forced to move to another

The Bogeyman (Also Boogieman)

"Be good, or the bogeyman will get you!" The warning is familiar to us all. A bogeyman is a supernatural being who lurks under the bed, in closets, down unlit stairways, and in any other dark and scary place. The bogeyman has no particular appearance. Rather, like the Hogwarts boggart, he takes whatever shape will terrify you the most.

The bogeyman is a descendant of two other malicious spirits, the Scottish bogle and the English bogie, both of which are closely related to the boggart. The bogle is a shape-shifter that can appear as anything from a dog to a cloud to a sack of corn. Bogles are known for playing tricks on travelers, but they cause serious harm only to villains who deserve a bad end. Bogies are described as small, black, and hairy mischief-making **goblins.** Like the bogeyman himself, bogies are often called upon to frighten children into good behavior.

town to escape one. Even that did not always work: One story tells of a farmer who was so fed up with the destruction caused by a boggart that he packed up his family and all of his possessions and headed for a new home. Just as he passed through his front gate, a surprised neighbor asked if he was moving away. Before he had a chance to answer, a voice from deep within his suitcases said happily, "Yes, we're leaving!" The farmer and his family sadly turned around and went home, realizing there was no escape from the wily boggart.

 PA 7/133

Broomstick

No one loves a broomstick quite like a **witch**. Harry's great affection for his Firebolt makes it tempting to include **wizards** in this statement as well. Historically speaking, however, almost every person reported to soar through the sky on a broom was a woman. When the occasional wizard or warlock did lay claim to flying skills, he was more likely to travel on a pitchfork!

Although popular illustrations today invariably show a broomstick as the witch's mode of transportation, this was not always the case. Between about 1450 and 1600, when belief in the power of witchcraft was widespread in Europe, witches were reported to take to the skies and head to their midnight gatherings astride goats, oxen, sheep, dogs, and wolves, as well as on sticks, shovels, and staffs. Broomsticks ended up as the preferred vehicle, some scholars suggest, because of women's traditional role as housekeepers.

According to popular lore, much of it invented and circulated by professional witch hunters, witches usually left their homes via the chimney. Once airborne, flying was said to be relatively easy—except in two cases. A novice witch might have trouble staying on her broomstick, which was likely to be swift but unstable. Additionally, witches could be brought down—or prevented from taking off—by the sound of church bells. In the early seventeenth century a town in Germany was so fearful of witches on broomsticks that for a time the city council ordered all churches to ring their bells continuously from dusk to dawn.

Whether witches could really fly was a subject of serious debate among scholars and religious authorities, especially during the

Witches were reputed to rub "flying ointment" on their skin before leaving through the chimney for their midnight gatherings.

most intense years of **witch persecution.** According to the *Malleus Maleficarum* (1486), the most widely followed guide to the discovery and punishment of witches, flying was an incontestable fact. For one thing, many women had confessed to flying, and some had even boasted of their ability to take to the air. Furthermore, a passage in the biblical Book of Matthew described Satan's power to transport Jesus through the air, and if the Devil could make Jesus fly, some churchmen pointed out, he certainly could bestow that ability on the witches who served him. Other scholars rejected the notion of flying as a physical impossibility and argued that the Devil merely caused women to think they had flown by filling their heads with delusions.

A more scientifically minded group of thinkers offered yet another explanation. Witches were known to prepare for takeoff by rubbing their brooms and their bodies with a special "flying ointment" made of plants and herbs (among them henbane, **mandrake,** monks-hood, and nightshade) grown in their gardens. Physicians who experimented with flying ointment in the sixteenth century found that it contained powerful chemicals that entered the body through the skin and caused deep sleep and hallucinations—including a sensation of flying. As they explained it, witches who believed they "flew" actually fell asleep in their own kitchens and awoke with vivid memories of a fantastic flight that had occurred only in their **dreams.**

 SS 9/146

Cat

enign as old, gray Mrs. Norris might appear to an outsider, no Hogwarts student can quite feel comfortable in the presence of Argus Filch's pet cat. She's always on the lookout for bad behavior, and she seems to have an uncanny ability to share information with her master without so much as a meow.

Cats have long been associated with magic and the supernatural. In the sixteenth century, they were widely known as the companions of **witches** and, like Mrs. Norris, were suspected of being able to communicate with their owners. In parts of Scotland, this belief was so strong that many people refused to discuss important family business when a cat was in the room, for fear that what they revealed would later be used against them by a witch.

According to some theories, however, cats were more than just witches' spies—they were actual witches in disguise. Nicholas Remy, a sixteenth-century judge who presided over hundreds of witchcraft trials, claimed that almost all of the witches he had come across easily transformed themselves into cats when they wished to enter other people's homes. But unlike Professor McGonagall, who can turn herself into a cat as often as she likes, historical witches were said to be able to perform this feat only nine times—once for each of a cat's reputed nine lives.

The most common role for a witch's cat was that of *familiar* (see **witch**). More servant than pet, a familiar was reputedly a minor **demon,** provided by the Devil to do any evil errand a witch might devise, from souring milk to destroying livestock to bringing chronic illness or even death to her enemies. In one sixteenth-century trial, a confessed witch claimed that her cat, Sathan, spoke to her in a strange hollow voice, found her a wealthy husband, caused him to go lame, and murdered her six-month-old baby at her command. In western England, witnesses claimed to have seen a woman known as "the Wicked Black Witch of Fraddam" riding through the air on a huge black cat whenever she went looking for poisons and magical herbs. With stories like these running wild, it's not surprising that people were as terrified of cats as they were of witches, and treated them every bit as badly.

Before cats were feared, however, they were revered. The ancient Egyptians were the first people to keep cats as pets, and eventually cats became the object of religious devotion. It began about 2000 B.C., when the goddess Bastet, usually portrayed with the body of a woman and the head of a cat, was worshipped as the personification of fertility and healing. According to the Greek historian Diodorus Siculus, cats designated to live in temples were pampered with meals of bread and milk and slices of Nile fish, and even their caretakers had high status in the community. Eventually all cats came to be regarded not merely as symbols of Bastet's goodness but as gods themselves. Killing one, even by accident, was punishable by death, and when the family cat died of natural causes, everyone in the household shaved their eyebrows in mourning. Cat **amulets** were made and sold by the thousands. And

Cat Tales

Many people find cats fascinating, and folklore abounds with stories that attribute meaning to just about any little thing a cat might do. One legend has it that rain may be expected when cats are frisky; another claims this is true only if a cat passes a paw over both ears while washing. Guests can be expected when a cat trims its whiskers, but when it stretches its paws toward the fire, those approaching the house are strangers. A cat sneezing near a bride on her wedding day predicts a happy marriage, but three sneezes mean colds for everyone in the house. And in case you're wondering whether keeping company with a black cat really will bring bad luck, it depends on where you live. Americans tend to shun black cats, but in England, they're considered lucky. And in Elizabethan times, neither black nor white but brindled (tabby) cats were most often associated with witches, like the famous three in Shakespeare's *Macbeth* who take the fact that "thrice the brindled cat hath mewed" as a signal for action. No one can fully account for the way cat colors have gone in and out of style over the centuries. So perhaps it's safest to follow Welsh tradition, which holds that those who keep both a coal black cat and a snowy white one are the luckiest of all.

reverence toward cats didn't end when they died. It was important to bury a cat with the greatest respect, which in those days meant wrapping them as **mummies** (mummification was believed to enable the dead to return to life). In the summer of 1888, an Egyptian farmer digging on his land unearthed a group of 2,000-year-old cat mummies lying just under the desert sand—300,000 of them! This proved to be only one of many ancient cat cemeteries in Egypt.

Why have cats been so passionately loved and hated? Many cat superstitions can be traced to observations that reflect some pretty basic truths about cats. Like Hermione's cat Crookshanks, most felines have a strong dislike of rats. Some say Egyptian cat worship stemmed from the fact that cats protected granaries and other places where food was stored from becoming overrun by rodents. And having observed cats killing deadly vipers, Egyptians came to believe the cat was the natural enemy of the **snake,** a traditional symbol of evil. The cat's excellent night vision, and the way its eyes can eerily reflect light, led to the idea that cats were clairvoyant: If they could see in the dark, why couldn't they read minds or look into the future? The static electricity in cats' fur—which changes in quality when the air is particularly dry or moist—was translated into an ability to forecast the weather. And the tendency of many cats to appear aloof and indifferent to humans caused some people to regard them as "otherworldly" creatures with secret lives, or as scheming tricksters just waiting for the right moment to pounce on a sleeping baby or report an overheard conversation. So if you sometimes like to pat the head of a soft, purring cat and whisper a secret into its ear, you might want to consider telling a dog instead.

31

 SS 8/132

Cauldron

At first glance, a cauldron may appear to be just an oversized cookpot. But in the right (or wrong) hands, it can be a magical artifact of extraordinary power. With a cauldron, a skilled **witch** or **wizard** can brew **potions,** predict the future, provide an endless supply of food to an unlimited number of guests, grant youth and strength, or bestow knowledge and wisdom.

Early cauldrons came in many shapes and sizes and were made of bronze, copper, pewter (like Harry's), stone, and later of cast iron. In medieval times, the cauldron was at the center of almost every household activity. It was used for cooking, brewing medicines, washing and dyeing clothing, making soap and candles, and transporting both water and fire. A large family might own only a single cauldron, used for all of these purposes.

In some cultures, cauldrons were part of religious rituals. The ancient Celts kept their gods content with offerings of fine gold and silver jewelry, which they placed in a cauldron that was then sunk in a body of water. One such cauldron was later found in a lake in France and plundered by some very happy Romans. The famed Gundestop cauldron, which was discovered in a peat bog in Denmark in 1891, is made almost entirely of pure silver and features depictions of gods, plants, and fantastic animals. It dates from the first century B.C. and was probably used for human sacrifice.

The best-known use for cauldrons, however, is as a tool for witches. The association dates back to ancient times. In Greek mythology, the witch Medea promised her husband that she would extend the life of his aging and debilitated father. She mixed magic herbs with

The association between witches and cauldrons dates back to ancient Greece and Rome. Here, an old witch instructs her apprentice in the art of brewing potions.

parts from "animals tenacious of life" (notably tortoises) in a cauldron, then cut the old man's throat and poured her concoction into his wound. Medea's potion restored her father-in-law to the vigor of his youth.

Perhaps the most famous cauldron of all belonged to the trio of witches that helped lead Shakespeare's famous character Macbeth to his doom. Accosted by Macbeth with demands that they predict his future,

the witches prepared a most unappetizing brew, tossing into their cauldron a **dragon**'s scale, a wolf's tooth, a lizard's leg, and those old favorites, eye of newt and toe of frog. Using this unique stew and the famous incantation "double, double, toil and trouble, fire burn and cauldron bubble," the witches called forth three spirits that offered accurate—if cleverly misleading—prophecies.

The cauldron also figures prominently in Irish, Welsh, and Celtic mythology, in which it is considered a magical object holding power over life itself. The mouth of the cauldron is viewed as a gateway to the underworld, from which new life emerges and to which the dying return. The cauldron of Pwyll, Welsh lord of the underworld, was said to grant immortality. Some legends suggest that King Arthur and his knights once attempted to steal this cauldron. Legend also holds that the Irish hero Bran had a cauldron with the power to bring the dead back to life, which he gave to the king of Ireland. The corrupt king then used this magical vessel to create an inexhaustible supply of undead soldiers. These soldiers were mute, in order to prevent them from revealing the secrets of the afterlife. Accounts of battles describe how various body parts from soldiers cut down in battle were tossed into the cauldron, from which the bodies immediately emerged, whole and ready to fight another day. The Irish king was defeated only when Bran's half-brother leapt into the cauldron, sacrificing his own life to destroy the vessel, which was not meant to hold living beings.

An army mustered in this way might never be conquered, for new warriors could continually be created out of the remains of the fallen. It can be hard enough for decent wizards to defend themselves against the forces of evil that live and breathe. How much greater the danger when long-vanquished foes might even now be waking, slowly returning to life in the confines of some dark cauldron?

Centaur

$\mathfrak{U}$nlike the brooding and philosophical centaurs that roam the **Forbidden Forest,** the original centaurs of Greek mythology were a rowdy lot. Living in herds in the mountains of northern Greece, they pursued a wild and lawless lifestyle. Half man and half horse, the centaurs were beautiful to behold, but they were always ready to drink, fight, and seduce human women. Once invited to attend the wedding of their neighbor, King Pirithous of Laipithae, the drunken centaurs assaulted the female guests, tried to abduct the bride, and started a bloody battle with their host and his supporters—a contest they lost, to the great relief of all who lived nearby.

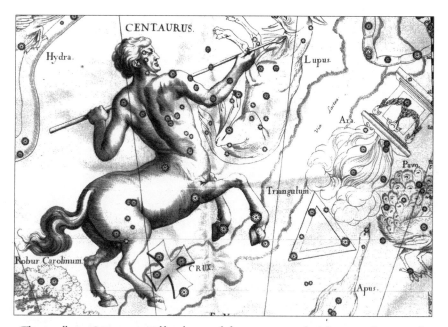

The constellation Centaurus is visible only to people living near or south of the equator. It contains the third brightest star in the night sky, Alpha Centauri, which is also the closest star to our own sun.

As in any large family, there were a few centaurs who rebelled against the wild ways of their kin, preferring a life of virtue and scholarly contemplation. The most famous is Chiron, who served as teacher and mentor to many young men destined for greatness, including Hercules, Achilles (the hero of the Trojan war), Jason (captain of the *Argo*), and Asclepius, god of medicine. Known for his wisdom and sense of justice, Chiron was skilled in medicine, hunting, **herbology,** and celestial navigation. He also practiced **astrology** and **divination.** Based on the ability of Ronan, Bane, and Firenze to read the future in the sky, we suspect these centaurs may have descended from Chiron's side of the family.

The myths tell us that Chiron might have gone on teaching young heroes indefinitely, for he was born immortal. But he chose to give up his immortality after he was accidentally wounded by a poisoned arrow belonging to his friend Hercules. When the pain became unbearable, he asked Zeus to allow him to die. Zeus granted Chiron's request but immortalized him nonetheless by placing him in the sky as the constellation *Centaurus.*

Charm

When we use the word "charm" in everyday conversation, we're usually referring to a certain sense of social grace, a rare enchanting quality that makes some people more alluring and persuasive than others. But the term "charm," which derives from an old Latin word for "song" or "ritual utterance" (*carmen*), has many different meanings, most of which are totally unrelated to a person's appearance or social skills. In the world of witchcraft and sorcery, a charm is usually a phrase that is recited or written down to achieve a particular magical effect. Thus, Harry utters a special summoning charm (*Accio Firebolt!*) when he wants to call his broomstick to his side, while Hermione uses a levitation charm (*Wingardium Leviosa!*) to make a feather float.

As the students in Professor Flitwick's charms class quickly learn, there are charms for almost every occasion. If you know the right words, you can charm your way into riches and fame, conquer your enemies, or capture men's hearts. One Old English charm even confers protection from malevolent dwarfs. But charms are most commonly associated with medieval wise women, who used them for fairly humble tasks, such as healing the sick, protecting crops and livestock from disease, and defending the local villagers from **curses.**

Although a few charms involve combining words with actions (such as spitting or waving a **magic wand**), most require no special ritual or magical tools to be effective. Charms are even said to work in purely written form. Some of the earliest known charms were simply scraps of parchment or paper, inscribed with a **magic word** like *abracadabra,* and then worn as protective **amulets** around the neck.

Simple spoken charms became especially popular in Europe around the twelfth century, when the Catholic Church began to place great emphasis on the power of spoken prayers and papal blessings. Throughout the Middle Ages, it was common for **witches, wizards,** and even local Church officials to adapt Christian prayers for magical purposes. The Lord's Prayer was routinely rewritten and used as a charm against disease, pestilence, and personal misfortune. One thirteenth-century French memoir actually describes how a parish priest used this prayer "to deliver Arnald of Villanova from the warts on his hands!" Other charms mixed magic words with the names of saints and were used to treat maladies such as snakebites and burns.

Some poorly trained witches and wizards—and most nonmagical folk—also use the word "charm" to describe any small, portable object with magical properties. Rabbits' feet, four-leaf clovers, and iron horseshoes are all frequently called "lucky charms," but any serious magician would scoff at such a claim. These sorts of magical artifacts can be more precisely identified as either **amulets** (objects that provide magi-

"Charmed, I'm Sure"

The notion that a charm can affect us in a magical or enchanting way has given rise to many "charming" phrases and expressions. A smooth operator can "charm the pants off" someone or "charm a bird from a tree." Quaint towns have "Old World charm," and music, according to the English playwright William Congreve, "has charms to soothe a savage breast." Prince Charming usually gets what he wants, and those who often escape from danger are said to lead a "charmed life." "How charming" is usually a sarcastic remark, but "the third time's a charm" shows that persistence pays off. And any particularly effective technique for getting what you want—a word, a smile, or a bill slipped into the hands of a maitre 'd—is said to "work like a charm."

cal protection) or **talismans** (objects that endow a person with some new magical ability). The so-called charms that hang from modern "charm bracelets" are usually purely ornamental symbols of love or friendship, possessing no magical powers.

As Hermione would be happy to tell you, the best place to find authentic charms is in books. So if you find yourself wanting a cheering charm for a friend who's feeling blue or a scouring charm to take care of a really nasty mess, just check the Hogwarts library for a copy of *Olde and Forgotten Bewitchments and Charmes*. But make sure you've picked just the right charm for the job and that you know how to pronounce every word. Otherwise, you may end up like Professor Dumbledore's ne'er-do-well brother, Aberforth, who was publicly humiliated for practicing inappropriate charms on a goat.

Circe

Beautiful and deadly, charming and cruel, Circe is one of the great **witches** of Greek mythology. Aided by her wand, **potions,** herbs, and incantations, she transformed men into animals, caused forests to move, and turned day into night. The ancient writers Homer, Hesiod, Ovid, and Plutarch all chronicled her exploits, ensuring her place in legend—and as a Chocolate Frogs trading card.

The daughter of the sun god Helios and the ocean nymph Perse, Circe lived on the island of Aeaea off the coast of Italy, where she spent her days weaving dazzling fabrics on her loom and singing in a most enchanting voice. She was occasionally visited by travelers who happened upon her island, or by those who knew of her magical powers and came to her for aid. But Aeaea was far more perilous than your typical island resort. The sea god Glaucus discovered this when he came to Circe for a love potion to help him win his heart's desire, a nymph named Scylla. Circe fell in love with Glaucus and asked him to stay with her. When he refused, she threw poisonous herbs into the water where her rival was bathing, turning Scylla into a hideous monster with dogs' heads and serpents protruding from her body. Another man foolish enough to reject Circe spent the rest of his days as a woodpecker.

The best-known visitors to Circe's island were the Greek hero Odysseus and his crew of sailors, who landed on Aeaea on their return from the Trojan War. Seeing a wisp of smoke in the distance, Odysseus sent half of his men to investigate. They soon came upon the home of the enchantress, a marble palace in the middle of a forest clearing surrounded by tame bears, lions, and wolves that had been human until they met Circe. Always the welcoming hostess, Circe appeared at the

Circe's wand and potions were powerless against Odysseus.
This illustration comes from an 1887 edition of The Odyssey.

door and invited the men to lunch. But the barley and cheese she served contained a powerful potion that deprived the men of both their memories and their desire to return home. As they sat in a contented stupor, Circe tapped each man with her **magic wand,** turned them into pigs and led them off, weeping, to the pigsty.

Circe planned the same fate for Odysseus, but on his way to find his men he was met by the god Hermes who gave him an herb called *moly* to neutralize the effect of her **spells** and potions. Powerless to work her magic against him, Circe instead befriended Odysseus and restored his sailors to human form. From then on she acted as his advisor, forecasting the dangers that lay ahead and explaining how to communicate with the **ghosts** he would meet in his journey to the underworld.

Myths about Circe, along with stories about the sorceress Medea (Circe's niece) and the Greek goddess and witch Hecate, formed the basis for many popular beliefs about witches and witchcraft. During the Middle Ages, it was common for those who heard these myths to believe that Circe had been a real person and that her magical feats were within the realm of possibility.

 SS 6/103

Crystal Ball

et me look into my crystal ball. . . .
Today these words are often heard as a sarcastic response to questions about the unknowable future. For those who practice the many arts of **divination,** however, crystal-ball gazing is serious business. At Hogwarts, Professor Trelawney instructs her third-years in the proper method of peering into the misty orb—assuring them that patience and relaxation will reward them with a view of things to come. Harry, Ron, and Hermione are skeptical at best, but those who believe in the revealing powers of the crystal ball are certainly not alone.

Although actual crystal balls were not used until the Middle Ages, *crystalomancy*—the art of gazing into natural or polished crystal in an attempt to see the future—is part of a much older tradition. It's a form of *scrying*—a method of divination that involves staring at a clear or reflective surface until images begin to form, either within the object itself

In the 1920s and 1930s, the vaudeville entertainer and mind reader Claude Alexander Conlin used a crystal ball to symbolize his ability to "know all, see all, and tell all."

or else within the mind of the practitioner. All cultures seem to have practiced a form of scrying. In ancient Mesopotamia, diviners poured oil into bowls of water and interpreted the shapes that appeared on the surface. The biblical prophet Joseph carried a silver goblet, which he used for both drinking and scrying. The ancient Egyptians, Arabs, and Persians gazed into bowls of ink, while the Greeks stared at shiny mirrors and burnished brass in the hope of receiving enlightening visions. The Romans were the first true cystalomancers, preferring to peer at polished (though not necessarily round) crystals of quartz or beryl.

Even back then, a skeptic like Hermione would have made a poor crystal gazer, since sincerity, a positive mental attitude, and faith in the process were said to be the keys to success. The ideal crystalomancer was supposed to be spiritually and physically pure, preparing for each reading with a few days of prayer and fasting. A special room with a solemn and ceremonial atmosphere would generally be used for the

reading. Such preparation and attention to detail was intended to help the seer to reach a trancelike state while gazing at the crystal, making it more likely that images would appear in his or her mind. The ancients recognized that whatever crystalomancers saw came from their own minds and did not really form within the crystal itself. Nonetheless, these visions were treated as true prophecies and not mere daydreams.

In some traditions, children were thought to be the best scryers, since they were spiritually pure and likely to be more open to the imagination than adults. This theory was generally accepted in Renaissance Europe, where a child might be employed to foretell the future through a crystal-gazing ritual similar to that of the ancients, involving prayers, incense, and **magic words.** During this period, both children and adults also began peering into crystal balls for more practical purposes, such as discovering the identity of criminals or locating lost or stolen property. An account from 1671, for example, tells of a merchant who, upon finding himself constantly robbed of his goods, elected to wander the nearby streets at midnight with a young boy and girl, instructing them to gaze into a crystal until they saw the likeness of the thief. Whether he caught the right man, we'll never know.

Undoubtedly the best-known crystal ball of the Renaissance belonged to John Dee, a highly respected English mathematician and astronomer who was hired to calculate the astrologically correct time for Queen Elizabeth I's coronation in 1558. Dee was passionately interested in scrying as a way of contacting the world of angels and spirits, whom he believed possessed knowledge unavailable elsewhere. He owned a crystal ball, which he described as "most bright, most clear and glorious, of the bigness of an egg." Unfortunately, however, no matter how many hours Dee spent gazing into his ball, he could see nothing. Rather than give up, he hired Edward Kelly, a professional scryer whom many scholars believe was a swindler. For years, the two men worked together, Dee asking questions while Kelly peered into the crystal ball and reported the answers. Together, Dee and Kelly produced volumes of spirit messages, including one predicting the execution of Mary, Queen of Scots, which took place in February 1586. Dee's crystal ball now resides in the British Museum in London, England.

Like Dee, some modern crystal-ball readers use their globes to attempt to communicate with the spirit world. Others tell fortunes or try to locate missing persons. Most use procedures similar to those followed in earlier times, although their preparations are not as rigorous. Careful attention is given to the appearance of the room, and the reading is usually performed under subdued lighting. The crystal ball is usually a perfect sphere of about four inches in diameter and may be white, blue, violet, yellow, green, opalescent, or transparent. Traditionally, the ball rests on a stand of highly polished ebony, ivory, or boxwood. When a reading is given, the seer may place the ball on a table or hold it in the palm of the hand against the background of a black cloth.

Today, crystal balls are often associated with the commercial storefront studios of self-described psychics or itinerant fortune-tellers who, like Professor Marvel in *The Wizard of Oz*, claim to be able to "see all and know all." Although the art of scrying no longer has the universal respect it did in ancient times, it still plays an important role in many cultures. Most notably, the current Dalai Lama was discovered through scrying by a committee of monks who searched for his identity by gazing into Lake Lhotso in Tibet.

 PA 15/296

Curse

When our parents told us not to curse, we didn't consider it a matter of life and death. And, of course, it wasn't. In modern usage, "cursing" generally means saying something vulgar or profane.

While it may be offensive, and it is certainly bad manners, it is hardly fatal. In earlier centuries, however, a curse was much more than a swear word; it was considered one of the most powerful and dangerous forms of **magic,** intended to bring pain, suffering, illness, or even death to an enemy. That's undoubtedly why the Ministry of Magic recommends that curses not be taught until the sixth year of a wizard's education. After all, the last thing a teacher would want is a young hothead uttering curses against a classmate who got better grades.

The practice of cursing enemies has existed in cultures around the world for thousands of years. Curses can be spoken or written. A typical form of oral curse involved calling on the aid of a supernatural being such as a **demon** or god and then outlining each grim detail of the victim's intended fate, as in this spiteful curse from the fourth century: "I call thee, evil spirit, who sittest in the cemetery and takest away healing from man. Go and place a knot in [the victim's] head, in his eyes, in his mouth, in his tongue, in his throat; put poisonous water in his belly. If you do not go and put water in his belly I will send against you many evil angels. Amen." Such curses were thought to be effective whether yelled in someone's ear or whispered from hundreds of miles away. Written curses, however, were usually considered more powerful than the spoken variety, since they could live on long past the moment of their creation.

Ancient curses have survived from as far back as the fifth century B.C., though presumably their intended victims are long dead. They were inscribed on "curse tablets"—sheets of lead, pottery, or wax bearing the victim's name, the desired outcome of the curse, some **magic words,** and the names of demons who were to assist in carrying out the curse. A simple curse tablet might be inscribed with the words "As this piece of lead grows cold, so will John Smith." The tablet would then be buried in the ground, and as it cooled to the temperature of the earth, John Smith was expected to feel his own body temperature drop until he died. The most powerful places to bury curse tablets were believed to be places of death: fresh graves, battlefields, and sites where executions were held. They could also be dropped into wells, which were thought to be entrances to the

Licensed to Curse

From ancient times to modern, those wishing to harm an enemy often sought help from a professional—a village wizard or witch with a reputation for creating and delivering effective curses. People who knew they had been cursed often felt symptoms, probably because the fear and anxiety instilled by the very notion of a curse were enough to bring on nausea, vomiting, headaches, insomnia, and other ills. If the victim was not too incapacitated, he or she might seek out another wizard to undo the curse and perform a countercurse. In villages where there was just one wizard, however, he would get the business of both parties, earning a tidy sum.

underworld. For additional potency, a nail was often driven through the victim's name, or the tablet might be bound tightly in wire.

Curse tablets were widely used in ancient Greece and Rome. Archaeologists have uncovered various types of tablets, some requesting the painful death of an enemy, others aimed at merely muddling the brains and tying the tongues of political opponents or legal adversaries. One tablet was intended to ensure the outcome of a chariot race by cursing the horses and drivers of the opposing team! Although curses were officially disapproved for private use, they were apparently acceptable when administered by public officials against criminals, enemies of the state, or military opponents.

During the Middle Ages, the use of governmental curses declined, but curses delivered by the poor and downtrodden were believed to be quite powerful, especially when the anger that inspired them seemed

The Mummy's Curse

One of the most famous curses of all time—the "Mummy's Curse" on the tomb of King Tut in Egypt—is probably no more than a myth. Legend has it that when the British archaeologist Howard Carter opened King Tut's tomb in 1922, he ignored an inscription reading: "Death Shall Come on Swift Wings to Him Who Disturbs the Rest of the King." Only a few months later, Carter's financial backer, Lord Carnarvon, died unexpectedly of an infected mosquito bite. (Death on swift wings indeed!) Five more people who had been present at the opening of the tomb also passed away during the next twelve years.

However, there is little evidence to support the idea that a curse was ever laid on this tomb. Although many folktales describe elaborate curses promising a swift and terrible death to anyone who disturbs a **mummy**'s grave, archaeologists have actually verified the existence of protective curses at only two Egyptian tombs, and both of these simply threaten graverobbers with harsh judgment by the gods. The curse inscribed on King Tut's tomb—if there ever was one—has mysteriously vanished. Howard Carter himself lived for another seventeen years after disturbing Tut's rest, eventually becoming one of the world's most famous and admired Egyptologists.

justified. The Beggar's Curse, uttered against those who refused to give alms to the poor, was widely feared for centuries.

In sixteenth- and seventeenth-century England, public cursing was commonplace. It was not unusual, for example, to see someone in the town square fall to his knees and call upon God to burn his enemies' houses, blight their crops, kill their children, destroy their possessions,

and bring down on their heads "all the plagues of Egypt." While such rants might seem harmless, cursers were well advised to exercise some caution. If the intended victim did become ill and the curser developed a reputation for success, he or she could well end up in jail, accused of witchcraft.

 GF 14/211

Dark Arts

Wander off the familiar sidewalks of Diagon Alley into a dingy side street near Gringotts Bank and you'll find yourself in Knockturn Alley, home to purveyors of shrunken heads, hangman's rope, poisonous candles, and other such sinister goods. Although Hagrid ventures here in search of flesh-eating-slug repellent, most visitors to this part of town are practitioners of the Dark Arts—the branch of magic devoted to causing harm to others.

Like every other kind of magic, the Dark Arts (also known as black magic) have been around for thousands of years. While some members of early civilizations developed **spells** and **magic words** to try to cure disease, bring rain to parched fields, or protect a village from enemy invasion, others were working on **curses** and other supernatural means of inflicting pain and misfortune on their neighbors. Such methods might be used to exact revenge for a personal insult, to eliminate a business competitor, or to get the better of a political op-

Protected by a magic circle, sixteenth-century necromancer Edward Kelly and his assistant, Paul Waring, conjure a spirit in a churchyard in Lancashire, England.

ponent. When the Roman general Germanicus died in A.D. 19, evidence that someone had used black magic against him was found in the form of human bones, written curses, and pieces of lead (then known as the metal of death) hidden under the floor and behind the walls of his bedchamber.

At Hogwarts, young students learn about the Dark Arts by studying the wicked ways of **red caps, kappas, werewolves,** and other menacing creatures. More mature pupils are taught to defend themselves against the curses of evil **wizards** and **witches** who use these illegal means to gain total control over others, to inflict torture without ever laying a finger on the victim, or even to commit murder. Many other practices that have traditionally been considered Dark Arts are not part of the Hogwarts curriculum, as far as we know. However, rumor has it they may be taught at Durmstrang, and it never hurts to know what devices an aspiring Dark wizard may have at his disposal.

One of the oldest and most widely practiced forms of black magic is *image magic,* in which a drawing or a clay or wax model of the intended victim is created and then purposefully harmed or destroyed. Any damage inflicted on the model—also known as an effigy—is supposed to hurt the victim as well. In ancient India, Persia, Africa, Egypt, and Europe, doll-like wax effigies were common, since they were easy to create and could be destroyed by melting, a method alleged to cause the victim to die of a wasting illness. Small dolls might also be made of clay, wood, or cloth and painted to look like the victim. Other common methods of harming an effigy included sticking it with pins or knives (believed to cause a person pain or sickness) or, if it was made of animal or vegetable matter, burying it in the ground so it would decompose.

Another ancient form of black magic was *necromancy* (from the Greek *nekros,* meaning "corpse," and *mancy,* meaning "prophecy")—attempting to raise the spirits of the dead for purposes of **divination.** No longer bound by the earthly plane, the dead were believed to have access to information about both the present and the future that was unavailable to the living. Necromancy appears in the Bible, was practiced in ancient Persia, Greece, and Rome, and experienced renewed

popularity in Renaissance Europe. While some necromancers tried to raise actual corpses (and a few were accused of trying to send those corpses to attack the living), most were content to summon only the spirit of the dead person by performing rituals over the grave, uttering incantations, and drawing magic words and symbols on the ground. Often the necromancer would surround himself with skulls and other images of death, wear some clothing stolen from a corpse, and concentrate all his thoughts on death as he waited for the spirit to appear. Once it did (any small sign, such as the flickering of a candle, might be taken to indicate the spirit's presence), he would ask it questions—sometimes about life's great mysteries, sometimes about the future, and sometimes about more mundane concerns, like where to find buried treasure. Although the purpose of necromancy was not always to harm people, the process of calling upon (and perhaps disturbing) dead souls has generally been considered immoral and despicable, earning its place among the Dark Arts.

Some writers have suggested that all magic is really "colorless": Whether a practice is "black magic" or "white magic" depends upon its intention. For example, melting a wax effigy in order to kill a cruel dictator might be considered white magic by the people being oppressed by the dictator, but black magic by the dictator himself. Others have suggested that the war between black magic and white magic is an ongoing expression of man's dual nature—our capacity to do good, but also to harm. Wizards, like the rest of us, can use their powers to create, help others, and contribute to the world. Or, like the Death Eaters, they can give rein to a different aspect of human nature—to be selfish, domineering, power-hungry, and capable of terrible atrocities. As Dumbledore tells Harry, which side you're on is not a matter of destiny but a matter of choice.

CS 4/53

Demon

Demons—malicious spirits of world folklore, mythology, and religion—come in all shapes and sizes and are almost always up to no good. The vicious English **grindylow** that attacks Harry in the Hogwarts lake is a demon. So is the Arabian **ghoul** in the Weasleys' attic and the Japanese **kappa** studied in Defense Against the Dark Arts. Terrifying tales of demons and their wicked ways can be found in most cultures. Although they are now recognized as creatures of the imagination, demons were once considered quite real and were held responsible for much of the evil and suffering in the world.

The earliest accounts of demons can be found in the ancient cultures of Mesopotamia, Persia, Egypt, and Israel, where a variety of evil spirits were blamed for disease, crop destruction, floods, fires, plagues, hatred, and war. Demons with names like "the Croucher" and "the Seizer" were thought to lurk anywhere and everywhere—in the deserts and forests, in cellars and on rooftops, and inside homes that had not been properly protected by **amulets** or magical incantations. Capable of assuming many forms, ancient demons were often said to appear as flies, dogs, bulls, or many-headed monsters.

The European conception of demons evolved from these traditions, as well as from the *daimons* of ancient Greece. These invisible spirits, described as intermediaries between man and the gods, could be either good or bad. Bad *daimons* led men astray and en-

The triple-headed demon Asmodeus was said to specialize in destroying marriages and sparking anger and revenge.

couraged evil acts, while good *daimons* were thought to offer positive guidance and protection. The philosopher Socrates claimed that a good *daimon* watched over him throughout his life, whispering advice into his ear and warning him of dangers. Because *daimons* were thought to communicate with the gods, people often tried to summon them for help with magical activities such as casting **spells** or working **curses**. The presence and influence of *daimons* were accepted by everyone in the classical world.

By the late fourth century A.D., *daimons* had evolved into demons. Christianity had become the official religion of the vast Roman Empire, and Church leaders taught that the true spirits that occupied the realm between god and men were angels. All pagan spirits—including both good and bad *daimons*—were regarded as fallen angels, or demons, who led men into evil. As in antiquity, demons were held responsible for any kind of misfortune, whether it was an accident, an illness, or even a bad **dream**.

As Christianity grew and spread during the Middle Ages, the many demons of the Middle East were absorbed into Christian lore. All were described as servants of the Devil, but each had his own name, physical description, and particular talents. Asmodeus, for example, was a demon of jealousy, anger, and revenge who specialized in destroying marriages. He was portrayed as having three heads (those of a man, a ram, and a bull), the feet of a goose, and the tail of a snake. Belial was a deceptively handsome demon with a soft voice, who delighted in causing men to become wicked and plagued by guilt. Some of the greatest painters of the Middle Ages and Renaissance let their imaginations run wild in depicting demons in religious paintings, on church walls, and in illuminated manuscripts. By the sixteenth century, the lore of demons had become so elaborate that a detailed catalog of all of Satan's helpers placed their number at 7,405,926.

All those demons floating around could hardly be good news. During the era of **witch persecution** in sixteenth- and seventeenth-century Europe, demons became widely associated with witchcraft. Both witches and demons were servants of the Devil, and witches were said to use demons to perform many of their wicked deeds. Most alarming, demons were believed to enter people's bodies and "possess" them, causing the kind of symptoms that would now be diagnosed as epilepsy or a form of mental illness. Often, demonic possession was attributed to a witch who had placed the demon on a morsel of food eaten by the victim.

Because they were once wise angels, demons were also believed to possess a storehouse of valuable knowledge about such diverse subjects as mathematics, medicinal herbs, geometry, flying, and how to become invisible. This made it extremely tempting for would-be **sorcerers** to try to contact them and gain access to their secrets. But demons were quite wily, and according to popular lore had many ways to harm or destroy those foolish enough to attempt to communicate with them. Summoning demons was a highly illegal activity, and in many parts of Europe was punishable by death.

How to Recognize a Demon

If you're worried that demons lurk in every dark alley, you may be able to draw some comfort from the ability to recognize one when you see it. Although demons hail from many lands, they do share a number of physical characteristics that make them hard to miss.

Most demons walk upright and combine recognizable human features with those of a beast. More than one head is common, as is either an abundance or a shortage of fingers and toes. Many demons sport batlike wings, tails, talons, and horns—though they usually tuck these appendages out of sight when they go out stalking prey. Their mouths are often grotesque and distorted, with jutting fangs and long curly tongues. Some have no skin, and almost all have half their bodies covered by scales or feathers.

The dead giveaway for most demons, however, is their feet. While the rest of the creature may resemble a beautiful woman, a three-headed tiger, or anything else you might imagine, the feet will always be those of a goat, pig, rooster, or goose, or in the case of a water demon, the tail of a fish or snake.

Still, not all demons are associated with Dark forces. In some cultures, demons aren't interested in leading men into the ways of evil; they merely want to have them for supper! In other cases, they attack only to defend their territories—the woods, mountains, deserts, lakes, and rivers where they commonly dwell—from human invasion. But throughout the world, demons represent all that is scary, both in the natural world and inside ourselves. Like people, demons will rant and rage, scheme and plot, deceive and seduce, and display boundless energy (they "work like

demons") to get what they want. Fortunately, in almost all cases, demons can be outwitted—the most powerful weapons against them being human ingenuity, truth, love, and in many cases, laughter.

Divination

Who will I marry? How long will I live? What's the winning number? Will this product sell? Will this plane crash? Will we win the war? Everyone from lovestruck teenagers to world leaders wants to know what lies ahead. That's why divination—the art of foretelling the future—has existed in some form in every culture in recorded history. Today, one can find practitioners of the most popular forms of divination— **astrology,** tarot card reading, **crystal-ball** gazing, palm reading, numerology, and **tea-leaf reading**—in most any city. And these examples are only a tiny sample of hundreds of divinatory systems that have been developed over the centuries.

Many methods of divination began in ancient Mesopotamia more than 4,000 years ago. There, the divinatory arts were practiced by the priests, who studied the movements of the stars and planets and examined the entrails of sacrificed animals for clues to the welfare of the king and community. Some diviners sought clues to future events by going into a trance and seeking guidance from the spirit world. Others looked for omens in nature. An eclipse, a hailstorm, the birth of twins, or the way smoke drifted through the air—almost anything might be interpreted as a sign of things to come.

In ancient Greece and Rome, there were two levels of divination: Professional, highly trained diviners worked for the government, while ordinary fortune-tellers worked for anyone who could afford them. Of the official diviners, the most esteemed in Greece was the Oracle of Delphi, to whom petitioners would bring their questions (which were often multiple choice) and receive an answer directly from the god Apollo, as channeled through a priestess. Royal emissaries from neighboring lands consulted the Oracle on such important matters as where to construct a new temple or whether to go to war. In Rome, the state-appointed diviners were known as "augurs," from the Latin *avis*, meaning "bird" and *garrire*, meaning "to chatter." Indeed, their highly regarded counsel to the empire was based on bird watching. Of all earth's creatures, birds were the closest to the heavens, so it's understandable that they were regarded as good indicators of what might or might not please the gods. Interpretations were based on many kinds of observations, including the number and species

The hat, robes, wand, and books of the fortune-teller made him instantly recognizable. This seventeenth-century diviner holds an astrolabe to symbolize his knowledge of astrology.

People from all walks of life consulted professional fortune-tellers. Here a young nobleman learns what the cards reveal about his future.

of birds and their flight patterns, calls and songs, direction, and speed. Julius Caesar, Cicero, Mark Anthony, and other eminent Romans all served as augurs.

Less noteworthy diviners were available to most everyone (even slaves were sometimes permitted a consultation), and fortune-telling was a booming business throughout the ancient world. **Dream** interpretation and

The Mantic Arts

What does the fearsome green predator of the insect kingdom known as the praying mantis have in common with systems of fortune-telling? Not much, really, except for an interesting connection in language: the Greek word *mantikos,* which means "prophet." Because of the prophetic nature of fortune-telling, diviners are sometimes said to practice "the mantic arts," and dictionary makers use the word ending "-mancy" to indicate any form of divination. Palm reading is chiromancy (*cheiro* is Greek for "hand"), dream interpretation is oneiromancy (in Greek *oneiros* means "dream"), and so forth.

The voracious garden mantis derives its name from the typical upraised position of its forelegs, which suggests a prophet with his hands held together in prayer. Usually, however, the praying mantis is more concerned with "prey" than with either fortune-telling or heavenly supplication.

astrology were the most venerable systems, but also popular were **arithmancy,** scrying (a relative of crystal-ball gazing), and **palmistry,** as well as systems involving birds, dice, books, arrows, axes, and other surprising items. Popular fortune-tellers, many of whom also sold **talismans** and **amulets,** were not afforded the respect given official diviners. They were more likely to be deliberate frauds, and humorists enjoyed poking fun at those who flocked to them for advice on every trivial matter.

Many ancient divinatory systems survived into the Middle Ages, despite opposition in Europe from the Church. Professional seers con-

tinued to work in major cities, traveling fortune-tellers moved from town to town, and village **wizards** and wise women served as diviners for their communities. Village wizards, it should be noted, were expected to look toward the past as well as the future. They were frequently asked to find lost objects, identify thieves, discover the whereabouts of missing persons, and locate buried treasure (centuries ago, when banks were few and far between, many people buried their valuables in a hole in the ground, a practice which led others to try to locate them and dig them up). Ordinary folks were also able to practice some do-it-yourself divination, which they learned from the cheap illustrated booklets on palmistry, astrology, and other subjects that could be purchased as early as the sixteenth century. For the most part, however, divination remained in the hands of professionals who claimed to have information, training, and "a gift" not available to others.

Two additional systems of divination were added to the fortune-teller's arsenal in later centuries. Cartomancy—divination using playing cards—was developed around the mid-seventeenth century, about 150 years after playing cards first appeared in Europe, and soon became the trademark system of wandering gypsy fortune-tellers. Tasseomancy—divination by tea leaves—although practiced in China from about the sixth century, did not appear in Europe until the mid-eighteenth century. These new systems quickly became quite popular, perhaps because card playing and tea drinking were already part of everyday life. Although many ancient systems of divination have now been abandoned, all of those taught at Hogwarts remain in use to this day.

 PA 6/102

A Divination Glossary

Hundreds of systems of divination have been devised over the centuries. Here are a few of our favorites.

AEROMANCY: Rather than forecasting the weather, in this ancient system of divination the weather is the forecaster. Believers saw omens of the future revealed in atmospheric conditions such as thunder, lightning, the shapes of clouds, the direction and strength of the wind, and the presence of halos around the sun or moon. Aeromancy was practiced by the priests of Babylonia and is one of the oldest divinatory systems.

ALECTROMANCY: A rooster (*alektor* in Greek) was the key to this ancient form of divination. The letters of the alphabet were drawn within a large circle and grains of wheat placed on each letter. The order in which the rooster ate the grains spelled out a message. If the words made no sense the diviner interpreted them. Grains were immediately replaced as they were consumed so that any given letter could appear as many times as the message required.

ALOMANCY: In many parts of the world, salt was once believed to have magical properties. In this system of divination, the practitioner would toss a handful of salt onto a surface and then interpret the patterns that appeared. This ancient practice may be related to the superstitions that spilling salt is unlucky, or that tossing it over one's shoulder, usually the left shoulder, brings good luck or deters bad.

APANTOMANCY: Chance encounters with animals were once believed to be full of meaning. In medieval Europe, accidentally meeting up with a goat or a hare foretold imminent good luck, especially if the hare was escaping from hounds. Seeing a bat, a raven, or an ass foretold ill. Interpretations of the same encounter vary among cultures. In the United States, a black cat crossing one's path is often considered a sign of bad luck, while in Britain it can have the opposite meaning.

ASTRAGALOMANCY: Divination by throwing dice dates back to ancient Egypt, and many systems have been passed down through the centuries. (In case you're wondering where it got its name, it's from the Greek word *astragalos*, which refers to the knucklebone or vertebra of an animal, the original material from which dice were made.) A simple system, explained in a medieval booklet, involved three dice. Tossing three sixes meant your wishes would come true. Two sixes and a two indicated success, but with hardship. A six and two fours meant forget it—what you wished for was a bad idea and should be abandoned.

BIBLIOMANCY: All you need is a book. The diviner poses a question, opens a book at random, and, with eyes closed, points to a spot on the page. The sentence or paragraph where the finger rests is then taken as an answer—or at least a commentary on the question. The Bible was the book of choice for centuries, but later the classics—Homer, Virgil, and Shakespeare—became more popular. Most any book is worth a try—even this one.

CEROMANCY: This ancient and widely practiced system relies on wax melted in a brass bowl. The hot wax was slowly poured into another bowl filled with cold water. As the wax hit the water it congealed into various shapes that were interpreted by the seer. Standard interpretations were compiled over the centuries, resulting in a system anyone could learn. The same interpretations were later applied to tasseomancy, the reading of tea leaves.

GEOMANCY: A handful of loose dirt is cupped between the palms and gently tossed to the ground. The seer interprets the patterns it forms. In a later version, called paper geomancy, the diviner poses a question and, with eyes closed, taps the point of a pencil onto a sheet of paper, making random marks. After whatever feels like the appropriate amount of time, the procedure is ended and the patterns are interpreted.

HYDROMANCY: Water was an important element in several forms of divination. In one method, practiced in ancient Greece, three stones were dropped one at a time into a pool of still water. The first stone was round, the second triangular, and the third square. The diviner studied the patterns of concentric ripples and looked for images or reflections that could be interpreted.

MYOMANCY: Divination based on the appearance, color, and sounds of mice. A wide variety of predictions, from wars to famines, were based on the direct observation of mice and sometimes rats, as well as on the telltale signs of their presence, such as footprints or teeth marks. The Roman historian Herodotus reported the defeat of an army following an infestation of rats. This seems to have been more a practical matter than a prediction, however, since the rats ate through the quivers and bows of the soldiers, leaving them virtually weaponless.

PADOMANCY: Similar to palmistry, except that it is the soles of the feet that are interpreted. This system of divination was widely used in ancient China.

XYLOMANCY: Patterns made by fallen tree limbs, branches, twigs, or other pieces of wood lying on the ground were studied and interpreted by the seers of biblical times. At first, only branches that had fallen naturally were used. In a later system, branches were stripped of half of their bark and tossed to the ground, forming a random pattern. Those that fell bare wood up were interpreted.

A Brief History of Tarot

Although the striking appearance and mysterious images of tarot cards might make you think they were made for telling fortunes, they were originally just a pretty deck of playing cards. Created in the fifteenth century, they were used to play a popular game called *tarrochi* (thus the name *tarot*), a distant relative of the modern game of bridge. The cards' colorful depictions of such varied characters and scenes as the Hermit, the Juggler, the Hanged Man, the Chariot, the Priestess, and the Castle suggest that they may also have been used to tell stories.

Tarot cards first became associated with fortune telling in the 1770s, after a Frenchman named Antoine Court de Gebelin came up with a very elaborate and completely mistaken theory about their origin and meaning. De Gebelin believed tarot cards had been created in ancient Egypt and were a source of secret wisdom. Although any connection to Egypt was later disproved, this fanciful theory brought new attention to the tarot. In 1785, a professional card reader named Jean-Baptiste Alliette published the first complete system for telling fortunes using tarot cards. He also produced an original deck of his own design and assigned specific meanings to each of the cards. Alliette taught his method to more than 150 students and helped to launch the tarot on its way to becoming one of the best-known systems of divination in the world.

Swiss tarot cards from about 1800: the Chariot, the Tower, and the Hanged Man.

Dragons

The heroes of Western legend have faced a vast assortment of fiends and monsters, but only a select few have dared challenge the mightiest of them all—the enormous fire-breathing dragon. More than just another conquest, in many tales the dragon represents the ultimate step in a hero's quest for greatness. Facing the temperamental Hungarian Horntail is thus a truly fitting challenge for Harry in his pursuit of the Triwizard Championship.

Dragons have been featured players in myth and folklore for most of recorded history. In the West, they appeared in the early literature of Babylonia, Egypt, Greece, Rome, Germany, Scandinavia, and the British Isles. The list of warriors who've done battle with dragons reads like a *Who's Who* of heroes. The Greek and Roman hero Hercules slew several dragons in his long career, most notably the Hydra, who had nine venomous heads. Various Babylonian warriors battled Tiamat, a dragon known as the Queen of Darkness, who had the head and forelegs of a lion, the hind legs of an eagle, feathery wings, and a scaled body impervious to all weapons. The Norse thunder god Thor succumbed to the venom of the Midgard Serpent, a huge dragon that encircled the entire Earth, but not before dealing the creature a fatal blow. Beowulf, considered one of the first heroes of English literature, also met his death while slaying a dragon, and medieval knights made dragon hunting a fairly common pastime.

Physical descriptions of dragons remain fairly consistent from tale to tale. Generally depicted as enormous serpents (the Greek word *drakon* means "huge serpent"), dragons tended to be armored with impenetrable scales and equipped with one or two pairs of legs and a set of batlike wings. Most had wedge-shaped heads and long, sometimes poisonous, fangs. Some also sported twin horns, enormous claws, and a forked or barbed tail. Welsh dragons were often red, German dragons were white, and others came in black or yellow.

Almost all dragons had one thing in common—their scorching breath. The enormous fireballs the creatures could unleash at will were more than just a hazard for brave knights: They were said to devastate entire countries! And when a hero was clever enough to avoid the flames and slay his foe, a dragon could prove dangerous even after death. Dragon's blood was said to be deadly to the touch, and dragon's teeth, if planted in the earth, were alleged to grow a crop of armed and bloodthirsty warriors. (The modern expression, "sowing dragon's teeth," means causing a war.)

Such a threatening beast was bound to be perceived as the natural enemy of mankind. Dragons were said to be crafty, gluttonous, and cruel creatures who lived in huge caves or the craters of volcanoes, as well as in lakes and oceans. Periodically, they would satisfy their hunger by feasting on livestock or people. In many legends, a dragon would kidnap a young maiden and spirit her away, sometimes to make a meal of her, sometimes simply to share her company. Although they had no need for money, dragons were also famous for their greed, maintaining enormous hoards of gold, silver, and other treasures. (Sea dragons were apt to hoard pearls.) A dragon was said to know the exact composition of its stash, and to realize instantly, and react violently, if even a single coin was taken.

During the Middle Ages, dragons came to be associated with the biblical serpent responsible for the expulsion of mankind from the Garden of Eden and were portrayed in art and literature as representatives of sin, wickedness, and sometimes even the Devil himself. The classical struggle of knight against dragon therefore represented the larger battle of good against evil. Many Christian saints were said to have encountered dragons. One of the

Dragons of the East

Any dragon to wing his way from Europe to China or Japan would experience some serious culture shock. Instead of finding himself loathed, feared, and attacked, he'd be welcomed with a smile. For in the East, the dragon has always been viewed as a benevolent creature and sign of good fortune.

Unlike their Western cousins, Eastern dragons don't breathe fire or have wings, although they can usually fly by magic. A typical Eastern dragon has the horns of a stag, the head of a camel, the neck of a snake, the claws of an eagle, the ears of a bull, and long whiskers on his face. In Chinese legends, there are dragons who guard the skies, dragons who bring rain, and dragons who control rivers and streams. In Japan, where they are widely considered to be wise, kind, and helpful, dragons have served as the official emblem of the imperial family for centuries.

most famous was St. George, who was reportedly traveling near Silena, Libya, when he heard of a dragon that lived in a local lake. Like many of its kind, the dragon enjoyed feasting on maidens, and it refused to allow the townspeople access to their only water supply unless they fed it a maiden each day. Entire armies had been slaughtered trying to fight the creature. On the day St. George arrived, the king's daughter, the only remaining maiden in the land, was to be sacrificed. St. George gallantly offered to fight the dragon and succeeded in killing it with a single strike of his lance.

The success of St. George was much admired, especially after he was made patron saint of England in the fourteenth century. Dragons

became associated with chivalry and romance, and any literary knight worth his salt had to slay a fire-breathing beast and rescue a fair maiden to be considered a true hero. In the legends of King Arthur, both Lancelot and Tristan, sometimes cited as the most gallant knights of the Round Table, were dragon slayers. Tradition holds that such brave souls, eager to prove their Christian faith and heroism, were responsible for the eventual extinction of dragons. Charlie Weasley would no doubt tell you otherwise.

 SS 14/230

Dreams

Some people have trouble remembering their dreams, but that's never a problem for Harry. Whether he's sleeping soundly on Privet Drive or dozing off during Professor Trelawney's class, Harry has dreams that give him plenty to ponder during waking hours. Vivid and frightening, some seem to foretell future perils; others offer an unwanted glimpse of horrific events occurring at the very moment Harry has the dream. Such nightmares are not easily ignored.

From the Bible to the epic poems of India, early writings suggest that people have always been fascinated by their dreams. In antiquity, it was widely believed that dreams contained important information, often in the form of predictions about the future of the dreamer, his or her family or village, or—especially if the dreamer was a king—the fate

of an entire nation. Sometimes a dream's message is perfectly clear, as it is with many of Harry's most intense and scary dreams. But often, the meaning is hidden or disguised, requiring the services of an interpreter.

Dream interpretation, or oneiromancy (from the Greek *oneiros,* meaning "dream," and *mancy,* meaning "prophecy") is one of the oldest systems of **divination.** In ancient times, it was always considered a job for a professional—usually a priest or priestess or someone known simply as a dream interpreter, whose only job was to listen to people's dreams and explain their meanings, sometimes offering advice on what course of action, if any, the dreamer should take. Systems of dream interpretation are referred to in the earliest of all recorded literature, the myths of the Assyrian hero King Gilgamesh, which were inscribed on clay tablets around the seventh century B.C. In ancient Egypt, dream interpreters were known as "the learned men of the magic library" and resided in temples where the god of dreams, Serapis, was worshipped.

Special locations were designated not only for dream interpretation but also for dreaming itself. Many people hoped that solutions to problems that eluded them during their waking hours might be revealed in a dream sent by the gods, provided the right procedures were followed. In an effort to receive helpful dreams, ancient Egyptians were known to sleep in the shadow of the **Sphinx** or spend the night in one of the temples of Serapis. In the event that a dream seeker couldn't make the journey himself, it was permissible to hire a surrogate dreamer to sleep at the temple and have a dream on his employer's behalf! Similarly, a citizen of ancient Greece seeking relief from poor health might travel to one of several temples dedicated to Asclepius, the god of medicine, in the hope of receiving a dream that would diagnose his illness and suggest a cure. In medieval Japan, a pilgrim could stay at a dream shrine for one hundred days or more, adhering to a restricted diet and a rigid schedule of prayers in hope of receiving an enlightening dream.

Investigating the meaning of one's dreams became much simpler when books on the subject became available. The first comprehensive dream guide was the *Oneirocritica,* or *The Interpretation of Dreams,* written in the second century A.D. by the Greek dream interpreter Artemidorus of Daldianus. It contained the meanings of hundreds of different dreams and dream symbols and remained the most important book on the subject for more than a thousand years. Some of the interpretations sound quite sensible even today, for example, "all tools that cut and divide things in half signify disagreements, factions, and injuries. . . ." Others, such as the warning that it's bad luck to dream of winged ants or quail, probably reflect the superstitions of the time.

Dream interpretation has gone in and out of fashion over the centuries, and it's always had its skeptics, among them the philosopher Aristotle, who asserted that when dreams come true, it's only due to coincidence. And while many citizens of ancient Rome were busy buying **amulets** and magic **potions** and telling their dreams to turbaned diviners, the orator Cicero complained that dream divination was nothing but superstition, and that the public had been "betrayed . . . into endless imbecilities." Still, many people throughout history have reported dreams like Harry's that do come true, or appear to reveal information the dreamer could not possibly have known through normal channels. Indeed, one of the characteristics of legendary magicians and tribal shamans is that they can supposedly see what's going on elsewhere, either in dreams, by entering a visionary trance, or through the use of a **crystal ball.**

But regardless of whether dreams truly reveal the future, or allow us to mystically travel to distant places to eavesdrop on our friends or enemies, they can be valuable in other ways. Many famous people have found their dreams to be a wellspring of creative ideas and brilliant solutions to problems. The writer Mary Shelley claimed that the immortal characters of Dr. Frankenstein and his monster came to her in a dream; the novelist Bram Stoker said the same thing about his most famous creation, the **vampire** Count Dracula. And the nineteenth-century chemist Dmitri Mendeleyev, after struggling unsuccessfully with a system for categorizing the chemical elements, "saw in a dream a table where all the elements fell into place as required" and, on waking, came up with the periodic table of the elements every chemistry student studies today.

Modern thinkers, such as Carl Jung and Sigmund Freud, argued that the true significance of dreams lies not in what they reveal about the outside world, but in what they can tell us about ourselves. Freud believed dreams express our deepest wishes, while Jung said all the fascinating, scary, or helpful characters in dreams are aspects of our own minds. In any case, you don't have to be an accomplished dream analyst to realize that the dream world, like the wizarding world, is a unique place where anything can happen. We can experience scenes of dazzling splendor or monstrous horror and everything in between. In dreams we fly, hover in the air, achieve feats of superhuman strength, or experience transformations as amazing as those produced by Professor Snape's most powerful potions. Which may be why, when we read about magic, or watch as it's performed on stage, it sometimes seems strangely familiar. And for good reason. We've seen it all before in our dreams.

 GF 2/17

Dwarf

Delivering singing valentines to teenaged **wizards** is hardly the usual line of work for a dwarf. Legend holds that these bearded little tough guys spend most of their days laboring underground, where they mine for iron and precious metals. Since they take pride in hard work, it's no wonder they go about their frivolous business at Hogwarts with the air of children being forced to eat Brussels sprouts.

In the folklore of Germany and Scandinavia, dwarfs are a race of small supernatural beings who guard magnificent treasures buried deep

inside the earth. Although they have the power to become invisible or assume any shape, they usually look like small men with large heads, wizened faces, long gray beards, and misshapen legs and feet. Social creatures, they live in communities inside mountains, caverns, or dazzling underground palaces. Because they dress in drab colors, they blend in easily with rocks and shrubs, enabling them to come and go from their subterranean homes unseen by human eyes. In the lore of certain regions, dwarfs, like **trolls,** turn to stone if exposed to sunlight.

Dwarfs are gifted metalworkers, and their magic powers lead them to the richest lodes of precious metals for their craft. The more artistic dwarfs work in fine gold and silver, fashioning jewelry and decorative objects said to be more beautiful than any made by human hands. Others forge iron into dangerous weapons endowed with magical powers. Thor, the Norse god of thunder, wisely chose dwarfs to manufacture his most important tool—a mighty hammer that, when thrown, caused lightening to flash and then returned to its owner's hand. Dwarfs also worked for Odin, the supreme Norse god, for whom they created a magic spear that always hit its target.

In some parts of Germany, miners are said to encounter dwarfs on occasion, usually when they break through an underground wall into a dwarf workshop or palace. Provided the humans aren't rude, dwarfs take no offense at such intrusions, and may even provide some advice on where to find the best veins of ore. Dwarfs may also sound the alarm when there is danger in the mine from a build-up of noxious gases or a collapsing roof. However, if the little men have not been shown proper

respect, they may actually *cause* such catastrophes. Should a miner be so foolhardy as to steal from the dwarfs' hoard of gold and jewels, not only will he suffer great misfortune, but when he gets home and opens his bag, all the treasure will have turned to leaves.

Because they live for several hundred years and can see the future, dwarfs are thought to be very wise. According to legend, in some German towns dwarfs once shared their wisdom with humans, offering advice, telling stories, and lending a hand with household chores in exchange for a warm place to sleep during the long winter months. They abandoned this practice, however, when the villagers got too curious about their tiny guests' feet, which were always kept hidden beneath floor-length coats. Wanting to know what the dwarfs were hiding, homeowners dusted their floors with ashes, hoping the little men would leave telltale footprints. Instead, the dwarfs, who were very sensitive about their appearance, got angry and left town, returning forever to their underground homes. We've heard some say that dwarfs have the feet of a goose, a crow, or a goat; others claim they have human feet put on backward—but these are only rumors.

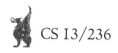 CS 13/236

Elf

Alternatingly infuriating and endearing, Dobby the house elf is a credit to his species. When Harry first sees the tiny figure clothed in nothing but a tea towel, he isn't very impressed. But when Aunt Petunia's cake lies smashed to bits on the kitchen floor and there's no one but Harry to take the blame, Harry quickly learns that elves can work some powerful magical mischief.

Because elves appear in the folklore of many nations, they come in all shapes and sizes. Most are said to resemble slender humans in their

natural state, but they can change shape or vanish in the blink of an eye. An elf may be small enough to sleep under a toadstool or large enough to pass for human. The dark elves of Germany are said to be hideous, while Danish elves are renowned for their beauty. In English folklore, male elves are usually described as wizened old men, yet females are lovely, golden-haired maidens.

Elves of all nations specialize in using their supernatural powers to intervene in human lives. Although we've never heard of any quite like Dobby and his friends, who are bound to serve human masters and beat themselves up for disobedient behavior, many elves willingly devote themselves to helping out around the house. In the fairy tale "The Shoemaker and His Elves," for example, two elves come to the aid of a poor, hungry shoemaker by fashioning beautiful shoes each night from the leather the cobbler lays out before going to bed. But when the shoemaker and his wife show their gratitude by leaving out a set of tiny new clothes for each elf, the elves squeal with delight, don their new outfits, and promptly depart, never to be seen again.

The Elf's New Clothes

Why does the "gift" of a dirty old sock set Dobby free? While we don't claim to know all the rules governing human—house elf relations, we do know that household fairies have always had a strong reaction to new clothes. Some, like the shoemaker's elves, are overjoyed at the sight of fancy duds, while many others seem to find such gifts offensive. Either way, the result is the same: Leave out a new shirt or shoes for your elf, **pixie,** or brownie (see **boggart**), and you guarantee he'll be gone by morning, never to return.

Explanations for this odd behavior vary from place to place. In some British folklore, household fairies are said to be free spirits who simply don't want to be encumbered by earthly belongings. In the English county of Berwickshire, they say that brownies leave when given any gift because God appointed them as the servants of mankind, bound to work without payment. But in Lincolnshire the opposite is true; there brownies are proud creatures who will depart when gifts don't measure up to their expectations. One story tells of a brownie who took to the road after receiving a shirt of coarse fabric, but not before making it known that he'd have stayed if the shirt were linen! Clearly, Dobby has no such reservations.

This may seem like a rude response to a kind gesture, but it's mild compared to some of the tricks elves play. Indeed, it's hard to find an elf (even a house elf) without a mischievous streak, and some are downright mean. In the folklore of Iceland and Germany, elves steal babies, rustle cattle, pilfer food, and cause diseases in humans and livestock. They also sit on people as they sleep, causing bad dreams (the

German word for "nightmare" is *Alpdrücken,* or "elf pressure"), and enchant young men, sometimes holding them spellbound for years on end. The well-known American story of Rip Van Winkle, who sleeps for two decades, is based on this old folk belief.

In England, malicious elves were blamed for so many ills that a whole vocabulary developed to describe their evil deeds. During the Middle Ages, people or animals who died suddenly from mysterious ailments were said to have been "elf shot," or struck by the arrow of an elf. Proof that such vicious attacks did occur was offered in the form of "elf arrows," small flint arrowheads found in the countryside (which we now know were made by Stone Age men, not elves). People born with birth defects were said to be "elf marked," and someone who suffered a paralyzing or deforming stroke was "elf twisted." Even tangled hair was blamed on elves, who were said to turn smooth tresses into knotted "elf locks."

 CS 2/12

Fairy

The **pixies** who run rampant in Gilderoy Lockhart's classroom, the **leprechauns** who shower the Quidditch field with gold, and the house **elves** who labor in the Hogwarts kitchen all belong to a larger family known as fairies. Frequently referred to as the "little people," the "wee folk," the "good folk," or the "good neighbors," fairies make up a vast international community of immortal, supernatural beings who are only occasionally seen by humans. Although they are best known in their British forms, these magical creatures figure prominently in the folklore of countries throughout the world, from Sweden to Iran to

The Tooth Fairy

Today, no fairy is better known or loved than the Tooth Fairy. In the United States and parts of Great Britain, Canada, and Spain, she is said to visit in the night, leaving money or small gifts in return for "baby teeth" placed under a child's pillow.

Although tales of the Tooth Fairy have only been around since the early twentieth century (and no one knows quite where they began), the association of teeth with treats is much older. More than a thousand years ago, Viking children received a "tooth fee"—a present of some kind—when their first tooth grew in. A more recent predecessor to the Tooth Fairy was the Tooth Mouse, a creature beloved by nineteenth-century European children, who placed their teeth inside mouse holes, under kitchen shelves, and anywhere else a mouse might find them. Not only did these lucky children receive candy or coins from the Tooth Mouse, but legend held that their new teeth would be as sharp as those of their tiny benefactor!

China. Many of us are familiar with fairies from modern children's stories, where they most often appear as tiny, good-humored people with generous hearts. In centuries past, however, fairy beliefs encompassed a great range of beings large and small, nasty and nice, frightening and funny, beautiful and ugly—from the murderous **red cap** of the Scottish borderlands to Cinderella's kindly fairy godmother.

The word for "fairy" comes from the Latin *fata*, or fate, referring to the mythical Fates, three women who spin the threads of life, controlling each person's destiny from birth to death. Like the fates, fairies were thought to be active participants in the lives of mortals, helping

them out when they were so inclined but also delivering large doses of pain and misery. During the Middle Ages, fairies took the blame for a wide array of physical ailments, from skin rashes to tuberculosis. Bruises, cramps, and the pains of rheumatism were attributed to the pinching fingers of angry, invisible fairies. Those struck down by heart attacks, paralysis, or mysterious illnesses were said to have been "elf shot," as if wounded by an invisible elf arrow. Mothers were warned to never leave their newborns out of sight, lest a fairy steal the infant and leave a sickly fairy baby, known as a changeling, in its place.

By the mid-sixteenth century, fear of fairies had been replaced by fear of **witches,** and fairies, while they could be mischievous pranksters like the **hinkypunk,** were more often thought of as benevolent and usually imaginary fun-loving creatures who were well disposed to humans. Fairy lore, which is vast and varied, tells of woodland kingdoms inhabited by tiny creatures clothed in exquisite fabrics of blue, green, and gold. Although they usually resemble the fairest of humans, fairies can shift shape to look like animals or become invisible at will. Great lovers of music, they dance round mushrooms and toadstools by the light of the moon, accompanied by tiny flutes and harps. Several old Scottish folk songs are said to be fairy tunes that were taught to mortal pipers lured into Fairyland by the beautiful melodies. Humans who are enticed to enter a fairy kingdom usually become lost in time, so that when they emerge, years have passed in the blink of an eye. But mortals who set out to search for Fairyland rarely find it, for legend has it that the realm of fairies is discovered only by chance.

Not all fairies favor an idyllic life of leisure. Many folktales tell of household fairies—brownies, pixies, and some elves—who prefer living among humans and are glad to assist with chores in exchange for a nightly bowl of cream or a morsel of cake. Knowledge of fairy etiquette is essential to anyone who lives with the little people, since they are easily offended. If you fail to keep your hearth clean or try to pay

your fairies for their services, they may express their displeasure by over-turning garbage pails, smashing dishes, or causing the cow to go dry. Such temper tantrums are best overlooked, however, since—then, as now—good help is hard to find.

PA 10/189

The Cottingley Fairies

In July 1918, two young girls from rural Cottingley, England, produced what appeared to be the world's first photograph of actual fairies. The picture, taken by sixteen-year-old Elsie Wright, showed her cousin, Frances Griffiths, sitting in the forest with several tiny, winged people flitting about her. Elsie's father, who developed the film, did not believe in fairies and told the girls so, suggesting gently that they had staged the scene. But the girls insisted that they had seen fairies in the woods many times. A month later, they produced a second picture, this time of Elsie posing with a **gnome**.

Elsie's father remained skeptical, but her mother mentioned the pictures to friends who had an interest in the supernatural. From there the story spread quickly, ultimately coming to the attention of one of the most famous writers of the era—Sir Arthur Conan Doyle, creator of the great detective Sherlock Holmes. Fascinated by the possibility that fairies were real, Doyle and other interested parties consulted a variety of experts to find out if the photographs had been faked. Although some commented that the fairies' hairstyles looked too "modern," no one could produce conclusive evidence of fraud. In December 1919, Doyle published an article in the *Strand* magazine entitled "Fairies Photographed—An Epoch-Making Event," which met with tremendous excitement from believers, as well as brutal criticism from skeptics. Further fuel was added to the fire when, in 1920, the girls took three more fairy photographs.

The debate over the authenticity of the Cottingley fairies raged for the next several decades. At last, in the early 1980s, both Elsie and Frances admitted that the pictures were a hoax. They had constructed the fairies out of paper and used hatpins to secure them to tree branches or to the ground. Frances remembered being shocked that anyone had believed their stories. After all, she pointed out, the pins were visible in some of the pictures—yet somehow no one noticed.

Frances Griffiths and her fairy friends, photographed by her cousin Elsie Wright in 1918.
It was not until the 1980s that the cousins admitted they had perpetrated a hoax.

Fairy Rings

It's long been said that fairies leave evidence of their nightly revelry. According to British folklore, when fairies dance under the stars, in the morning the spot will be marked by a circle of bright green or matted-down grass known as a "fairy ring." A wish made while standing in the center of a fairy ring under a full moon is guaranteed to come true.

But beware of stepping into a fairy ring while the fairies are still celebrating! Any human who does so will be compelled to dance to the point of exhaustion. The only means of escape is to be rescued by a friend, who, keeping one foot firmly on the outside of the ring, reaches in and pulls the captive out.

Mysterious rings of discolored grass really do exist across Europe and North America, often appearing after heavy rains. They can range in diameter from a few inches to as much as two hundred feet. However, scientists insist that they're caused by a class of fungi known as *Basidomycetes*, and not by fairies after all.

Flying Carpet

Flying carpets may be outlawed by the Ministry of Magic, but that hasn't kept these wondrous tapestries out of the hands of some of the Far East's most powerful **wizards** and **magicians**.

The earliest stories about magic carpets appear in connection with King Solomon. The son of David (of David and Goliath fame) and Bathsheba, Solomon is traditionally regarded as ancient Israel's greatest ruler. According to the Old Testament's Book of Kings, he was both a skilled politician and a ferocious warrior. With his mighty armies, he carved out an empire that stretched all the way from Egypt to the Euphrates River in Iraq. An unusually wise and just king, he cherished beauty, wrote exquisite poetry, and built spectacular temples and palaces.

Solomon's achievements were so impressive that, after his death, many ancient Jewish and Islamic writers came to believe he was a powerful magician. The Muslim holy book, The Koran, claims that Solomon could "speak the tongue of birds" and command the actions of angels and genies (known as *jinn*), and "was endowed with all good things." Later Arabic storytellers expanded on this tradition, giving the Israelite king a magic ring and **cauldron,** the power to control the wind, and a magnificent flying carpet that would carry him wherever he desired.

Descriptions of Solomon's flying carpet vary greatly from story to story, but most writers agree that it was made of fine green silk and was very, very large—perhaps as wide as sixty miles across. According to the nineteenth-century explorer and scholar Richard Burton, "its length and breadth were such that all the Wise King's host could stand upon

it, the men to the left and Jinns to the right of the throne." Once Solomon's army was comfortably settled on the rug, "the Wind at royal command, raised it and wafted it whither the Prophet [Solomon] would, while an army of birds flying overhead canopied the host from the sun."

Solomon's miraculous carpet was clearly the inspiration for the later, more modest flying tapestries found in many Arabic folk tales, such as "The Story of Prince Ahmed and the Fairy Paribanou." In this popular Persian fable from *The Arabian Nights*, a young prince named Houssain accidentally stumbles across an amazing "piece of tapestry" that can transport its owner anywhere in the world. With this carpet Houssain is able to save the life of his beloved princess, instantly delivering a magical apple to her bedside when he learns that she lies dying hundreds of miles away.

Perhaps because carpets were not widely used in Europe and North America until the late nineteenth century, the flying variety have never played a central role in Western mythology and folklore. (Indeed, most Westerners mistakenly associate flying carpets primarily with the story of Aladdin, a tale in which they never actually appear.) Instead of flying rugs, Western magicians and heroes have relied on a host of other levitating objects ranging from winged sandals to hovering suitcases to great glass elevators. One popular American children's story even features a flying sofa. And then, of course, there are **broomsticks,** such as Harry's beloved Firebolt, which could probably fly rings around any carpet foolish enough to float onto a Quidditch field. It's just too bad most broomsticks are single-passenger vehicles. If Harry ever amasses an army like King Solomon's (or gets a date with Cho Chang), he'll have to borrow the keys to Mr. Weasley's flying car.

GF 7/91

Forbidden Forest

Each time Harry enters the Forbidden Forest, he feels a certain sense of dread. And well he should, for he and his classmates have been warned repeatedly of the dangers that lurk within the dark woods. Just as the forests of our favorite fairy tales are populated by **witches** and ogres, **goblins** and **trolls,** so the Hogwarts wood is alive with monsters of every description. What makes these places so frightening—and also so exciting—is that you never know what lurks behind the next tree.

The forest has always been associated with risk—the perils of getting lost, encountering evil strangers, or being devoured by wild beasts. In the first century B.C., Julius Caesar wrote of travelers who walked through a terrible forest for sixty days without ever coming to its edge, eventually emerging to describe encounters with bizarre creatures that had long been extinct elsewhere. To the ancient Romans, the clearing and cultivation of land and the construction of cities represented the triumph of civilization over barbarism. A pleasing landscape was one that had been shaped by the hand of man, while the untamed wilderness was viewed as ugly and frightful. The best way the Roman historian Tacitus knew to distinguish his cultured countrymen from the Germans they despised was to note that their foes were "forest dwellers."

Centuries later in England, views of the forest were much the same. The woods were thought to be the proper home of animals rather than men, and any man who dwelt in them was assumed to be crude and brutal. A seventeenth-century philosopher contrasted "civil and rational," city dwellers with the "irrational, untaught" inhabitants of woods and forests. (Some folks at Hogwarts seem to hold the same opinion about Hagrid, who is in many ways a creature of the forest and lives on its edge.) The forest stood for all that was strange, suspicious, and outside the boundaries of normal human experience. Indeed, the English words "foreign" and "forest" both derive from the same Latin root, *foris,* meaning "outside."

To those of us who enjoy a pleasant walk in the woods or a camping trip now and then, such negative assessments of the forest may seem harsh. But they did have some basis in reality. In medieval and early modern Europe, forests were often populated by vagrants and outlaws who had little respect for life or law. For anyone who wanted to hide from the authorities or conduct illicit business, a densely wooded area provided an ideal place to avoid detection. This bit of history helps to explain why so many fairy tales contain characters like the witch who captures Hansel and Gretel or Little Red Riding Hood's big bad wolf—sinister villains who lurk in the woods, waiting to prey upon the innocent. It is therefore very much in keeping with tradition that Lord Voldemort chooses to dwell in the forest while regaining his strength.

85

 SS 7/127

Ghost

Have you ever wondered where ghosts really come from? Or why some dearly departed souls, like Moaning Myrtle and Professor Binns, float about the earth, while others simply slumber away in a nice, peaceful grave? If you have, you're not alone. Ghosts and ghost stories have played an important role in the folklore, literature, and religion of virtually every civilization.

Ghosts manifest themselves in many forms. The most basic and universal type of ghost is the apparition, or disembodied spirit. Some apparitions appear to be composed of a pale mistlike vapor; but many others resemble perfectly normal, flesh-and-blood human beings. European folklore is filled with tales of all-too-human-looking ghosts, who eat, drink, and carry out most of the standard bodily functions of living people. Often, the ghostly nature of such specters is revealed only by their uncanny ability to vanish into thin air, or by the odd musty or rotting odor that some ghosts leave behind.

In ancient Greece and Rome, the spirits of the dead often took the form of dark shadows, strange black patches, or invisible, **poltergeist**-like presences. The ancient Egyptians believed the dead could return in their own reanimated bodies, and many other cultures have believed that ghosts could appear as **demons,** animals, and even plants.

Most ancient societies, in both the Eastern and Western world, took it for granted that ghosts were a very real—and very natural—phenomenon, and many cultures held festivals throughout the year to maintain good relations with the dead. Perhaps the strangest ancient festival of the dead was the Roman feast of Lemuralia, held every spring. During Lemuralia, Roman homeowners would get up in the middle of night and march around their living rooms, strewing a trail of black beans behind them. "With these beans," the men would intone seriously, "I buy back myself and my family." They would circle the room, trailing their beans and repeating this phrase nine times, to ensure that the spirits of the dead had plenty of time to gather up their offerings. Then the homeowner performing the ritual would clash a heavy bronze cymbal and cry out "spirits of my ancestors depart," after which all restless ghosts were believed to go quietly away until the following year.

As the relatively friendly character of this ritual indicates, most ancient ghosts were not so much feared, as honored. Today, however, most ghost lore—whether presented as fact or fiction—depicts ghosts

as frightening, unnatural creatures, who only appear when the spirit of
a dead person is restless or uneasy for some reason. Some restless spirits, like the character of Jacob Marley in Charles Dickens' *A Christmas
Carol,* are doomed to haunt mankind because of the sins they committed in life. Others walk the Earth because they have met with some sort
of violent or unexpected end. Beamish Hall, in County Durham, En-

gland, for example, is said to be haunted by the ghost of an unfortunate young woman who suffocated to death while hiding in a trunk. (Legend has it she was trying to avoid an unwanted, arranged marriage. One can only hope that her fiancé was really as bad as she thought!)

Most of the ghosts at Hogwarts clearly suffered similarly brutal or tragic ends. Nearly Headless Nick's gruesome demise may actually have been inspired by the case of the fourteenth-century Earl of Lancaster, who is said to haunt England's Dunstanburgh Hall in retaliation for his own botched beheading. According to witnesses, it took an inexperienced executioner eleven ax strokes to sever the Earl's head from his body, and even hardened soldiers fainted at the sight!

Once a ghost has been set loose on the world, it is usually required to roam around, haunting houses or loitering in cemeteries, until its spirit has been avenged or set free. The most popular way to get rid of an unwanted spirit is to hire a professional exorcist, or "ghost releaser," but some ghosts will disappear if you simply rebury their bones at a crossroads. Since ghosts have a notoriously poor sense of direction, this little trick will usually disorient them for eternity. If all else fails, you may eventually get used to having a ghost around. After all, there are far worse things than getting invited to a good deathday party once in a while.

SS 7/115

Ghoul

Someone who loves the loathsome, revels in the revolting, and delights in the disgusting may properly be said to have "ghoulish" tastes. That's because ghouls are best known for digging up corpses and eating rotting human flesh. That said, we can't imagine why a ghoul chooses to hang out in the Weasleys' attic. It makes you wonder what they keep up there.

Although they have a home in Western folklore, ghouls (or *ghuls*) first sprang to life in the ancient legends of the Arab Muslim world, where they belonged to a rebellious breed of evil spirits. Primarily desert dwellers—though they also lurk in caves, wander in the wilderness, and sniff out sites where humans have recently died—ghouls and their cannibalistic, grave-robbing ways are feared throughout northern Africa, the Middle East, and India. While they eagerly consume any corpses they come across, most ghouls are not truly happy unless they do a little killing of their own.

A ghoul can't be described with any precision. Some tales say it looks like a camel, an ox, a horse, or a one-eyed ostrich. Others tell of a creature with shaggy, matted hair covering its eyes. Its "true" appearance matters little, however, since the ghoul is a constant shapeshifter and can easily transform into any guise that will attract the human eye. Sometimes it takes the form of a solitary traveler who claims to know a shortcut, thus enticing a real traveler into the desert, where he may be easily killed and eaten. The ghoul's favorite trick, however, is to appear as a beautiful woman, the ideal lure for a wandering male.

The truly vigilant traveler can protect himself by looking out for

the one ghoulish trait that can never be disguised—the feet. No matter what shape it takes, the ghoul will have the hoofs of a goat, camel, or donkey. Unfortunately, by the time a potential victim gets close enough to notice any mismatched body parts, the ghoul is usually ready to rip him apart and have him for supper. The traveler's only chance of escape will be to kill his attacker with a single blow to the head. A second blow, oddly enough, will only revive the ravenous ghoul, and it will not be pleased that its dinner plans were interrupted.

 CS 3/29

Giant

It can be hard to live down the reputation of your ancestors. No doubt that's why the enormous Madame Maxime insists that she's no giant—she just has "big bones." Giants have an age-old reputation for mindless cruelty, and as Hagrid discovers, most humans have little tolerance for their kind.

Giants feature in the earliest creation myths of many cultures, often as a race of enormous beings that existed even before the gods. Greek mythology tells of the Titans, giants as tall as mountains and tremendously strong. Born of a union between Earth and Sky, they were hideously ugly, with hairy faces, scaly feet, and in some cases multiple heads. In a struggle for supremacy, the Titans waged a war against the gods of Olympus that was so violent it almost destroyed the uni-

verse. With the help of Hercules, the mortal son of Zeus, the gods eventually won the battle and killed or imprisoned all of the Titans.

Giants play a similar role in Norse mythology, where the Frost Giants, led by the vicious Thrym (whose name means "uproar"), were the primary enemies of Thor and the other gods. In Celtic legend, evil giants called Fomorians were said to have been the first inhabitants of Ireland, and in some tales were associated with winter, fog, storms, disease, and poor crops. The Old Testament also mentions a race of giants, said to be the product of an unnatural union between fallen angels and humans. Biblical giants are not, however, quite as large as those of myth; the giant Goliath, who was famously killed by David with a slingshot, stood a mere nine and a half feet.

English folklore has long held a special place for giants, perhaps because of their importance in the nation's foundation myths. Geoffrey of Monmouth's *History of the Kings of Britain* (which is not a true history, but rather an account of the legendary beginnings of Britain) tells of a race of twelve-foot giants who could rip oak trees from the ground as if they were garden weeds. According to Geoffrey, these giants ruled England until they were defeated by the armies of Brutus, the mythical founder of the British race and great-grandson of the Trojan hero Aeneas.

During the Middle Ages, giants ranked with **dragons** as worthy opponents for chivalrous knights seeking adventure and glory. In the legends of King Arthur and other epic tales, giants represent all that is evil in the world: They are bloodthirsty, avaricious, gluttonous, and cruel. They kidnap women, steal from their neighbors, murder children, and sometimes even eat people. To kill a giant is thus an act of honor and goodness. In Sir Thomas Malory's *Le Morte d'Arthur* (*The Death of Arthur*, published in 1485), Sir Lancelot proves his honor at a young age by slaying a pair of vicious giants who have kept three damsels as their slaves for seven grueling years. The knight Marhaus wins riches and the gratitude of his peers by killing the giant Taulard and rescuing no fewer than twenty-four maidens and twelve knights from imprisonment. And King Arthur himself proves the most talented giant-killer of them all, besting the giant of Mont Saint-Michel, a cannibal who had vanquished fifteen kings and wore a coat embroidered with hair from their beards.

Giants continued to loom large in the popular imagination long after the age of chivalry had passed. In the eighteenth and nineteenth centuries, enormous men with enormous appetites—and in many cases a longing for ordinary-size wives—became a staple of European fairy tales. None were better known than those involving a brave, if somewhat foolhardy, young man named Jack. In "Jack the Giant-Killer," a tale that first appeared in print in the nineteenth century but was set in the time of King Arthur, Jack is an English farmer's son who makes a career of outwitting hapless giants. His first victim is an eighteen-footer named Cormoran who's been terrorizing nearby Cornwall, stealing and devouring so many sheep, hogs, and oxen that the people are left poor and starving. Jack digs a very deep hole in the ground, covers it with branches and leaves, and taunts the giant until he approaches and falls in, whereupon Jack strikes him dead. A series of similar triumphs earn Jack many rewards, including a large estate and the hand of a duke's daughter. In "Jack and the Beanstalk," a different Jack faces a giant who lives in a castle in the clouds (at the top of the beanstalk, of course), and famously mutters, "Fee, fi, fo, fum, I smell the blood of an Englishman," while a trembling Jack hides nearby.

Such a long history of bad behavior surely can't be attributed to just a few rotten apples, so it's hard to blame Hogwarts parents if they worry about their children taking lessons from a half-giant. But as Albus Dumbledore seems to know, judging an individual on the reputation of his or her kin can be misleading. In many modern stories, giants are actually kind beings who befriend and protect normal-size humans, especially children. They may suffer from painful physical ailments as result of their size, or feel isolated, awkward, or embarrassed because of it. We already know of some good giants, and there may well be more out there. If Dumbledore has his way, we may soon find out.

 GF 23/428

Gnome

These days, if you're looking for a gnome, you may need to go no further than the neighbor's front lawn. In Europe and in the United States, "garden gnomes"—cheerful plaster statues of bearded little men with pointed red hats—are popular outdoor ornaments. If your neighbors happen to be **wizards,** however, their gnomes will be far more animated than the plaster versions. In fact, as visitors to the Weasleys' vegetable patch know, gnomes can be giggly little pests who must be driven off like any other backyard intruders.

No one knows exactly how gnomes came to be associated with gardens. Some suggest that, as statuary, they first appeared as welcom-

ing figures at the entryways to grand buildings and then were adopted for more personal use. Another possibility is that the link emerged from folklore, where gnomes were traditionally associated with the earth.

In German lore, gnomes, like **dwarfs,** live underground, where they mine for precious metals and guard treasure. Remarkably, they can move through the earth in any direction without the benefit of a tunnel, just as a fish moves through water. Industrious and good-natured, they are usually depicted as being old and hunchbacked or otherwise misshapen. Their skin is always earth-toned (gray or brown), so they blend easily with their surroundings. If threatened, a gnome can literally dissolve into the ground or into a tree trunk.

Although there are plenty of tales of gnomes who enjoy the outside world, some authorities claim that gnomes turn to stone if exposed to the light of day. If that's the case, perhaps some of those decorative garden gnomes are simply the victims of too much sun.

 CS 3/36

Goblin

Open up the dictionary and you'll find "goblin" defined as a "mischievous and ugly **demon.**" Take one look at the clever and efficient goblins who run Gringotts Bank, however, and you'll know these magical beings have not always been cast in such an unflattering light. In medieval English folklore, goblins are usually portrayed as

helpful, if temperamental, imps or household spirits. Like Scottish brownies, French *gobelins*, and German *kobolds*, they frequently attach themselves to a specific person or family and move into their home. They are particularly fond of isolated farmhouses and cottages in the countryside.

Although goblins vary greatly in size, most are thought to be about half the size of an adult human. They have gray hair and beards, and their bodies or facial features tend to be grotesquely distorted in some way. They may have extra fingers or toes, missing ears, upside-down eyelids, or jointless limbs. Some goblins also have unusual speech defects, strange lisps or high-pitched, squeaky voices.

If they are well fed and well treated, most household goblins devote themselves to keeping things neat and orderly. They have a soft spot for children and will bring gifts to well-behaved youngsters. But beware the angry goblin! Once offended, they go to great lengths to seek their revenge. Some of the goblin's favorite pranks include stealing gold and silver, riding horses into exhaustion during the night, and altering signposts. According to many European fairy tales, a goblin's bitter smile can also curdle human blood, and his laugh can sour milk and cause fruit to fall from the trees. The only way to get rid of a household goblin is to cover your floors with flax seed. When he shows up ready to make trouble, he'll be compelled to first pick up all the seeds—a task that will be impossible to complete before dawn. A few nights of this tiresome business will be enough to convince him to find someone else to bother.

In their guise as bankers and moneylenders, the goblins of Harry Potter's world bear a striking resemblance to a mythical Scandinavian creature known as the *Nis*. According to Scandinavian folklore, these ugly little members of the **dwarf** family are especially skilled at handling money. When a Nis is angry with his human hosts, he often attacks whatever is most essential to their livelihood (killing off the cows on a dairy farm, for example). When he wants to reward them, he presents them with a chest of gold.

It was only in the seventeenth century, when anti-witchcraft hysteria swept across much of England and Scotland, that goblins became routinely associated with the forces of darkness and evil. Some later English fairy tales try to distinguish between good and bad household spirits by identifying to them as either goblins (who are clearly malicious) or hobgoblins, who are more benign and playful. The most famous hobgoblin by far is the literary character of Robin Goodfellow, also known as Puck, who appeared in dozens of stories and folktales from the late fifteenth century onward.

Well known as a friendly prankster who inhabited households and occasionally performed domestic tasks, in some tales Robin Goodfellow is also the personal servant and errand boy of the **fairy** king Oberon. He is blessed with the power of shape-shifting (see **Transfiguration**) and making wishes come true, and he uses his powers to punish the wicked and reward the good. Puck's most celebrated appearance is in Shakespeare's comedy *A Midsummer Night's Dream*, where he plays cupid to a group of star-crossed lovers lost in an enchanted forest. Laughing at the ridiculous antics of his victims, Puck merrily observes, "Lord, what fools these mortals be!"

SS 5/72

Grim

When Harry finds himself being followed around by an enormous black dog, he suspects the creature may be a grim, a spirit in the form of a menacing dog that has long been known in the

British Isles as an omen of death. Luckily, however, the beast turns out to be none other than Harry's godfather, Sirius Black, who can conveniently transform himself into a dog at will.

Unless there's a graveyard we don't know about at Hogwarts, Harry's fear that a grim was following him was probably unwarranted, for by most accounts grims never leave the churchyards or burial grounds they inhabit. In both British and Scandinavian folklore "grim" can be a general term for a household spirit, but it is more commonly used to refer to the "church grim," a guardian of dead souls that in England takes the form of a big, shaggy, black dog with fiery eyes. In Scandinavia, the church grim may also appear as a horse, lamb, or pig.

According to English tradition, the church grim bears the heavy responsibility of protecting a graveyard from the Devil and witches. In the early Christian era, many people believed that when a new churchyard was created the first person buried there would have to guard it against satanic influence. But some also believed that if a pure black dog

was buried in the northern part of the churchyard, the animal could stand guard instead, freeing a human soul to go on to the afterlife.

Grims are usually invisible, but during stormy weather they can be seen roaming about the churchyard. They may also appear at midnight on the night before a death, or standing in the church tower during a burial. It is said that the clergyman delivering a funeral service can tell from the grim's appearance whether the soul of the deceased is destined for heaven or hell.

 PA 6/107

Grindylow

Little does Harry realize when he first encounters a grindylow—pressing its hideous green face against the glass of the aquarium in Professor Lupin's office—that this experience will turn out to have a practical use. For these water **demons** of English folklore inhabit the Hogwarts lake, and Harry must face them as part of his second task in pursuit of the Goblet of Fire.

As genuine as grindylows may be in the wizarding world, no child over the age of ten in Yorkshire, the only region of England where grindylows are part of local folklore, would admit to believing in the nasty creatures. That's because grindylows fall into a special category of supernatural beings known as "nursery bogies." Never really taken seriously by adults, nursery bogies have been invented to scare children

away from dangerous or forbidden activities. *Don't go too close to the water, or the grindylow will pull you under and have you for supper!*

Because the grindylow is part of oral, rather than written, tradition, its physical characteristics are hard to pin down. However, if the grindylow looks anything like the water spirits Jenny Greenteeth and Peg Powler—its counterparts in other parts of England—then it has the face of a **hag,** with long green hair, green skin, pointy green fangs, and a gaping mouth. Perhaps it's Harry's advanced age that allows him to realize that despite such gruesome features, all it really takes to get rid of one of these pests is a swift kick in the head.

 PA 8/154

Hag

The British Isles are said to be populated by a great variety of hags. Some are benevolent spirits associated with harvests and spinning, others are witchlike figures who torment and even eat people. One is an ancient nature spirit, responsible for changing the weather and fashioning the natural landscape. But all of them have a few things in common—they are women, they are old, and they are hideous.

Hanging out with hags like those who frequent the Leaky Cauldron can be a dangerous business, since most have malice on their minds. They enjoy sitting on sleeping humans, causing nightmares and depriving their victims of breath. Someone who is "hag ridden" in this manner will awaken exhausted—if he is lucky enough to wake up at all. A flour sifter placed under the head prevents hag riding, since the hag is forced to pass through each hole in it, a feat that will take her all night.

The most famous hag in England is Black Annis, a one-eyed cannibal with blue skin, long white teeth, and claws of iron. She is said to dwell in the hills of Leicestershire, in a cave she carved from the rocky terrain with her own fingernails. In front of her cave stands a great old oak tree, in which she sits to survey the countryside in search of prey. When a tasty-looking child comes into sight, she swoops down and has a feast. When not in her tree, Black Annis is often seen sitting at the mouth of her cave, perched atop a pile of her victim's bones.

A Scotsman is more likely to recognize the Storm Hag, an ancient Celtic goddess also known as the Cailleach Bheare. Like Black Annis, the Storm Hag has a blue face and only one eye. She is distinguished by her white hair, which resembles dry, gnarled branches, and by the gray plaid dress she always wears. Closely associated with winter, she is said

Black Annis in her tree.

to usher in the season by washing her clothes in the Corrievreckan (literally "the speckled **cauldron**"), a great whirlpool off Scotland's western coast that can be extremely hazardous for ships. She also carries a **magic wand** or staff, with which she strikes the grass and crops, covering them with frost each year after Halloween. Legend holds that the Storm Hag created the islands of the Inner Hebrides by dropping rocks and peat into the sea. Many Scottish lakes and mountains are also attributed to her artistry.

 PA 4/49

Herbology

Having a green thumb can be mighty handy for a **wizard**. Many of the ingredients for magical **potions** can be found in the well-stocked garden, as can remedies for all kinds of maladies both natural and supernatural—from acne to snakebite to **petrification**. Certain herbs may even protect you from the magical machinations of your enemies. The secret lies in knowing which plants do what, and how best to grow and harvest them. That's what herbology is all about.

Herbs have been used in both magic and medicine for thousands of years. The systematic study of herbs dates back to the ancient Sumerians, who described medicinal uses for caraway, thyme, laurel, and many other plants that could be growing in your backyard today. The first known Chinese herb book (or "herbal"), written in about 2800 B.C., describes medicinal uses for 366 plants. The ancient Greeks and Romans used plants for medicine, seasoning, cosmetics, scents, and dyes. The more superstitious among them also used herbs as amulets that were worn in small cloth bags tied round the neck to ward off evil spirits, disease, or the **curses** of an angry neighbor. In Homer's *Odyssey*, the hero is given an herb called *moly* to protect him from the **spells** of the sorceress **Circe**. Elsewhere in mythology, magic herbs are associated with **witches** such as Hecate and Medea, who used them to create **potions** that bestowed great gifts on those they favored and terrible agony on those they wanted to destroy.

During the Middle Ages, most everyone knew of a local "wise man" or "wise woman" who used herbs to treat injuries and ailments and provide solutions to all sorts of personal difficulties, from a dry well to an overbearing mother-in-law. These prescriptions drew on folk beliefs about the medicinal and magical properties of plants that had been passed

A fifteenth-century illustration of one of the basic rules of herbology: A plant's appearance shows how it can be used. Plants that look like teeth cure toothache; those shaped like hearts are good for heart ailments; those that resemble eyes sharpen the eyesight; and hairy plants offer a cure for baldness.

down for generations. Many cures were based on the principle that every plant had been stamped by God with a visible image of its role in medicine, so by simply looking at a plant you could tell what it was good for. The color of the flowers or fruit, the shape of a root or leaf, the texture of a petal or stem—all might hold clues to a plant's medicinal properties. For example, yellow-flowered plants such as goldenrod were said to cure the yellow complexion caused by jaundice, plants with red leaves or roots were used to treat blood disorders or wounds, and the purple petals of the iris were made into poultices for bruises. If a plant resembled a human organ, it was thought to be beneficial in treating that organ. Lungwort, so named because of the lunglike spots on its leaves, was used to treat pulmonary complaints, while the three-lobed leaf of hepatica (or liverwort), said to resemble the human liver, was used for liver disorders. Quaking aspen leaves were used to treat the shaking symptoms of palsy, and flowers that resembled butterflies were recommended for insect bites.

Many ailments were believed to be caused by supernatural forces, but there were herbal treatments for those, as well. The local wise woman or herbalist might advise you to hang a blackberry wreath to ward off evil spirits, to stuff your keyhole with fennel seeds to keep out the **ghosts,** and to spread the juice of the foxglove plant on your floor to protect yourself from **fairies**. Herbs were also expected to work their magic on a variety of more down-to-earth problems. A traveler who feared falling asleep at the wagon reins, for example, would be instructed to carry mugwort, which was reputed to drive off sleep by its mere presence. A treasure seeker might be given chicory, said to be capable of opening locked doors and chests. A woman eager to bear children might be advised to plant parsley around her home, and a young man who hoped to win the girl of his dreams might be told to pick some yarrow while reciting a love charm.

Knowing which plants were useful for what purpose was only half the battle. It was also crucial to know the proper time and manner for gathering each plant. Many herbalists believed that the properties of plants, like the characteristics of people, were directly influenced by the movements of the stars and planets. One enthusiast of astrological botany insisted that "if a plant be not gathered by the rules of astrology, it hath little or no virtue in it." Thus plants believed to be associated with Saturn, such as hemlock and belladonna, were to be gathered when Saturn was in the appropriate position in the sky, and so forth. A more basic rule of thumb was that it was best to gather herbs at night, preferably when the moon was full and the plants were thus at their most potent. No doubt that's why Hermione had to follow careful instructions when gathering fluxweed for Polyjuice Potion.

But many plants had rules all their own. If you expected the simple blue chicory to open any locks, for example, you had to cut it using a gold blade at noon or midnight on St. James Day, July 25. If you spoke a single word during this process you would supposedly die on the spot. And if you hoped to use peonies to protect your livestock and crops from stormy weather, you had better be sure there were no woodpeckers around when you did your harvesting. Legend held that if one of these birds caught you in the act you'd go blind. With all these rules, and so many mortal dangers, its no wonder Hogwarts students are required to spend so many years studying herbology.

Hex

When Hermione's teeth suddenly grow past her chin, she knows she's been hexed by the spiteful Draco Malfoy. A hex is an evil **spell** or **curse** placed upon a person or object and intended to cause harm. Among those who don't have Madam Pomfrey around to reverse the ill effects, being hexed is considered very dangerous indeed.

The word "hex" comes from *Hexe*, the German word for "witch," and a hex is generally considered to be a form of witchcraft. Although the practice of hexing probably originated in Europe, it is most closely associated with the folk magic of the Pennsylvania Dutch, people of German ancestry who first settled in colonial America during the seventeenth century. Hexing was the specialty of "hex doctors," whose services for casting and removing hexes were available for hire to anyone in the community.

Among the early Pennsylvania Dutch farmers, a mild nuisance, such as the inability to churn cream into butter or a more serious concern, such as diseased livestock, might have been attributed to a hex. Hexing would be suspected if an animal's fur fell out, or if it stopped eating, or it became uncommonly restless. Even more grave was the hexing of a human being. A person who had been hexed might experience incurable insomnia, wasting away due to loss of appetite or inability to keep down food, a persistent uncomfortable or painful physical sensation, or general bad luck.

A number of options were available to anyone eager to protect his family and livestock from being *ferhexed* (hexed or bewitched). Drawing a five-pointed star on a door frame or windowsill was said to prevent a hex doctor from entering a building. A hex letter—a short declaration

A traditional Pennsylvania Dutch hex sign.

of animosity toward the hex doctor—could be hung from the rafters of a barn to protect its occupants. Animals could also be protected from, or even cured of, hex-induced illnesses by hanging small cloth bags containing mercury over their stalls.

Additional protection from hexes and other evil spells may have been offered by hex signs—colorful geometric figures traditionally painted on the sides of houses or barns. Like hexing itself, the custom of drawing hex signs probably originated in Germany, but by the nineteenth century the signs were much more common in eastern Pennsylvania. Today they are considered folk art, but some experts believe hex signs were originally used to protect both animals and humans from becoming hexed and to ward off the evil eye (see **amulet**). Although they are most often seen on buildings, hex signs are sometimes painted on cradles, household tools, and wooden or metal disks designed to hang in windows.

GF 23/405

Hinkypunk

Ron Weasley isn't the only wayfarer to have found himself waist-deep in mud after an encounter with the wispy one-legged spirit known as a hinkypunk. In the folklore of England's West Country, the hinkypunk is said to lurk in remote areas at night, waiting for an approaching traveler before he lights a lantern and steps into view. The weary pedestrian, overjoyed to see a flicker of light in the distance, heads toward it, mistaking it for his destination or for a fellow traveler up ahead on the trail. The next thing he knows, he falls in a ditch, sinks into a bog, or tumbles off a cliff—much to the amusement of the hinkypunk.

Many similar spirits—characterized by flickering flames and the desire to lead gullible travelers into peril—are said to roam the English

A traveler has a near miss as one of the hinkypunk's close relatives,
the Welsh pwca, tries to lure him over a cliff.

countryside. English folklore abounds with tales of travelers who wander around in circles, fall into ditches, lose their bearings, and end up north when they were headed south. Perhaps this is because so much of the English countryside is covered by marshes, bogs, and moors, which are treacherous to negotiate, particularly at night. Rather than blame the landscape itself, centuries of tradition have pointed the finger at supernatural beings. Some are said to be **demons,** some are thought to be **ghosts** whose souls cannot rest, and still others are rumored to be guardians of treasure, teasing humans with a vision of wealth that is forever just out of reach.

Interestingly, in many parts of England, strange lights with no human attached to them *are* frequently seen flickering in the distance. But according to the scientific view, what travelers are actually seeing is the spontaneous ignition of marsh gases commonly emitted from boggy areas. For centuries, however, people believed the lights were caused by malicious spirits, and wherever such lights have regularly appeared a version of the hinkypunk is part of the local lore.

 PA 16/319

Hippogriff

ittle did Harry and Hermione know what a noble tradition they joined when they mounted Buckbeak, Hagrid's beloved hippogriff. The offspring of a rare union between a male griffin (itself half

eagle and half lion) and a female horse, the hippogriff is said to have been the favored mount of the knights of Charlemagne, warriors of the eighth and ninth centuries whose adventures were recounted and highly romanticized by later writers.

Although the hippogriff was presented in these heroic tales as a rare but real animal, the winged beast was invented around 1516 by Ludovico Ariosto, author of the Italian epic poem *Orlando Furioso*, which chronicles the exploits of several of Charlemagne's knights. Like a griffin, Ariosto's hippogriff has an eagle's head and beak, a lion's front legs with talons, and richly feathered wings, while the rest of its body is that of a horse. Originally tamed and trained by the **magician** Atlante, the hippogriff can fly higher and faster than any bird, hurtling back toward Earth with the speed of a thunderbolt when its rider is ready to land. Even normally fearless knights find this a little scary, but they are delighted by the steed's ability to soar easily from one side of the globe to the other.

Although the hippogriff likes to tease people who are trying to catch him, flying just out of reach the moment someone is about to grab his bridle, once mounted he proves a cooperative and loyal companion. In the hands of the knight Rogero, he flies over the Alps from Italy to England, where he astounds and delights a field of soldiers and noblemen by landing in their midst. Taking off again, Rogero and his mount head for Ireland, where they discover the fair maiden Angelina in the clutches of a terrible sea monster. Seeing the shadow of the hippogriff's wings upon the water, the monster abandons his prey in favor of something larger and more tasty. As the hippogriff deftly jumps out of the way, Rogero disarms the monster with the blinding glare of a magic shield. Rogero and Angelina hop on the hippogriff's back and—much like Harry and Hermione—sail off in search of new adventures.

 PA 6/114

Animals on Trial

Much as we may disapprove of the Committee for the Disposal of Dangerous Creatures for putting poor Buckbeak on trial, we can't hold them responsible for dreaming up this curious practice. In medieval and early modern Europe, domestic animals, as well as insects, rodents, and other common pests, were frequently charged with crimes (most often murder or destruction of property), arrested, imprisoned, tried, convicted, and sometimes executed. Carefully kept court records from as early as the ninth century and as late as the nineteenth reveal trials for caterpillars, flies, locusts, leeches, snails, slugs, worms, rats, mice, moles, doves, pigs, cows, roosters, dogs, mules, horses, and goats.

In the case of insects, the offense was usually destruction of crops. Since it was impossible to subpoena a swarm of locusts, one bug was captured, assigned a court-appointed attorney, and made to stand trial for the rest. If it was found guilty, all the locusts were ordered to leave town, which they usually did, eventually.

Animals that were large enough to imprison were confined in the same jails and received the same treatment as people. Like people, animals were even tortured to extort confessions. While no one expected an animal to confess to anything, such torture was part of the legal judicial process, and some judges believed they had an obligation to carry it out. This may actually have benefited some animals in the end, since accused criminals who did not confess their guilt under torture often got reduced sentences. Sentences might also be reduced or overturned as the result of an appeal made to a higher court. In one instance we know of, a pig and a donkey condemned to be hanged managed to get off with only a knock on the head after a new judge reviewed their case. Those animals whose appeals failed, however, had to hope that they, like Buckbeak, had a good friend to come to the rescue.

Horoscope

Sometimes, homework is just no fun. But it's especially trying when you're certain the assignment isn't worth the paper it's written on. That's how Ron and Harry feel about the horoscopes they have to prepare for **Divination** class. Unlike the millions of people who eagerly turn to the astrologer's predictions in the newspaper each day, these skeptical **wizards** seem convinced that the movement of the planets doesn't affect their future one bit.

Even worse, casting a horoscope of the sort Professor Trelawney demands is a lot of work. More than just a set of predictions, a horoscope is also a detailed chart or map showing what the heavens looked like at the moment a person was born. To cast his own horoscope, the budding astrologer must know the day, month, and year of his birth, as well as the location and the exact time of day. With these facts in place, he consults an "ephemeris"—a book that records the daily positions of the sun, the moon, and the planets—to determine where each heavenly body was located at the moment in question. Because an ephemeris lists positions for just one time of day and one geographical location (usually noon or midnight in Greenwich, England—the internationally agreed upon location for measuring time and longitude since 1884), each individual must perform a series of mathematical calculations to determine how the skies looked at his own hour of birth and from his own birthplace.

This information is then entered into a horoscope chart, which shows the location of each planet within the signs of the zodiac, the distances between the planets, and the angles formed by lines drawn between the planets. Using this information and a traditional set of

English astrologers earned a living casting horoscopes at carnivals and fairs. In this drawing from the seventeenth century, it's the bag of money, not the horoscope chart on the table, that has the astrologer's attention.

meanings associated with each planet and sign of the zodiac (see **Astrology**), the astrologer forms an assessment of his basic personality, talents, strengths, and weaknesses.

To make predictions, as Hogwarts students must do, it's necessary to again consult an ephemeris to determine the future position of the planets. A practicing astrologer will compare these planetary positions to those in the birth chart to assess what lies ahead. But a resourceful student may find it easier to follow Ron's advice and just make it up.

 GF 14/221

Invisibility Cloak

Sometimes clothes really do make the man—or woman. Just ask anyone with an invisibility cloak. These handy garments, which render their wearers invisible (to anyone but Mad-Eye Moody), have been helping heroes establish their reputations for hundreds of years.

The basic notion of invisible fashion accessories can be traced back to Greek mythology. Hades, the Greek god of the underworld, owned a miraculous "cap of darkness," which made anyone who donned it invisible. (Not coincidentally, *Hades* means "the unseen one" in ancient Greek.) This cap was very handy for outmaneuvering enemies, and it was frequently borrowed by other mythological figures. The young prince Perseus wore it when he went to slay the snake-haired monster Medusa, and the god Hermes used it in battle against the **giant** Hippolytus.

Other Greek legends speak of rings, arrows, and even clouds of mist that bestow the enviable ability to wander about unseen. An actual *cloak* of invisibility was unknown until the Middle Ages, when one appeared in the famous Austrian poem "The Song of the Nibelung." In this twelfth-century epic, loosely based on several tales from Norse mythology, a powerful **dwarf** magician named Alberich possesses a secret cloak (or *tarnekappe*) that can render its wearer invisible. An unusually potent garment, it also gives its owner the strength of twelve men. Alberich uses the *tarnekappe* to protect the underground treasure of the *Nibelung* (a mighty race of European kings) until he is defeated, and his cloak taken, by the great German folk hero, Siegfried. The story of Alberich and Siegfried is also told in the celebrated nineteenth-century German opera *Der Ring des Nibelungen*, by Richard Wagner.

*Before Harry Potter, the most famous owner of
an invisibility cloak was Jack the Giant Killer,
who uses his magic garment here to sneak past two griffins.*

By the eighteenth century, cloaks, coats, and mantles of invisibility had become standard garb in European folklore. The popular English hero Jack the Giant Killer is said to have worn a "coat of darkness" that allowed him to sneak up on his enemies without warning. (Never one to dress down, Jack also sported a cap of knowledge and shoes of swiftness in many of his adventures.) Invisibility cloaks also figure prominently in several of Grimm's fairy tales, such as the popular fable, "The Shoes That Were Danced to Pieces." In this lighthearted tale, a penniless soldier wins fame, fortune, and a royal bride by using his cloak to outwit twelve spoiled princesses. Despite his magical trappings, the soldier only narrowly avoids detection. He has trouble keep-

ing his hands and feet to himself, and at one point his unseen presence in a rowboat even prompts the question: "I wonder why the boat is so much heavier tonight?"

Of course, not all invisibility cloaks are created equal. Like any article of clothing, they come in various sizes, fabrics, and colors. Jack the Giant Killer's invisible garment is routinely described as a humble "old coat," while the cloak Harry inherits from his father is made of a supple, silver fabric that flows and shimmers like water. Some invisibility cloaks also confer additional powers on their wearer, like the flying cloak of invisibility that appears in a sequel to *The Wizard of Oz* that could whisk its owner wherever he wished.

There is, however, one quality that all invisibility cloaks share in common; they allow their wearers to do exactly what they want, without fear of judgment or reprisal. As Harry discovers when he uses his cloak to sneak out of Hogwarts after hours, the power of invisibility allows you to make your own rules and to go wherever you please. The idea of such boundless freedom once prompted the ancient Greek philosopher Plato to ask his students how they would behave if they were suddenly rendered invisible. What would *you* do? Would you slay terrible monsters, like Perseus, rule a hideous underworld, like Alberich—or just sneak out for some tasty Black Pepper Imps, like Harry and his friends?

 SS 12/201

Kappa

Although most Hogwarts classes appear to be geared toward the needs of European witches and wizards, the wise Professor Lupin knows that preparedness against the demons and monsters of faraway lands can never be a waste of time. In this spirit, we imagine, he offers his third-year Defense Against the Dark Arts students a lesson on the kappa, an amphibious water spirit of Japanese folklore that drags its human and animal victims into the water and drowns and mutilates them.

Kappas dwell in rivers, lakes, and ponds, but are never reluctant to wade ashore in search of prey. Stories have traditionally portrayed them as highly malicious, eager to suck the guts out of their victims and drink their blood. They are said to be especially fond of human liver.

Yet they are also portrayed as both intelligent and honorable. Mankind is said to have learned the art of setting broken bones from a kappa who traded his knowledge in return for his arm, which had been torn off during one of his marauding adventures. Kappa limbs, when reattached, are as good as new in a few days.

Fully grown, a kappa is about the size of a ten-year-old child. Its skin is scaly and yellow-green; it has the face of a monkey and the back of a tortoise; and its hands and feet are webbed, for ease of swimming. Perhaps its most distinctive physical feature is the saucerlike depression on the top of its head, which must always contain water if the kappa is to maintain its supernatural powers and superior strength on land.

The best method of subduing a kappa, therefore, is by bowing to it repeatedly. Being an unusually courteous creature, the kappa will feel compelled to bow back. After several bows, all the liquid will spill from the kappa's head and it will be forced to return to its watery home.

Another strategy for placating an ill-disposed kappa is to feed it cucumbers, widely known to be its favorite food. Carving the names of family members into cucumbers and throwing them into the water is said to protect those people from harm by kappas, who in accepting the cucumbers are honor-bound not to harm their namesakes. This legendary association between kappas and cucumbers has become such an entrenched part of Japanese culture that sushi stuffed with cucumber is today called *kappa maki*.

 PA 9/170

Leprechaun

The Quidditch World Cup may not be filled with gold, but it's worth a bundle to the Irish and Bulgarian teams as they battle it out at wizardry's premiere sporting event. When the Irish emerge victorious, they have no complaints about the performance of their exuberant leprechaun cheerleaders. By most accounts, however, encounters between humans and leprechauns are rarely so harmonious.

Although these **fairies** of Irish folklore spend most of their time making shoes, it's no secret that leprechauns also keep watch over ancient

stores of buried gold and other treasure. Legend holds that humans may share in this wealth, but only if they are clever enough to capture a leprechaun and force him to give up his riches in exchange for freedom. This is no easy feat, for these tiny men (all leprechauns are male) are extremely clever and will usually find a way to turn the tables on a human. A typical tale begins with a traveler who tracks down a leprechaun after hearing the faint sound of hammering coming from a secluded forest or meadow. When discovered, the leprechaun usually proves friendly enough until his visitor demands that he reveal the location of his gold. Then he may throw a tantrum, deny he has any gold, point to an imaginary swarm of bees or a tree about to fall, or do anything else he can think of to create a distraction. The instant the human looks away, the leprechaun will vanish. If this trick fails, there are plenty of others. The leprechaun may become surprisingly generous and, with a twinkle in his eye, hand over a weighty purse of gold coins. But as fans of the Quidditch World Cup learned when showered with leprechaun gold, it's best not to run up debts too soon, for this gift will soon turn to ashes or vanish altogether.

Modern depictions of leprechauns, especially those seen around St. Patrick's Day, usually show a little man dressed all in green. Traditionally, however, the dapper leprechaun might be seen in a red jacket with shiny silver buttons, blue or brown stockings, big shoes with fat silver buckles, and a high-crowned or three-cornered hat. Standing tall at six inches to two feet, leprechauns can look both mischievous and dignified. Many wear a beard and smoke a pipe. When on the job, a leprechaun often wears a leather cobbler's apron and carries a little hammer to make or mend a tiny, fairy-size shoe. Apparently, leprechauns don't treat their fellow fairies much better than humans, for they provide them with only single shoes, never

pairs. In fact, some scholars believe the word leprechaun is derived from the Gaelic *leith bhrogan*, meaning "maker of one shoe." But perhaps the leprechauns' failure to make pairs is merely an oversight, for they are frequently tipsy from drinking too much home-brewed beer.

The Farmer and the Leprechaun

This typical tale of leprechaun ingenuity has been told in Ireland for generations:

A farmer was laboring in his fields when he spied a tiny man hiding under a leaf. Knowing this must be a leprechaun, the farmer quickly scooped the man up in his hands and asked him where his gold was. The leprechaun seemed eager to get away and quickly revealed that his treasure was buried under a nearby bush. Carefully holding on to his tiny captive, the farmer set off to find the spot. As it turned out, the bush was one in a field of hundreds of identical shrubs. Having no digging tool at hand, the farmer removed one of his red socks and tied it to a branch to mark the bush the leprechaun had indicated. As he headed home to get a shovel, the leprechaun pointed out that his own services were no longer required and asked to be freed. The farmer agreed, but not before making the leprechaun promise not to move the sock or dig up the gold. Clever thinking, but not clever enough. When the farmer returned to the field just a few minutes later, every bush in the field was marked with an identical red sock!

Magic

At age eleven, Harry Potter receives the greatest surprise of his life. Unlike Aunt Petunia and Uncle Vernon, unlike horrible cousin Dudley and everyone else he's ever known, Harry can do magic. He can grow out a bad haircut overnight, make a plate glass window disappear at the zoo, and shrink an ugly sweater without the aid of a dryer. And as Hagrid is happy to inform him, a little training at Hogwarts School of Witchcraft and Wizardry will enable him to do much, much more.

In the wizarding world, magic is a way of accomplishing things that are impossible by the natural laws that bind the rest of us. **Wizards** can use magical Floo powder to get from one place to another, while non-magical folk are forced to walk or take the bus. Albus Dumbledore can point his magic wand and utter a few magic words to fill the Hogwarts hall with sleeping bags, while an ordinary person would have to drive to a store, buy the sleeping bags, load them in a van, drive them back to the school, and carry them inside. Sirius Black can use magic to turn himself into a dog, while a non-wizard can do nothing more than put on a costume.

Much as we delight in reading about the exploits of these fictional wizards, in the modern world most people don't believe in magic. We enjoy the performances of theatrical **magicians** who give us the experience of magic, but we don't really expect them to make the impossible occur. Nor do many of us believe in another once-common conception of magic—that the world is controlled by supernatural beings, whose powers may be harnessed and used by humans to achieve their goals.

Throughout most of Western history, however, people did believe in magic, and they did look to invisible, supernatural forces to exercise

power over others or control the natural world. People practiced magic to gain knowledge, love, and wealth, to heal illness and ward off danger, to harm or deceive enemies, to guarantee success or productivity, and to learn about the future. Magical practices involved many of the techniques taught at Hogwarts, such as **spells, potions, charms,** and **divination,** as well as elaborate rituals and ceremonies designed to summon gods, demons, and ghosts. Practicing magic helped people to relieve their anxieties and to feel they were doing something to control the course of their lives.

The Origins of Magic

The English word "magic" is derived from the name of the high priests of ancient Persia (modern-day Iran), who were called *magi*. In the sixth century B.C., the *magi* were known for their profound learning and gifts of prophecy. Followers of the religious leader Zoroaster, they interpreted **dreams,** practiced **astrology,** and advised rulers on important matters. When the *magi* became known in the Greek and Roman worlds, they were regarded as deeply mysterious figures who possessed profound secrets and supernatural powers. Exactly what these secrets were was unclear (after all, they were secrets), but for a long time anything regarded as supernatural was deemed to be a creation of the *magi* and became known as "magic." Indeed, Zoroaster himself was often called the inventor of magic.

Of course, no single individual or culture actually invented magic. The magical practices that have been handed down over the centuries originated in many civilizations, including those of the ancient Persians, Babylonians, Egyptians, Hebrews, Greeks, and Romans. The Western magical tradition as we know it today owes much to the exchange of ideas between members of different cultures. Such contact occurred with increasing frequency after the third century B.C., when the Greek general Alexander the Great conquered Syria, Babylonia, Egypt, and Persia and established the city of Alexandria, Egypt, as the intellectual crossroads of the ancient world.

Magic and Religion

In all early societies, magic and religion were intertwined. A multitude of gods and lesser spirits, both good and bad, were believed to control most aspects of life, causing both sunshine and rain, prosperity and poverty, sickness and good health. Magic was designed to appeal to or control these spirits. Like religious practices, magical practices involved rituals and ceremonies that called upon the gods, and, like priests, **magicians** were believed to have special access to the gods. But rather than worshipping these deities, magicians requested or even demanded favors from them.

Sometimes, magicians simply called upon the gods for assistance when they cast spells, or uttered curses. But often they also tried to make the deities appear "in person." After performing a special ceremony to summon, or invoke, a spirit, a magician of ancient Babylonia or Egypt might command the spirit to drive away disease, strike down an enemy, or ensure a political victory. A minor deity would typically be threatened with punishment by other, more powerful, spirits if the magician's demands were not met. Then the magician would dismiss the deity, sending it back to the spirit world. Hundreds of documents from antiquity confirm that attempting to raise spirits was a common, if often disappointing, activity in early Greece and Rome.

Nearly all forms of ancient magic depended upon knowing the secret names of the gods. Many deities were thought to have two sets of names, the common names everyone knew, and the secret names known only to those who studied the magical arts. In a sense, these secret names were the first **magic words.** Whether spoken or written, they were believed to possess great power, since knowing a god's true name was believed to enable a magician to summon all the powers that god represented. Egyptian priests gave their deities long, complex, often unpronounceable names so that they could not be easily learned by outsiders. It was said that Moses parted the Red Sea by speaking the secret seventy-two-syllable name of God known only to himself. And accord-

ing to the Greek writer Plutarch, the name of Rome's guardian deity was kept secret after the city's founding, and it was forbidden to ask anything about the god—even whether it was male or female—lest the enemies of Rome discover the name and appeal to the god for their own purposes.

As ancient civilizations came into contact with one another, it was common for the magicians of one culture to "try out" the names of the gods of another land. Some of the earliest known scrolls recording magical practices, written during the third and fourth centuries, contain long lists of the names of gods of many religions, which could be inscribed on **amulets** or **talismans** or incorporated into spells and incantations. One of the most famous incantations of third-century Greek and Egyptian magicians, which was alleged to be so powerful that "the sun and the earth cringe when they hear it; rivers, seas, swamps, and springs freeze when they hear it; [and] rocks burst when they hear it," was composed of the names of a hundred different deities strung together.

High Magic and Low Magic

Ancient magic is often divided into two categories—"high magic" and "low magic"—that can be distinguished primarily by the goals of their practitioners.

High magic, which had much in common with religion, was motivated by the desire to achieve wisdom not available through ordinary experience. When high magicians (who counted among their ranks such notables as the Greek philosopher and mathematician Pythagoras) petitioned gods or spirits, they had the loftiest of goals. They hoped to receive prophetic visions, become healers, achieve insight and self-knowledge, or even become godlike themselves.

Many systems of high magic also taught that every human being was a miniature version of the universe, containing within himself all of the elements of the outside world. By developing his inner powers of imagination and intuition, it was believed, the magician would eventually be able to cause real (and seemingly supernatural) changes in the world simply by focusing his emotions, will, and desire. Achieving the powers promised by high magic, however, was the work of a lifetime.

But most people who turned to magic did so with more immediate and practical goals in mind. They wanted to bring luck, riches, fame, political success, health, and beauty; to harm enemies and compel love, to win at sports, know the future, and solve everyday practical problems. The pursuit of these goals is generally known as "low magic"—a category which also includes popular fortune-telling, making potions, casting spells, and the use of **charms** and amulets. From the fourth century B.C. onward, hundreds, if not thousands of men and women went into business as professional **sorcerers** and diviners, offering magic for a fee. Although many had a reputation for fraud, historical records show that people of all classes consulted these professional magicians regularly, some openly and some in secret.

The Reputation of Magic

In general, magic in the ancient world was more feared than admired. Even those who knew nothing about it believed that they could be harmed or influenced by the magic of someone else. If a politician lost his place in the middle of a speech, or someone unexpectedly became ill, it was not uncommon to assume an enemy's **curse** was to blame. The sinister reputation of magic was enhanced by its associations with witchcraft in the popular imagination. Greek and Roman literature was filled with highly imaginative and often horrifying descriptions of **witches** and their despicable practices. Erictho, a witch created by the first-century Roman writer Lucan, uses human body parts in her potions, buries her enemies alive, and brings rotting corpses back to life. Although clearly a fictional character (and a memorable one at that), Erictho and witches like her had a strong impact on the popular view of what witchcraft and magic were all about.

Although magic was popular with a public who wanted to be able to consult fortune-tellers and purchase protective charms and amulets,

those in positions of authority were wary of astrologers who predicted their deaths and sorcerers who could be hired by their enemies to harm them with curses. In 81 B.C. the Roman dictator Cornelius Sulla ordered the death penalty for "soothsayers, enchanters, and those who make use of sorcery for evil purposes, those who conjure up demons, who disrupt the elements, [or] who employ waxen images destructively." A series of similar laws were passed in the following centuries, so that by the fourth century A.D., all forms of magic and divination were outlawed in the Roman Empire. At the same time, the Christian Church, which was rapidly growing in power, made a concerted effort to suppress magical practices, which were seen as competition to the Christian faith. All forms of magic were declared to be associated with **demons** (and thus the Devil) and were prohibited by Church law.

The Church and government continued to work together to oppose magic through the Middle Ages. Nonetheless, magical beliefs and practices, especially those associated with folk medicine (magical healing), were passed on secretly and became part of the repertoire of the "cunning men" or village wizards of later centuries (see **herbology**, **magician**).

Magic in Medieval Literature

Beginning around the middle of the twelfth century, magic began to be portrayed in a much more appealing light, at least by writers of fiction. First in France, and later in Germany and England, poets spun marvelous adventure tales that were set in the distant past and involved the magic-filled exploits of valiant knights, beautiful damsels, and heroic kings. These tales, which are now known as the "medieval romances," downplayed the negative associations of magic with demons and witchcraft. The word "magic" was often avoided, and authors spoke instead of "wonders," "astonishments," and "enchantments." Heroes were provided with swords that furnished superhuman strength, dishes that served themselves, boats and chariots that needed no pilot, and rings that made their wearers invulnerable to fire, drowning, and other catastrophes. **Fairies** and monsters from mythology also appeared with great regularity, and it was often a fairy who provided the hero with just what he needed to complete the task at hand. Potions, astrological divination, spell casting, and healing herbs were also prominently featured in these epic works. While the idea of "black" magic still lingered, with evil sorcerers and enchantresses appearing from time to time, most of these tales presented magic in a positive light and readers found them as delightful as we do today.

Natural Magic

Magic found a new respectability during the fifteenth and sixteenth centuries, due to the rise of "natural magic," which did not involve the aid of demons or supernatural beings. A kind of science of its day, natural magic was based on the belief that everything in nature—people, plants, animals, rocks, and minerals—teemed with powerful but hidden forces known as "occult virtues." Gems, for example, were believed to contain the power to cure disease, affect mood, and even bring good luck. Herbs had occult virtues that could promote healing, sometimes simply by being suspended over a patient's bed. Even colors and numbers had hidden powers. Furthermore, all of the elements of nature were connected to each other in meaningful but hidden ways. Natural magicians, who included physicians among their ranks, set themselves the challenge of discovering these forces and connections and putting them to use in positive ways.

But being a serious natural magician was no simple task; it required research, study, and careful observation of nature. Sometimes the "occult virtue" of a substance was revealed by its appearance. For example, the herb *scorpius* (named for its resemblance to a scorpion) was deemed an effective remedy for spider bites. Plants and animals with similar shapes were believed to share similar qualities. But especially important to the mastery of natural magic was the study of astrology, since many of the relationships and hidden properties in nature were believed to have emanated directly from the planets and the stars. The

Natural magic taught that plants and animals that looked alike shared the same magical properties.

gem emerald, the metal copper, and the color green, for example, all shared qualities derived from the planet Venus. Knowing this, the natural magician was able to use these elements in combination when trying to affect those areas of life "ruled" by Venus, such as health, beauty, and love. Using the metal lead, the onyx stone, and the color black was likely to have quite the opposite effect, since they were ruled by Saturn and were associated with death and depression. In addition, the practitioner was required to have extensive knowledge of anatomy and herbology, since curing disease was an important goal of natural magic, and a disease caused by one planetary influence might be cured by an herb regulated by the same planet or, in some cases, its opposite. The natural magician was a kind of wizard of the natural world and a master of combinations—mixing, matching, and exploiting the hidden properties of nature so as to achieve miraculous and beneficial results.

Whereas in the ninth or tenth century, a respectable person might have avoided any connection with magic, during the Renaissance natural magic was an appropriate area of study for intellectuals, physicians, clergymen, and anyone with a sense of scientific curiosity. Indeed, scholars of the time might have felt quite at home at Hogwarts, where many elements of natural magic—herbology, astrology, **palmistry, arithmancy,** and the casting of **horoscopes**—are all part of the curriculum.

Ritual Magic

The possibility of raising of spirits, however, was never entirely forgotten. Between the fifteenth and eighteenth centuries, a series of sensational books known as "grimoires" (or Black Books) appeared throughout Europe in many languages. Most were written anonymously, but were attributed to ancient sources (the older a book seemed to be, the more secret wisdom it was thought to contain) including Moses, Aristotle, Noah, Alexander the Great, and most famously, the biblical King Solomon. At first sold and circulated in secret, since owning and using one was a serious crime, these books taught procedures that would supposedly conjure up the spirits and demons of ancient times.

The grimoires promised magic for every imaginable purpose: gaining love, riches, beauty, health, happiness, and celebrity; defeating, cursing, or killing enemies; starting wars, healing the sick, and making the healthy ill, becoming invisible, finding treasure, flying, foretelling the future, and unlocking doors without keys. Not surprisingly, such promises made the books very popular, especially during the seventeenth century, when cheap editions of some grimoires became widely available. From college students to clergymen, devoted believers and the merely curious followed the instructions to see what would happen.

Because they involved elaborate ceremonies and rituals, the procedures taught by the grimoires were known as "ritual magic" or "ceremonial magic." Essentially, ritual magic followed the same steps used to

LES CLAVICULES

DE SALOMON

Traduit de l'Hébreux en Langue Latine,
Par le Rabin Abognazar,
ET
Mis en langue Vulgaire Par M. Barault Archevêque d'Arles.

Le Grand   Pentacule.

M. DC. XXXIV.

A seventeenth-century French edition of
The Key of Solomon, *the best known of all grimoires.*

summon gods and spirits thousands of years earlier. First, the magician drew a large circle on the ground, which he inscribed with magic words, sacred names, and symbols. Then he stepped into the circle (which protected him from the spirits he raised), uttered the incantations that would make the demon appear and grant his wishes, made his demands, and sent the demon on its way. That, at least, was what was supposed to happen.

But before any of this could be attempted, there were weeks, and even months of preparation to be undertaken. According to the many grimoires, all of the apparatus used during the ceremony—candles, perfumes, incense, the sword used to draw the magic circle, the magic wand—had to be brand new. Nor could you simply buy what you needed at Diagon Alley. Ceremonial candles had to be personally

A sixteenth-century ceremonial magician orders a demon to do his bidding.
The magic circle was supposed to protect the magician from harm.

molded by the magician using wax made by bees that had never made wax before. The **magic wand** had to be freshly carved from a hazel branch, hewn from a tree with one blow of a newly made sword. Colored inks used to draw magical **talismans** had to be freshly prepared and kept in a new inkwell; and, according to one of the best known of all grimoires, *The Key of Solomon*, the quill pen used to draw the talismans had to be fashioned from the third feather of the right wing of a male goose. Moreover, each step had to be carried out according to the principles of astrology, under the influence of the appropriate planets at the right times of year. The magician also had to prepare himself spiritually for the ceremony by special diet, fasting, ritual bathing, and other purifying practices.

None of this, of course, was any guarantee that anything would happen during the ceremony. In fact, instructions were so elaborate, so specific, and usually so bizarre that they were virtually impossible to actually carry out as described. It was no wonder, then, that despite repeated pleadings, incantations, and sincerity, spirits routinely failed to appear, except in the imaginations of some practitioners and grimoire writers. Failures, however, were also easily explained. With so many details, somewhere, somehow, something had been overlooked.

Magic Today

Belief in magic began to decline during the mid-seventeenth century as people began to discover more practical and effective ways to deal with their problems. Modern chemistry led to the creation of new medicines that replaced cures performed by the principles of herbology, astrology, and natural magic. With the rise of scientific thinking, ideas about how the world worked were tested by experiment, and the power of magic words, spells, amulets, and talismans, was increasingly called into question.

Today, the idea of obtaining extraordinary powers by conjuring spirits has disappeared from most parts of the modern world. Yet it's also true that the modern world is more magical than it has ever been. Things once thought to be impossible, like flying or talking to someone halfway across the world, are daily occurrences. The aspirations of natural magic—discovering and harnessing the hidden powers of nature—have been achieved by modern science. And while the principles of astrology have been disproved, it turns out, ironically, that all the occult virtues in nature *did* come from the stars, since we now know that all of the elements of the natural world, including ourselves, originated in the materials of exploding suns. As it was to the ancients, the universe remains an amazing place, filled with wonder, impossible possibilities, and magic.

The adventures of Harry Potter and his friends have been enjoyed

in exactly the same way that the medieval romances once were, except by millions of more people. Theatrical magic is more popular than at any time in history. Whether in literary or theatrical form, magic confirms our intuition of "another reality." Although magic may make no sense to our logical minds, it makes perfect sense to our creative and intuitive minds, which operate by a different set of rules. The appeal of magic seems to have nothing to do with whether it's "real." Magic came from the imagination and it feeds the imagination. And it seems to us, it always will.

Magician

Wizard. Witch. Sorcerer. Warlock. Enchantress. Conjurer. Charmer. Diviner. These are but a few of the many guises of the magician.

A magician is simply someone who does magic, whether it is "real" magic like that of Albus Dumbledore, or something that simply appears to be magical, like the spell casting of a village witch or wizard or the great escapes of a stage magician like Harry Houdini.

Almost every culture in the world has told tales of legendary magicians who could soar through the sky, disappear, or produce banquets from thin air. Each culture has also had its real, historical magicians who claimed to have special powers and used a variety of techniques to perform apparently magical acts. Although we cannot do justice to all the world's magicians, here are some of the basic types:

The Legendary Magician

The purest form of magic is done by the **wizards** and **witches** of myth, legend and fairy tales, who can do just about anything they want. They can fly, be in two places at once, disappear and reappear, produce any object desired, change their own shape or the shape of others, converse with animals, animate objects, foretell the future, cure illness, and travel through time. Some legendary magicians have great knowledge of **potions** and **spells,** but often these are unnecessary. Most of the time, a **magic word** and a wave of the wand are all it takes.

Tales of legendary magicians go back thousands of years. In ancient Egypt, where magic rituals were part of everyday culture, imaginative accounts of the powers of great wizards never failed to delight the listener. In one charming tale set in the time of King Cheops (2600 B.C.) the magician Jajamanekh comes to the aid of a young woman who has dropped her turquoise hair ornament overboard while boating on a lake near the royal palace. With a few magic words, Jajamanekh neatly picks up half of the lake, stacks it on top of the other half, and retrieves the hairpiece for the delighted young lady. In the literature of ancient Greece, where legendary magicians were usually women, the sorceress **Circe** and her niece Medea were able to turn men into beasts, return youth to the aged, and divine the future. The Roman poet Virgil tells of the wizard Moeris, who can move crops from one field to another, transform himself into a **werewolf,** and restore life to the dead.

During the Middle Ages, the most famous magicians of legend were found in wondrous tales of the adventures of gallant knights, virtuous maidens, and noble kings. **Merlin,** advisor to King Arthur, was the most famous of all, known for his power to turn night into day, produce phantom armies, foretell the future, and assume a variety of human and animal forms. Readers of *Orlando Furioso,* an epic Italian adventure written in 1516, knew a different set of magicians, sorcerers, and enchantresses, who seemed to be engaged in a never-ending battle to out-magic each other. In one episode, the wizard Atlante casts a spell on the knight Astolfo (rider of the famed **hippogriff**), causing him to appear as a beast, a giant, and a bird all at once, depending on who's looking at him. Later in the story, the enchantress Melissa transforms herself into the likeness of Atlante in order to rescue the hero of the story, Rogero, who has been enchanted by yet another wizard!

Today's readers, of course, are entranced by a new cast of legendary magicians whose powers are no less wondrous than those of the sorcerers of old. Like all great magicians, these modern wizards have the power to transform and enchant not only one another, but us as well. During the school year, they can all be found at the same address—Hogwarts School of Witchcraft and Wizardry.

The Shaman

The oldest type of historical magician is the tribal sorcerer, also known as a medicine man or shaman. Shamans were the first doctors, priests, and specialists in the supernatural. Their practices date back at least 30,000 years and still survive in some cultures today. In many tribal societies, the shaman occupied a position of power and prestige that was second only to that of the chief. His or her weighty responsibilities included healing and **divination;** communication with the spirit world; ensuring the food supply through hunting, fishing, and fertility magic; finding lost objects and missing persons; locating and identifying thieves; and protecting the village and thwarting its enemies. Shamans made **amulets** and **talismans,** performed rituals and cast **spells,** and understood the medicinal properties of herbs, plants, and minerals. They were also the keepers of the tribe's lore, traditions, and mythology.

In some cultures the shaman inherited his position; in others he was appointed by his predecessor. Sometimes a shaman was an apparently ordinary person who received a "calling" to the job through a **dream,** vision, or other unusual extraordinary experience.

Although shamanism can be found in many parts of the world, it was originally associated with Siberian and Eskimo cultures. This eighteenth-century engraving depicts a shaman of the Tungus people of Siberia.

He would then retreat to the wilderness and live alone like a wild animal, perhaps for weeks or months, as he learned to control his gifts. Often he would fast for long periods. If all went according to tradition, he would have a dream or vision in which he received instruction from a guardian animal spirit about his future, his powers, and his role in the community. He would then return to society and begin his new life.

Most of the shaman's powers were said to come from the invisible realm of ancestor and animal spirits, which he contacted by entering a trance. Shamanistic ceremonies were part of tribal life, and involved community chanting, dancing, and drumming during which the shaman

usually danced himself into a frenzy and was thought to leave his body, communicate with his spirit guides, and return with valuable information. Depending upon the culture, a shaman might wear ceremonial animal skins, put on a mask or a set of antlers, paint his face and body, or drape himself in a feathered cloak symbolizing his "flight" to the other world.

In many cultures, shamanic rituals were accompanied by displays of supernatural power that were actually accomplished by trickery. Using sleight of hand and other secret techniques, tribal magicians could apparently stab themselves without injury, walk on fire, escape from ropes, swallow knives, eat glass, and cause small dolls to dance. Using ventriloquism, they sometimes held public conversations with invisible spirits. These demonstrations must have had a profound impact on those who saw them and contributed to the psychological effectiveness of shamanistic medicine.

Interestingly, the use of trickery did not necessarily mean that the shaman's abilities to heal the sick were fraudulent. Most shamans believed in their powers, and so did the community at large. That's one of the things that made them effective. It never hurt to be able to display one's mastery of the supernatural, however, especially during important ceremonies.

The Cunning Man and the Wise Woman

From medieval times until well into the nineteenth century, nearly every European town and village had a resident magician whose role was similar to that of the tribal shaman. Known variously as a wizard, a wise woman, or a "cunning" man or woman (from the Old English root *cunnan*, meaning, "to know"), the village magician was consulted for healing and divination and all the other things for which ancient people had turned to the shaman. Unlike shamans, however, cunning men and wise women conducted their business privately, rather than in the public ceremonies typical of tribal magic, and although they sometimes dressed more eccentrically than their fellow citizens, they didn't wear animal

skins, perform ritual dances, or enter trances. But many of their practices were the same: They were knowledgeable about herbal medicine, used healing **charms,** and made talismans, amulets, and love potions. In smaller villages, cunning men and women served as doctors and even veterinarians. Some cunning men and women knew the basics of **astrology** and **palmistry** (subjects unknown to earlier tribal cultures), as well as dream interpretation, which they learned from popular booklets. But many cunning men and women were illiterate, and their knowledge of folk remedies and potions came from fellow practitioners or from friends and relatives. Some legends said that village magicians learned their secrets from **fairies.**

Although there were laws against practicing magic, most cunning men and wise women operated openly. The services they provided were in great demand and as long as they did no harm they were left alone by authorities. Many were regarded as "oddball" types who kept to themselves and lived on the outskirts of town where they maintained herbal gardens for their remedies. Their homes were rumored to be filled with strange items, such as **magic mirrors, crystal balls,** or other devices associated with divination. Cunning men and women were respected, feared, and often avoided. But most everyone knew where to find one when they needed to.

Cunning men also had practices in the larger European cities. Operating on a more sophisticated level than their country cousins, urban cunning folk charged higher fees and were often consulted by wealthy aristocrats. One of the best-known cunning men of his time was the London practitioner Simon Forman, who lived from 1552 to 1611. Unlike most of his peers, who feared leaving written evidence of their sometimes illegal activities, Forman kept detailed journals which reveal the types of matters on which he was consulted. Merchants

Village cunning men often dressed and acted strangely, but they knew things that ordinary people didn't.

wanted astrological advice about business matters; sailors' wives inquired about their husbands' safety; distraught patrons sought information about missing pets or stolen property; people wanted spells cast and spells removed; and many came to buy love potions, talismans, amulets, and herbal medicines. Forman was an astrologer and crystal-ball gazer, but he also considered himself a qualified doctor. Although he had no official medical training, he apparently produced many successful cures at a time when the accepted medicine of the day involved bloodletting and other therapies that are now known to be more harmful than helpful. Despite the opposition of the Royal College of Physicians, Forman was awarded a medical license from Cambridge University in 1603 and went on to become physician to many of Elizabethan London's wealthiest citizens.

According to popular lore, Foreman cast a **horoscope** in which he predicted the exact hour of his own death, which took place on September 8, 1611, while he was rowing on the Thames River. He left behind an estate worth £1,200, a considerable fortune for a man of his time.

The Scholar Magician

"Nowadays," wrote an Englishman in the year 1600, "[a man] is not adjudged any scholar at all, unless he can tell men's horoscopes, cast out devils, or hath some skill in soothsaying."

The idea that a learned man might occupy himself with these traditional magician's arts would have been unthinkable little more than a hundred years earlier. But during the late fifteenth and sixteenth centuries, magic had gained a new intellectual respectability. In Renaissance Italy, scholars had revived the ancient notion that magic could serve as a way of achieving spiritual goals and mastery over the natural world. Through diligent study, self-knowledge, and the power of imagination, he could learn to use magic words, incantations, and symbols to control the hidden forces of nature and achieve virtually anything.

These ideas soon made their way north, where they found a vocal proponent in a brilliant young German scholar named Cornelius

One of the best-known scholar magicians of the Renaissance, Agrippa spoke eight languages,
practiced law and medicine, and lectured on philosophy, astrology, and religion.

Agrippa. Although Agrippa is now familiar as Ron Weasley's missing Chocolate Frogs card, he was best known in his own time as the author of the three-volume *Occult Philosophy*, published in 1533. There he argued that all of nature—people, plants, animals, rocks, and minerals—contained hidden properties and powers that could be discovered and put to use. The task of the scholar magician, according to Agrippa, was to apply the tools of magic—divination, **arithmancy,** astrology, the study of **demons** and angels—to uncover the hidden connections and forces in nature and use them to solve problems and cure disease. In the process, Agrippa claimed, man could also discover that part of himself which was linked to the universe at large, and by the force of his own imagination and will, could attain supernatural powers.

Although, to the disappointment of his readers, Agrippa did not explain exactly *how* a magician could achieve his potential, this did not stop many people from trying. Among Agrippa's many devotees were college students who tried to raise demons in their dorm rooms, physicians who tried to harness the hidden forces of nature to cure their patients, and men of science with a yearning to unravel all the mysteries of the universe. The most famous of these was the English mathematician, astronomer, and astrologer John Dee, who gained a reputation as a magician early in his career and was even imprisoned in 1553 on a charge of attempting to murder Queen Mary by enchantment. Dee believed that he could learn many of the world's secrets from angels and spirits, whom he tried to contact by gazing into a crystal ball and a magic mirror. Although he rarely got any response from the spirit world himself, Dee had a series of partners who claimed to be able to see and hear the angels. Despite decades of trying, however, no one was ever able to convince these beings to reveal the secrets of God and the universe Dee sought so earnestly to discover.

Nonetheless, by the time of Dee's death in 1608, interest in magic was quite fashionable among English intellectuals. Throughout much of the seventeenth century, public debates were held at Oxford University on such topics as the power of incantations, the use of magic to cure disease, and the effectiveness of love potions. No doubt many an ambitious young scholar also fancied himself a magician.

The Performance Magician

Tricksters though they are, theatrical magicians may be the "realest" magicians of all. Storytellers create magic that goes from their imaginations to ours (a great trick in itself); performance magicians take the same impossible feats described in fiction and show them to us—live and in person. Like their legendary counterparts, stage magicians appear and disappear; levitate or fly; predict the future; walk through walls; create something from nothing; and change men into beasts, or ladies into leopards. Performance magicians also cast spells over their

This drawing from a German astrology book of 1404 includes the earliest known depiction of a street magician at work. His trick is the classic "Cups and Balls." Overhead are five of the twelve signs of the zodiac: Taurus the Bull, Leo the Lion, Cancer the Crab, Aries the Ram, and Capricorn the Goat.

audiences, causing them to see things that aren't there, and not see things that are. It's no wonder, then, that centuries ago, audiences at magic shows often felt as if they had been bewitched!

Although performance magic—the art of creating and presenting mystifying illusions—can be found in cultures throughout the world, the first magical entertainers in recorded history are the street conjurers of first- and second-century Greece and Rome. The Latin writers Seneca, Alciphron, and Sextus Empiricus all recorded descriptions of the performers they saw—and particularly of the trick known as "The Cups and Balls," which is still performed today by modern magicians. Usually done with three small cups and three small balls (no surprise

*At first glance this painting from about 1480 simply shows a crowd enjoying
a performance of "The Cups and Balls." But a closer look reveals a pickpocket in the audience.
Are the magician and thief partners?*

there), this one trick incorporates many of the most startling effects in
magic. Under the closest scrutiny of the audience—standing only a
foot or two away—the balls vanish into thin air, reappear under the
cups, travel impossibly from cup to cup, penetrate the solid tops of the
cups, and are sometimes produced from the ears and noses of the spec-
tators. For the grand finale the balls change into something else entirely—pieces of fruit, or sometimes mice or baby chicks!

By necessity, early performers were versatile. Not many tricks had
yet been invented, so in addition to performing what we'd describe as
"magic tricks" today, performers might also juggle, tumble, put on a
puppet show, or exhibit a trained animal such as a dog, monkey, or bear.
Schools for street performers existed in Athens, and many performers
were renowned for their abilities to astound and amuse even the most
sophisticated observers. Greek citizens appreciated skills of all kinds—

artistic, athletic, theatrical, musical, and rhetorical—and conjuring was no exception.

As the Roman Empire expanded, magicians began to appear in towns and cities throughout Europe. Some were solo performers, while others joined troupes of acrobats, jugglers, fortune-tellers, poets, and musicians, and traveled from town to town, entertaining royalty in feudal castles and appearing before the common folk in taverns, barns, and courtyards. Surprisingly few details are known about these conjurers, although we do know that many people, especially the clergy, didn't like them one bit. Though these harmless tricksters were known in England as jugglers and their art was innocently called jugglery, the Church considered conjuring immoral because it was based on deception. The same sleight-of-hand techniques employed in magic tricks could also be used to cheat in gambling, or to swindle the public with "miracle" cures. Others feared and mistrusted conjurers because they suspected a magician's illusions might rely on supernatural powers. Since the exact nature of a street magician's methods was usually kept secret, it was easy for those who believed in witchcraft and demons—as many did until the late seventeenth century—to suspect the worst. Furthermore, many performers played on popular magic beliefs by uttering magic words, spinning a **magic wand,** and pretending to cast spells and call upon supernatural powers.

During the eighteenth century, performance magic began to emerge as a form of entertainment in its own right, distinct from juggling, puppetry, and other circus arts. Thanks to new ways of thinking brought by the scientific revolution, conjurers were no longer suspected of having supernatural abilities, and their status as artists of illusion—or "magicians," as they began to be called during the late 1780s—became clear. Magicians began charging admission to their shows (previously they worked for tips, or sold small items like lucky talismans or medicinal tonics after their shows) and performed more frequently in royal courts. By the mid-1700s, magic shows had made their way to the theatrical stage. Giovanni Giuseppe Pinetti, regarded as one of the first great stage magicians, appeared in Europe's best theaters during the 1780s and 1790s, performing such feats as removing a man's

Giovanni Pinetti was one of the first great theatrical magicians. In one of his most famous feats,
a selected card was returned to the deck, the cards were tossed into the air, and the chosen
card was pinned to the wall with a nail fired from a pistol.

shirt without first removing his jacket, apparently reading the mind of a member of the audience, and shooting a nail through chosen card in mid-air, instantly pinning it to the wall.

Late-nineteenth- and early-twentieth-century magic was characterized by two-hour extravaganzas of illusion, filled with eye-popping wonders. Performers circled the globe with literally tons of apparatus, scenery, and costumes. Harry Houdini, who rose to stardom in vaudeville as a man who could escape from anything—including chains, handcuffs, and prisons—became the most famous and most highly paid entertainer of his time.

Today, people all over the world still stop in their tracks to watch a roving street performer or pay a hefty ticket price to take in a theatrical illusion show. Why? Everybody knows "it's just a trick." Are they trying to figure out the secrets? Actually, we think it's quite the opposite. It's not the secrets people want; it's the mysteries. Magic jolts our minds, turns the world upside down and fills us with wonder and astonishment. It also reminds us of something most witches and wizards already know—that the impossible is possible after all.

Magic Mirror

Most of us take mirrors for granted. We don't expect them to show us our heart's deepest desire as the Mirror of Erised does, or to speak to us, like the mirror owned by the evil queen in "Snow White." We use them for everyday tasks like brushing our teeth and combing our hair and don't give them a moment's thought. But the presence of mirrors in our midst has not always been accepted so casually.

In the earliest days of human history, the only place men and women could catch a glimpse of themselves was in still pools of water, and they seldom really understood what they were looking at. Many ancient cultures actually regarded reflections as human souls (which they believed could exist quite independently of a person's body). In some societies, including ancient Greece, it was even considered perilous to see your own reflection, since it meant that your soul had left your body and was in danger of being captured by evil spirits or water nymphs.

Not surprisingly, then, when the first man-made mirrors appeared some 4,500 years ago, they were perceived as miraculous magical objects. (The word "mirror" comes from a Latin term, *mirari* or *mirus*, meaning "marvelous" or "wonderful.") The ancient Greeks, Romans, Chinese, Egyptians, and Central Americans all believed that mirrors were potent **talismans,** capable of bewitching men's minds, befuddling evil spirits, and carrying off the souls of the living and the dead. The Aztec god of night, Tzcatlipoca, is even supposed to have carried a magic mirror that enveloped his enemies in clouds of smoke.

Until the seventeenth century, when they were gradually supplanted by **crystal balls,** mirrors were also routinely used to predict the future. The first recorded case of mirror divination (known as *catoptromancy*) can be traced back to ancient Rome, where small metal mirrors were used to predict the life expectancy of the sick and the elderly. According to one account, from the second-century Greek traveler Pausanias, ancient Roman seers (or "scryers") would lower their mirrors into a pool of water, and then hold them up to the face of the sick person. If the patient's reflection appeared normal, it meant they would recover; if it was distorted, they would surely die.

Catoptromancy reached the height of its popularity around 1200, shortly after Venetian glass makers perfected the craft of producing large, flat glass mirrors. European catoptromancers would tilt their mirrors towards the sun or some other light source, and then "read the future" in the cryptic patterns of light and darkness they saw reflected there. According to the fifteenth-century German scholar Johannes Hartlieb, some medieval scryers also claimed to be able to create enchanted mirrors that could show men whatever they most desired.

By the late thirteenth century, mirrors had become so closely associated with catoptromancy and other forms of magical practice that one of the first questions posed at medieval witchcraft trials was: "Have you conducted experiments with mirrors?" At the same time, however, the great Christian philosopher Thomas Aquinas saw mirrors as a tool of enlightenment and argued that studying one's image could increase self-awareness and help a person to better understand his place in the world. (In fact, Aquinas helped coin the word "speculate," meaning to guess or ponder. In Latin, it literally means to peer into a *speculum*, or looking glass.)

Many European folktales and works of literature also depict mirrors as tools of knowledge, presenting them as windows onto important truths, distant lands, and unimagined marvels. In the medieval tale *Parsifal*, the guardian of the Holy Grail is able to spot his enemies approaching in a "foe glass" much like the one belonging to Mad Eye Moody. Beauty, from "Beauty and the Beast," eases her loneliness by watching her family in an enchanted looking glass. Even the mirror in "Snow White" is an instrument of truth and self-knowledge, bluntly informing Snow White's enemy that she is no longer the fairest in the land. (Of course, some talking mirrors are more outspoken than others. The one in Harry Potter's room at the Leaky Cauldron doesn't bother with any cute rhymes or diplomatic phrases. It just takes one look at Harry's hair and tells him he's a lost cause!)

Perhaps the most popular story ever written about a magic mirror is Lewis Carroll's *Through the Looking Glass*, in which a little girl named Alice slips through her drawing room mirror into a magical looking glass world, where everything and everyone is backward. People walk backward, read backward, even prick their fingers and scream backward! Mirrors, of course, really do flip things around, which explains why, in the looking-glass world, the Mirror of E-R-I-S-E-D reflects D-E-S-I-R-E.

Mirror Superstitions

Today, the science of optics has taken most of the mystery out of mirrors. But a few popular superstitions still linger to remind us of their magic. Here are ten of the most common superstitions from yesterday and today.

1. Breaking a mirror will bring seven years of bad luck. This belief originated around the first century A.D. with the Romans, who added the seven years to an earlier Greek superstition. The bad luck can be avoided, however, by burying a piece of the mirror.

2. When a mirror falls from the wall it means someone will die soon.

3. Mirrors should be covered during thunderstorms lest they attract lightning.

4. **Vampires** and **witches** cast no reflections in mirrors because they have no souls.

5. Mirrors can trap a human soul and should be covered when a person has died.

6. A mirror that is framed only on three sides has been used by a witch to see over long distances.

7. A baby should not be allowed to look at its own reflection during the first year of life for fear that its young soul will be sucked into the mirror.

8. Once dressed for a wedding a bride should not look at herself until after the ceremony, otherwise bad luck will result.

9. It's unlucky to gaze into a mirror by candlelight, especially on Halloween.

10. To dream of your future love, sleep with a mirror under your pillow.

Magic Wand

Who among us hasn't wished, at least once, for a magic wand? Magic wands—simple, elegant, easy to transport—are recognized the world over as symbols of the ability to make things happen. A wave of the wand and *poof!*—the dishes are done, your room is clean, your bowl of ice cream has tripled in size, and Aunt Henrietta just called to say she's not coming after all. But, as we learn from Harry's experiences, maybe it's not quite so simple. Perhaps you need a little skill in **spells** and **transfiguration** to go along with your wand, plus some guidance on what kind of timber you should be toting. Mahogany, oak, holly, or hazel? And what about **unicorn** hair, **phoenix** feathers, or other enhancements for your wand's core? These details are not to be taken lightly.

Magic wands have been around for a very long time. They appear in prehistoric cave paintings and in the art of the ancient Egyptians. The **magicians** of the Druid society that flourished in pre-Christian Europe presided over religious rituals with wands fashioned from hawthorn, yew, willow, and other trees they held sacred. Wands were carved only at dawn or sunset—considered the best times to capture the powers of the sun—using a sacred knife that had been dipped in blood. In the Old Testament, Moses uses a magic wand in the form of a shepherd's staff to part the Red Sea and draw water from a rock. A fourth-century image shows Jesus raising Lazarus from the dead by touching him with a wand. As these examples suggest, historically wands served not only as conductors of supernatural forces but also as tools of religious ceremony and symbols of power.

In fiction, magic wands first appear in *The Odyssey*, written by the Greek poet Homer in about 800 or 900 B.C. The beautiful witch **Circe**

*Two different ideas of the magic wand appear on these tarot cards. On the left,
the street magician's wand serves as symbol of his profession and a useful device
for directing the attention of his audience. On the right, an authentic wizard uses his wand
to call down the powers of the heavens for use on Earth.*

uses her wand to transform the hero's crew of sailors into a herd of squealing pigs. Changing one thing into another is a classic literary use of the magic wand, depicted in countless fairy tales. The best-known example is the star-tipped wand used by Cinderella's fairy godmother to transform mice into horses and a pumpkin into a coach. Other fabled wands belong to **Merlin,** wizard and mentor to King Arthur, and to the Greek god **Hermes,** who uses his wand (or *caduceus*) to make himself invisible to mortal men.

In early modern Europe, many practitioners of **magic** regarded the wand as an essential tool. It was used by ritual magicians (see **magic**) for casting spells, as well as drawing "magic circles" that would protect the magician from the harmful influence of any **demons** or spirits he planned to conjure up. Lacking the convenience of Diagon

Alley shopping, aspiring magicians turned to spell books for instructions on how to design and manufacture a wand. According to *The Key of Solomon,* one of the most famous magic books of the Middle Ages, the ideal wand should be made of hazel and cut from a tree with a single blow of a newly made axe. Some authorities claimed that the potency of the wand could be kicked up a notch or two by adding magnetized tips to the ends, attaching crystals, or inscribing **magic words** or sacred names on the wand. As the wand was carved, the magician called upon the appropriate spirits, demons, or gods to endow the wand with its desired powers—to heal the sick, control the forces of nature, or grant the practitioner's every wish.

While ritual magicians took their work very seriously, by the early fifteenth century wands were also being used for more lighthearted ends—as a standard prop of the street entertainers who performed "magic" as a livelihood. From the performer's point of view, the wand served at least two important functions: It was the agent that apparently caused the magic to happen, and it helped fool the audience by directing their attention to one thing while the magician secretly did something else. Magic wands are, of course, a hallmark of stage magicians today. Several performers we know collect "trick wands" that collapse, bend, change color, shoot streamers, or break into pieces. This brings to mind those trick wands manufactured by the entrepreneurial Weasley twins, who seem to have used magic to make the same kind of gimmicked item a nonwizard would buy in a joke shop or conjuror's supply store—you wave it and it turns into a rubber chicken.

 SS 5/82

The Magic Club

Why did a wand and not, say, a feather, become the symbol of magic? What is it about this stick that represents the awesome powers of the magician? The answer, according to some scholars, can be traced back to prehistoric man's first instrument of power—the cave man's club. While not particularly "magical," the club, in the form of a hefty hunk of a tree branch, certainly did endow its user with an extraordinary amount of *power* he didn't have without it—power to defend himself, bonk his enemies into oblivion, and put dinner on the table. Indeed, in a confrontation with an enemy, even raising the club in a threatening gesture was recognized as a sign of power. As spears and swords replaced the club as weapons of choice, the theory goes, the club was retired from everyday use but lived on in reduced size and symbolic form. In one version it became a scepter, the king's or emperor's wandlike emblem of power; in another, the club took the form of a herald's staff, investing the bearer with the powers of the king he represented. And, in the hands of a magician, the mini-club took the form of the wand, symbolizing command of the powers of nature and the supernatural. While the wand no longer resembles the club it evolved from, in the wizarding world it continues to function as the most powerful of weapons.

The king's scepter, like the magician's wand and the cave man's club, is an emblem of power.

The Caduceus

One of the snazziest of all wands is the winged and **snake**-entwined caduceus carried by Hermes, the Greek god of communication and master of magic and trickery. Given to him by his brother Apollo in exchange for a flute, the caduceus became Hermes' badge of office.

The design of the Caduceus—two serpents entwined around a central rod—can be found in Mesopotamian art dating back as early as 3500 B.C. Centuries later, the Greeks added wings to the rod to represent Hermes' swiftness and placed an orb or globe on top. According to Roman legend, the Caduceus was formed when Hermes (called Mercury by the Romans) came upon a pair of fighting serpents. He placed his wand between them, whereupon the snakes became friends and coiled themselves around the rod, and have been together ever since. In this version of the story, the wand represents harmony through communication. During the Middle Ages, alchemists like **Nicholas Flamel** believed that the snakes represented the union of opposites.

The caduceus is sometimes used as a symbol of the medical profession, although the true medical symbol is the staff of Asclepius, Greek god of medicine: a long staff entwined by a single serpent. The serpent entwining the staff is said to represent rejuvenation, because the snake sheds its old skin every year. Thus it symbolizes the physical rejuvenation that comes through medicine and healing.

Physicians during the Middle Ages traditionally carried a staff or cane as sign of their profession, and many attributed magical healing powers to the rod. Because of years of confusion between the caduceus and the Staff of Asclepius, both wands are now associated with medicine, healing, and in some places, health insurance.

Magic Words

A wizard is as powerful as the words he knows. Words are the thread by which **spells** are woven and **charms** and **curses** held in place. As stories from around the world attest, there are magic words for most every occasion—to enchant a castle, fly on a carpet, become invisible, or convince a broom to cook dinner and clean up afterward. Naturally, not any words will do. They must be the right words for the task at hand, and as Professor Flitwick wisely counsels his first-year students in Charms class, they must be pronounced with perfect precision. Say it right and it works automatically, like turning on a light. Say it wrong and you may end up with three heads.

Many of the Latin-sounding words taught at Hogwarts mean exactly what they seem to say. *Petrificus totalus* totally petrifies its victim, and *riddikulus* makes a formerly frightening **boggart** look, well, ridiculous. But magic words don't have to mean anything. A medieval spell book tells us that the nonsense words *saritap pernisox ottarim*, for example, will open any lock, while *onaim peranties rasonastos* will guide you to buried treasure and *agidem margidem sturgidem* will cure a toothache if said seven times on a Tuesday or a Thursday. Where these particular words came from and why they were believed to work is almost anybody's guess. Some were no doubt invented by practicing **magicians** to impress their clients. Other magic words, however, seem to have originated thousands of years ago as the names of gods and supernatural beings that were garbled and mistranslated over time, ultimately becoming unrecognizable. Yet even without evident meaning, words were thought to have tremendous power, and could bring into being the intentions of the magician. In fact, the belief that words are the instruments of power is probably as old as language itself, and one of the most ancient of all beliefs is that to say a thing is to make it so.

A string of magic words, especially when pronounced in a ritualistic way, is called an "incantation," or magic formula, and is often used to cast a spell or charm. In many traditional tribal cultures, incantations were chanted or sung and accompanied by dancing and drumming (the words "chant," "enchant," "charm," and "incantation," all share a Latin root meaning "song" and "to sing"). In classical Greece and Rome, sorcerers often cast their spells by wailing or howling the magic words, like a dog baying at the moon. In certain Hindu and Buddhist traditions, extraordinary powers were often associated with the repetition of special words or phrases called mantras, which were secret and could be learned only from a special teacher or guru. One mantra was said to give the chanter the power to control nature if repeated 200,000 times and to be instantly transported to anyplace in the universe if repeated a million times.

Abracadabra, the most familiar of all historical magic words, was thought for centuries to be extremely powerful. It first appears in the book *Res Reconditae* (*Secret Matters*) by Serenus Sammonicus, a Roman physician who lived in the third century. Serenus recommends *abracadabra* as a cure for tertian fever, a terrible flu-like illness with symptoms that occur every other day. The word can be spoken, but according to Serenus, the treatment is most effective when *abracadabra* is written on a piece of parchment in the form of an inverted triangle and worn around the neck as an **amulet.**

```
ABRACADABRA
 ABRACADAB
  ABRACADA
   ABRACAD
    ABRACA
     ABRAC
      ABRA
       AB
        A
```

As the word *abracadabra* shrinks, by removing one letter each time the word is written, so, presumably, will the patient's illness. At the end of nine days the amulet is removed and tossed backward into a river flowing eastward, ending the treatment.

Abracadabra remained in use as a magic word well into the seventeenth century. In his *Journal of the Plague Year* (1772), the English novelist Daniel Defoe reported that many Londoners tried to protect themselves against the bubonic plague epidemic of 1665 by using "certain words or figures, as particularly the word 'Abracadabra' formed in a triangle or pyramid."

Some of the most potent magic words of the Middle Ages took the form of palindromes—words or phrases that read the same backward as forward. Particularly appealing were words that could be arranged to form a "magic square" in which the words read identically top to bottom, bottom to top, right to left, or left to right. The best known of these, going back at least to the eighth century, is the square formed from the palindromic phrase *sator arepo tenet opera rotas*.

SATOR
AREPO
TENET
OPERA
ROTAS

Again, the meaning of these words is obscure, but according to many spell books, this square possessed at least three remarkable properties: It was a reliable **witch** detector (any witch in the same room with it would be forced to flee); it served as a charm against sorcery and disease; and if written on a wooden plate and kept handy, it worked as a fire extinguisher when hurled into a burning building! Other magic squares, such as those recommended in the spell book *The Sacred Magic of Abremelin the Mage*, offered palindromes like *odac dara arad cado*, which would allow the user to fly "like a vulture" (a different palindrome was offered for those who preferred to fly "like a crow"), and *milon irago lamal ogari nolim*, which would, if inscribed on parchment and held over one's

A Little Hocus Pocus

There's at least one place where magic words have always seemed to work—in the performances of entertainment magicians. Seventeenth-century wonder-workers were particularly fond of *hocus pocus,* which was originally part of the larger incantation *hocus pocus, toutous talontus, vade celerita jubes.* Like other pseudo-Latin incantations, the words mean nothing, but they sound mysterious and were used by countless performers.

Hocus pocus was originally an entertainer's phrase. Unlike *abracadabra,* it never appeared on amulets or in spell books, but its origin is a mystery. Some conjuring historians trace it to *Ochus Bochus,* the name of a legendary Italian wizard. Another theory cites the Welsh *hocea pwca,* meaning "a goblin's trick." It has also been suggested that *hocus pocus* is related to the Latin *hoc est corpus meum* ("this is my body"), from the Roman Catholic mass. This seems unlikely to many scholars, however, since popular entertainers would hardly have risked offending the Church—whose antagonism to magic of every sort was well known—by borrowing "magic words" from a sacred service. About all we can say for certain is that *hocus pocus* was in common use by the early seventeenth century. The English playwright Ben Johnson reported a stage magician calling himself Hokus Pokus in 1625, and the word appears in the title of an early "how-to" magic book, *Hocus Pocus Junior,* published in 1634. Today, many conjurors have dropped the use of magic words altogether, and "hocus pocus" has come to mean, in a general sense, trickery or deception. It may be the root of the English word "hoax."

head, deliver knowledge of all things past, present and future, as whispered into one's ear by a **demon**.

Achieving the desired result, as might be imagined, was not always as simple as copying down the words. Squares had to be inscribed on the proper materials, under the astrological influence of the appropriate stars and planets, and at the proper time. And even then, the results were not guaranteed. When a magic square or word failed to work, however, the fault was often said to lie with the practitioner, who was either saying the word incorrectly, did not have the proper attitude, or had omitted some important procedure. On the other hand, when a patient recovered from an illness or demons kept their distance, the effectiveness of the word was proven.

Belief in the power of magic words has really not diminished much over the centuries. The notion that "please" and "thank you" will bring magical results is still taught to children (at least by some folks) and still works. College students and advertising mavens know that the right words (called "buzz words" these days) will produce good grades and spectacular sales. And major corporations pay tens of thousands of dollars to wordsmiths who can come up with the one "magic" name or word that will make them or their product a household word—and a fortune.

 SS 10/171

Mandrake

It's a rare plant indeed that requires the gardener to wear ear protection. While Professor Sprout's insistence that her **herbology** students don earmuffs to work with mandrake plants may seem batty, it does have the weight of centuries of popular folk belief behind it. Throughout Europe, tradition held that the mandrake would utter a shriek if pulled from the ground, and all who heard it would perish. Harvesting mandrake was well worth the risk, however, because the plant had several well-known medicinal uses and was also believed to be endowed with powerful magical properties.

The part of the mandrake plant that has generally been considered most valuable is the thick, brown root, which can grow three to four feet into the ground. The root is often forked, and to anyone with a little imagination can look like a person. Descriptive books of plants and herbs frequently depicted the mandrake (a member of the nightshade family) with human characteristics—as a male with a long beard or as a female with a bushy head of hair. The human likeness could be easily enhanced by carving the root with a knife. This close resemblance to human beings no doubt explains the belief that the mandrake would cry out when pulled from the ground, like a person suddenly yanked from a warm bed.

Despite any sympathy humans might have for the plight of the uprooted mandrake, it was pulled up with great frequency and applied to a wide variety of purposes. In ancient times, it was considered a painkiller and a sleeping aid, and in large doses was said to induce delirium and even madness. It was used to promote rest in those suffering chronic pain and was also prescribed to treat melancholy, convulsions,

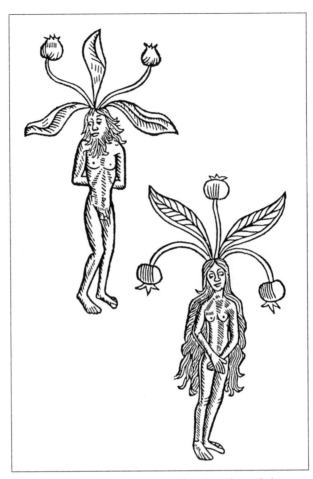

A fifteenth-century depiction of male and female mandrakes.

and rheumatism. The Romans used mandrake as an anesthetic, giving the patient a piece of the root to chew before surgery.

The ancients and their descendants in medieval Europe also valued mandrake for its supposed magical properties. It was a popular ingredient in love **potions** and was said to have been used by **Circe,** the best-known sorceress of Greek mythology, to prepare her most powerful elixirs. Anglo-Saxon lore held that the mandrake could expel **demons** from those who were possessed, and many believed it could ward off evil if prepared in a dried form and worn as an **amulet.** On the other hand, some folklore held that demons actually *lived* in mandrake roots, and possession of a carved mandrake root occasionally led

Mandrake Safety

Stories of the mandrake's fatal cry were well known in pre-modern Europe, and many who wanted to use the root for magic or medicine must have hesitated, fearing what might happen when they pulled the plant from the ground. Someone with such concerns might turn to an "herbal"—a book filled with information about the household and medicinal uses of plants. There they would find a solution to the dilemma. Most writers offered the same advice: Tie one end of a rope to the mandrake plant, while securing the other end around a dog's neck. After retreating to a safe distance, cover your ears and call the dog, who will run toward you, safely uprooting the plant.

A twelfth-century book on herbology illustrates the safest way to pick mandrakes.

to charges of witchcraft. Suspicious folk claimed that mandrake grew best under the gallows of executed murderers.

The mandrake was also employed for **divination**. Fortune-tellers insisted that the doll-like roots would nod their heads in answer to inquiries about the future. In Germany, peasants were known to take great care of their carved mandrakes, attaching bits of grain for eyes, dressing them, and tucking them into tiny beds at night—all to keep them ready and willing to answer any important question that might arise.

 CS 6/92

Manticore

If any beast could give us nightmares, the manticore would be the one. Not only is it the proud parent of Hagrid's feisty blast-ended skrewts, but its name means "maneater" in Persian, and its favorite activity—as you might guess—is devouring human flesh.

First described in the fifth century B.C. by the Greek physician Ctesias (who also gave us early **unicorn** lore), the manticore was said to inhabit the jungles of India, where its strength, speed, and sheer ferocity made it the most dangerous predator around. Although its reddish, hairy body resembled that of a lion, Ctesias reported, it had a human face, a melodious voice, and an extraordinary scorpion-like tail spiked with poisoned darts. The manticore could shoot these darts like arrows in any direction, striking prey at a distance of up to one hundred feet. Once a victim had succumbed to the fast-acting poison, the manticore was ready to get

down to business. Set in each of its enormous jaws and spanning the distance from ear to ear were three rows of razor-sharp teeth, perfect for reducing its favorite dish—humans—into bite-size morsels. Good eater that it was, the manticore devoured its victims entirely, including skull, bones, clothing, and possessions. When someone vanished from a jungle village without a trace, it was clear that a manticore was nearby.

Like so many fantastic creatures of antiquity, the manticore was thought to be quite real, and Ctesias's account was repeated by later authorities, among them Aristotle and the Roman naturalist Pliny. By the second century A.D., however, when a specimen of the manticore had yet to turn up, other explanations for alleged sightings of the creature were proposed. The Greek travel writer Pausanias offered the likely theory that the creature in question was really a man-eating tiger—now known as the Bengal tiger. While belief in the manticore did not survive, its legend inspired the imaginations of many artists and illustrators, and it became a recognized symbol of evil and malevolence.

Merlin

Merlin the Magician—**sorcerer,** prophet, and advisor to King Arthur—is probably the most famous **wizard** of all time. Much-loved English legends tell us that he could use his magic to win wars, transform himself into a greyhound or a stag at will, see into the future, and control the destinies of men.

Although Merlin and his life are the stuff of legend, he can be traced to a real historical figure—a sixth-century Welsh poet named Myrddin, who went insane in battle and fled into the forests of Scotland, where he made many predictions about the future. Myrddin's name was changed to Merlin by the historian Geoffrey of Monmouth, who introduced the **magician** to English folklore in his *History of the Kings of Britain,* an account of the legendary beginnings of Britain written in 1136. Over the centuries, Merlin's story was amplified by many writers, most notably Sir Thomas Malory, author of a fifteenth-century account of the Knights of the Round Table called *Le Morte d'Arthur* (*The Death of Arthur*).

Like many mythological figures, Merlin had extraordinary parents who bestowed him with special gifts. Geoffrey of Monmouth reports that the great magician's mother was the virtuous daughter of a king, while his father was a **demon** or evil spirit called an "incubus." Merlin inherited both his mother's goodness and his father's magical powers. He demonstrated his supernatural abilities while still a child, and in so doing, saved his own life.

The story begins with a fifth-century British king named Vortigern, whose efforts to construct a tower were a failure. No matter how much progress his workers made, each day's work would crumble to the ground overnight. Desperate, Vortigern consulted his magicians, who told him to strengthen the tower by mixing the mortar with the blood of a child who had no human father. Commanded to find such a child, Vortigern's emissaries soon discovered Merlin and brought him to the king. Although he was only seven years old, Merlin explained that the tower was unstable because it was built over an underground pool. He also predicted that if the pool were drained, two dragons would be found sleeping at the bottom in two hollow stones. When Merlin's words proved accurate, the king spared his life.

After Vortigern's death, Merlin became an advisor to three kings—Aurelius, Uther Pendragon, and, most famously, Uther's son, Arthur. Legend holds that during the reign of Aurelius, Merlin procured one of England's national treasures, Stonehenge, by using his magical powers to transport the enormous stones from Ireland. Aurelius wished to construct an impressive monument, and Merlin selected this circle of stones, known in Ireland as the Giant's Dance, because they were believed to have great healing powers. Although 15,000 English soldiers armed with cables and ladders were unable to budge the stones an inch, Merlin moved them in a flash. Made light as pebbles by his magical assistance, the stones were carried to boats and brought to the plain of Salisbury in England, where they remain today. (In reality, Stonehenge was erected around 2100 B.C., thousands of years before the earliest of the Merlin stories. However, there are a few bluish stones at Stonehenge known to have come from Wales, so the idea that the stones were quarried elsewhere and brought to Salisbury by way of water may have a grain of truth in it after all.)

During the reign of Uther Pendragon, Merlin performed a feat that was even more remarkable. Uther had fallen in love with a married duchess named Ygerna. As a result, her husband Gorlois, the Duke of Cornwall, locked her up in a heavily guarded castle. But Merlin cast a spell to make Uther look exactly like Gorlois, allowing Uther to gain entrance to the castle. The guards were fooled, as was Ygerna. That night, Arthur, the heir to Uther's throne and the future king of Britain, was conceived. Years later, after the real Gorlois was killed in battle, Ygerna and Uther married.

Merlin succumbs to Vivien's charms.

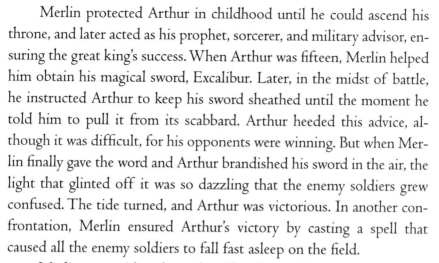

Merlin protected Arthur in childhood until he could ascend his throne, and later acted as his prophet, sorcerer, and military advisor, ensuring the great king's success. When Arthur was fifteen, Merlin helped him obtain his magical sword, Excalibur. Later, in the midst of battle, he instructed Arthur to keep his sword sheathed until the moment he told him to pull it from its scabbard. Arthur heeded this advice, although it was difficult, for his opponents were winning. But when Merlin finally gave the word and Arthur brandished his sword in the air, the light that glinted off it was so dazzling that the enemy soldiers grew confused. The tide turned, and Arthur was victorious. In another confrontation, Merlin ensured Arthur's victory by casting a spell that caused all the enemy soldiers to fall fast asleep on the field.

Merlin was said to have the gift of **transfiguration,** and could turn himself into a child, an old man, a woman, a dwarf, or an animal as it suited him. He could control the raging sea and make the walls of Arthur's castle, Camelot, throw off enemies who tried to scale them. But despite such extraordinary abilities, the great magician made a foolish mistake that resulted in his downfall. He became infatuated with the sorceress Vivien (sometimes called the Lady in the Lake) and revealed his magical secrets to her. Using this knowledge against him, she cast a spell that imprisoned him forever inside an oak tree.

Nevertheless, Merlin's place in literature and legend is so significant that no other magician approaches him in prominence. His combination of wisdom and magical prowess has appealed to artists of all kinds, and he has been a prominent character in countless works of fiction, theater, and film. No wonder Albus Dumbledore acknowledges his election to the Order of Merlin on his official Hogwarts correspondence. It's an honor any magician would be proud to receive.

 SS 4/51

Mermaid/Merman

We were as surprised as Harry to learn that the gray-skinned, yellow-eyed merpeople at the bottom of the Hogwarts lake are actually relatives of the beautiful, blonde mermaid whose picture hangs in the prefects' bathroom. As these dissimilar sightings illustrate, the familiar "bathing beauty" is just one member of a whole family of merfolk—a population that consists of not only mermaids and mermen, but dozens of cousins from around the world, among them the Cornish merrymaid; the Irish merrow; the blue men of Scotland; the neck, havfrue, and havmand of Scandinavia; the meerfrau, nix, nixe, and lorelei of Germany; and the Russian rusalka. Like humans, merpeople come in all shapes and sizes; some are kind, some evil, some are beautiful, and some hideous. In fact, the only traits all merfolk seem to share are a human form above the waist and a fish tail below.

The first merpeople were gods and goddesses of ancient civilizations. Ea (or Oammes in Greek) was a sea god that the Babylonians began to worship around 5000 B.C. He was credited with teaching them the full spectrum of arts and sciences, and with civilizing the Babylonians at a time in history when there were no laws and people often behaved like beasts. The first female of the species was a goddess known as Atargatis by the Syrians and Derceto by the Philistines. Because she ruled the seas, the priests of her temple apparently set up a lucrative business selling fishing licenses to her worshippers!

The well-known image of the beautiful, long-haired mermaid originated during the Middle Ages. Usually depicted seated on a rock, she sings an irresistibly sweet song while combing her hair and gazing dreamily into a mirror. Several theories have been offered to explain the mermaid's obsession with grooming. Some people believe it's because an unknown artist, copying an age-worn mermaid picture, made some mistakes, and all artists thereafter followed suit. According to this theory, her "comb" may actually have been a plectrum (a pick used for plucking a stringed instrument), while the "mirror" was the instrument itself, perhaps a lyre. Another explanation suggests that the mirror and comb symbolize vanity and female beauty, traits that were believed to lead to the destruction of men.

Indeed, despite her pleasing appearance, the mermaid was often portrayed as a wicked enchantress who lured sailors to their deaths with her beauty and song and kept the souls of her drowned victims prisoners beneath the waves. The most malevolent mermaids even ate their human prey. Thus it was considered a very bad omen to see a mermaid. Her very presence heralded storms, shipwrecks, and drownings. And, in addition to inciting natural disasters, a mermaid who was offended, hurt, or rejected might drive the wrongdoer mad, drown him, or wash away his family, house, and entire village.

Fortunately, not all mermaids behaved so badly. Some were believed to have a vast knowledge of herbal medicine, which they could be persuaded to use to cure human illnesses. Supernatural abilities allowed them to predict storms, foresee the future, grant wishes, and raise sunken treasure. Because of these powers, mermaids of fable were often captured by humans and forced to grant wishes and share their wisdom. Catching a mermaid was not as difficult as it might sound. You only had to steal one of her possessions—her comb or mirror, or perhaps the belt or cap she sometimes wore. Once captured, a mermaid could not escape unless she reclaimed her stolen property.

Mermaids were also coveted by men who wanted these beautiful and enchanting women for wives. Conveniently, mermaids were said to desire human husbands, not only for love but also to acquire a soul, which all merpeople lacked. Whether or not these "mixed marriages" would actually help mermaids obtain eternal salvation was an issue debated by the medieval Church. Regardless, legend holds that the children of such marriages could be identified by their webbed feet and hands, but were otherwise indistinguishable from human children.

Stories of marriages between mermen and human women also exist, but these are less common, probably because unlike their female counterparts, mermen are known to be grotesquely ugly. In fact, some cultures describe great differences between mermen and mermaids, claiming that mermen loathe mankind, do not desire souls, make brutal husbands, and even eat their own children.

Despite centuries of belief in merpeople, no such creature has ever been found. From medieval times until quite recently, mermaid sightings were reported by many respectable gentlemen, including sailors in the employ of Christopher Columbus and Henry Hudson, but no physical evidence has ever been produced. Some enterprising con men have exhibited so-called mermaids, but these have all turned out to be fakes. P. T. Barnum, for example, constructed the "Feejee mermaid" by sewing the top half of a monkey to the bottom half of a large fish. As for mermaid sightings reported by responsible citizens, scholars attribute these to mistakenly identified seals, walruses, manatees, or dugongs (Asian cousins of the American manatee). All of these animals frequently float upright and breast-feed their young like human mothers. Of course, if you've seen any of these creatures, you know they are not easily mistaken for the beautiful hair-combing, song-singing women of myth. But the people who most often spotted "mermaids" were sailors who'd been at sea for months or years. So maybe it's not so hard to understand why their eyes rewarded them with an image of a beautiful woman instead of yet another chubby dugong.

 GF 26/497

Mermaid Relatives

Many supernatural beings of folklore and myth are closely associated with water, yet not classified as merfolk. The best known of these creatures are naiads, sirens, and selkies. Although often mistaken for or confused with mermaids, each possesses distinctive and remarkable characteristics.

Naiads originated in Greek mythology and comprise one of the three main classes of water nymphs. (The other two are nereids, who dwell in the Mediterranean Sea, and oceanids, who live in the oceans.) Naiads inhabit bodies of fresh water, such as rivers, lakes, fountains, and springs. In ancient times, every major spring was believed to have a resident naiad, who gave the water special healing or prophetic powers. People were welcome to drink from the spring, but bathing was forbidden. Those who ignored this restriction were punished with illness or were driven mad. Although the naiads lived exclusively in water, they resembled humans and did not have tails or fins like mermaids.

Sirens also originated in Greek mythology, and, like naiads, inhabited rivers. However, when they offended the goddess Aphrodite, she turned them into malicious creatures with a bird's body and a woman's head and they went to live on an uninhabited island off the southern coast of Italy. Despite their anatomical differences, sirens are often confused with mermaids because of their similar seductive musical abilities. Sailors who passed the sirens' island and heard their beautiful song were inevitably lured off course and fatally dashed against the rocks. Legend holds that the hero Odysseus was able to save himself from this doom by ordering his men to stuff their ears with wax and lashing himself to the mast of his ship as they passed the sirens' island.

Selkies are creatures that look like seals and are said to live near the British islands of Orkney and Shetland. Female selkies can shed their sealskins and come ashore in the guise of beautiful women. If a human male finds the skin, he can force the selkie-woman into marriage. If she is able to locate her skin again, she will return to the sea, leaving her husband and children behind. Like mermaids, selkies will avenge any harm or insult by causing fierce storms or sinking ships.

Morgana

The ability to conjure and enchant, fly through the air, appear as an animal, and heal with magic herbs all earn the sorceress Morgana her place on a Chocolate Frogs trading card. Also known as Morgan le Fay, sister or half-sister to King Arthur, Morgana is a versatile fictional character who appears in the literature and legends of Britain, Italy, and France. Sometimes she's a goddess, sometimes a **witch,** a **hag,** an enchantress, or a **fairy.** Whichever guise she takes, her strong personality and supernatural skills make her a figure to be reckoned with.

Morgana makes her first appearance in Arthurian legend in the thirteenth-century writings of Geoffrey of Monmouth, who refers to her as Morgan le Fay (the fairy) and describes her as a learned and beautiful woman with healing powers and the ability to fly and change shape. She lives with her eight sisters on the island of Avalon. When King Arthur is wounded in his final battle, Morgan brings him to Avalon, lays him on a golden bed, and restores him to health. In many later accounts, Morgan is said to have learned her healing and other magic from **Merlin.**

In the late Middle Ages, when **witchcraft** was becoming a matter of grave concern in Europe, a powerful woman who could perform magic was an object of suspicion, even if she was merely a fictional character. As a result, new versions of Arthurian legend began to portray Morgan le Fay in a negative light. In Thomas Malory's *Le Morte d'Arthur,* Morgan appears as a thoroughly evil character, bent on using her magic to destroy her brother, his queen, and his court. Knowing

A nineteenth-century depiction of Morgan le Fay casting a spell.

Arthur is vulnerable without his magic sword, Excalibur, she steals it and gives it to Arthur's enemy in the hope that it will be used to kill the king. On another occasion, Morgan gives her unwitting brother an enchanted cloak, apparently as a peace offering. He is saved at the last moment from putting it on and being reduced to smoldering coals. Pursued by Arthur's men, Morgan escapes by turning herself into a stone.

Beyond Arthurian legend, Morgana appears in Irish folklore as a wicked fairy who enjoys frightening people and in Scottish folklore as the mistress of a castle inhabited by a band of evil fairies. In the Italian epic poem *Orlando Furioso,* Morgana is an enchantress who lives at the bottom of a lake, dispensing treasure to those who please her. She is also related to the Morganes or Morgens—**mermaids** said to live off the coast of France. It is perhaps a testament to the dual nature of Morgana's character that in some tales the sailors who encounter these mermaids are doomed; in others, they are welcomed into a magnificent underwater paradise.

 SS 6/103

The Fata Morgana

Morgana gives her name to one of the most famous mirages in the world, the *Fata Morgana* in Italy. Positioned over the Straits of Messina between mainland Italy and Sicily, this optical illusion first appears as a group of turreted castles that rise from the sea out of the fog. Look long enough, and you may see a tower turn into a figure—said to be Morgana herself—floating above the waves. This startling sight is believed to be caused by a complex interaction between layers of moist sea air, which distort and magnify the image of cliffs and houses on the shores of the straits.

Mummy

Parvati Patil's worst fear is having to confront a mummy, and we can't blame her one bit. After all, her idea of a mummy isn't the sort you might see lying peacefully in its sarcophagus at a museum, but the kind most of us know from horror movies—a lumbering monster that chases its victims with arms outstretched and bandages unraveling at every step.

Although "mummy" is a very general term that can be used to describe any dead body that's been preserved for an unusually long time, our popular conception of bandage-wrapped mummies was inspired by the ancient Egyptian practice of mummification, in which a body was drained of all its fluids, embalmed using a special chemical compound called natron, and then wrapped in fresh linen. Between 3000 B.C. and A.D. 200 the ancient Egyptians preserved millions of human and animal corpses this way, interring their remains in pyramids, underground tombs, and elaborate cities of the dead known as necropolises. The Egyptians went to so much trouble because they believed that the souls of the dead required an intact body to complete their journey to the afterworld. They also thought that during certain important religious celebrations the spirit, or *ka*, of a dead person could reenter its mummy and interact with the living again.

Even though the Egyptians stopped mummifying their dead around the first century, mummies never disappeared from the popular imagination. During the

Middle Ages, ground-up mummy powder was a popular ingredient in many medicines and magic **potions.** After Napoleon's invasion of Egypt in 1798, mummies also became much sought after as historical curiosities and collectors' items. The Italian adventurer Giovanni Belzoni made a small fortune raiding ancient Egyptian tombs, collecting mummies, and putting them on display throughout Europe. In the 1830s, Belzoni's friend Thomas Pettigrew began selling tickets to mummy-unwrapping ceremonies, and these events proved so popular that, on at least one occasion, even the Archbishop of Canterbury had to be turned away at the door. By the end of the nineteenth century, it was possible to purchase an authentic Egyptian mummy at almost any British auction house, and many fine English gentlemen kept a mummy or two hidden away in the attic (just for the heck of it, as far as anyone can tell)!

It didn't take long for such gory activities to inspire the fertile imaginations of fiction writers, who began to publish bestselling tales about mummies being brought back to life. In Edgar Allen Poe's humorous short story "Conversations with a Mummy," written in 1845, a group of Egypt-obsessed gentlemen sneak into a museum late at night and resurrect an ancient Egyptian corpse by electrocuting it. They receive a nasty shock of their own when they discover that their newly resurrected friend is not the primitive, uneducated monster they expected, but a suave three-thousand-year-old nobleman who knows more about astronomy, engineering, and science than any of the eminent Victorians who awaken him. The only modern invention that really impresses this mummy is a small peppermint breath mint, the likes of which he has never seen before!

The single most influential mummy story ever written in English is probably Sir Arthur Conan Doyle's 1892 work, "Lot Number 249." In this memorable tale about an ancient Egyptian brought back to life to commit murder and mayhem, Conan Doyle describes his mummy as "a horrid, withered thing" that stalks its enemies "with blazing eyes and stringy arms outthrown." This description proved powerful enough to inspire a thousand imitators and firmly established the modern image of the mummy as a monster.

Today, there are almost as many movies, books, and short stories about mummies as there once were actual mummies. But don't tell that to Parvati Patil. She's got enough to worry about just fighting one monster at a time.

 PA 7/137

Nicholas Flamel

Nicholas Flamel is best known to Harry Potter fans as the medieval alchemist who created the **Sorcerer's Stone**—a miraculous substance that could change lead into gold and produce an elixir of immortality. At the time of Harry's first term at Hogwarts (where the Stone is hidden away and guarded by **spells** and **charms**), Flamel is alive and well and residing with his wife Perenelle in Devon, England, at the ripe old age of 665. That's just about how old the historical Nicholas Flamel would be were he alive today. For Flamel was indeed a real alchemist, he did have a wife named Perenelle, and if the writings he left behind are to be believed, he created the legendary Stone in his alchemical laboratory on January 17, 1382.

Much of what we know about Flamel comes from his book *Heiroglyphica*, in which he

Nicholas Flamel.

tells how, almost by accident, he became an alchemist. When he was born—around 1330 in the small town of Pontoise, France—alchemy was already being practiced throughout Western Europe. Based on the practices of ancient Greek and Egyptian metalworkers, the secrets of alchemy were passed along through the Arab world and became available in Europe in Latin books around 1200. These books described sophisticated laboratory equipment, chemical ingredients, and complex procedures by which one could create the Sorcerer's Stone and acquire enormous wealth, not to mention the promise of everlasting life. Alchemy was also said to be a spiritual practice, so that with a humble attitude and devotion to the task, the alchemist himself might be elevated to a state of new purity and nobility. While many people were skeptical of both claims, countless others set up homemade laboratories and devoted their lives to trying to manufacture the Stone.

As a young man, however, Flamel seemed to have no particular interest in alchemy, although he had no doubt heard of it. He was well educated for a man of his era, literate in both Latin and French, and when it was time to set off on his own, he moved to Paris and went into business as a professional copyist, notary, and book dealer. Many of Flamel's contemporaries could neither read nor write, and when they needed some important transaction recorded, they went to a professional scribe. Flamel also copied books and manuscripts (the printing press would not be invented for another hundred years), and earned additional income by giving writing lessons to the wealthy, teaching them, among other things, how to sign their names. His first shop was located in a tiny wood stall on the Street of Notaries, but as his successful business grew he hired a staff of apprentices, bought a nearby house, and relocated his store to the first floor. He also met and married Perenelle, an attractive and wealthy widow.

Until this point the young scribe's life was ordinary enough. But all that changed when a stranger appeared in his shop and sold him a book that would change his life forever. "There fell into my hands," he wrote, "for the sum of two florins, a gilded book, very old and large. It was not of paper or parchment as other books are, but made only of thin bark. The cover was of copper, very delicate, and engraved all over with strange fig-

Alchemical processes often took weeks or months to complete.
Nicholas Flamel had only one assistant, his wife Perenelle.

ures." Flamel studied the book and became convinced it contained the secret of making the Sorcerer's Stone—if only he could understand it. But
like all alchemical books, much of it was written in a deliberately cryptic language. And the deepest secrets of all were contained not in words
but in mysterious symbolic pictures. One drawing, for example, showed
a painted desert filled with beautiful fountains overflowing with serpents.
Another depicted a windblown bush atop a mountain surrounded by
griffins and **dragons.**

Flamel copied the drawings (no one but Perenelle was ever allowed
to see the actual book), showed them to his colleagues and hung them
in his shop, hoping someone could explain what they meant. But no
one could. It was possibly at this point that Nicholas set up an alchemical laboratory and began experimenting, basing his procedures on
those parts of the book that he did understand. But nothing worked.
The alchemical tradition required that those who would learn "the art"
must first be initiated into its secrets by a master. And so, after many
failed experiments, Flamel finally sought out and found such a teacher
living in Spain. With the *real* secrets of the book at last at hand Flamel
returned to Paris where, after three years of intensive labor, he achieved
his goal. "I made projection of the red Stone upon a quantity of mer-

cury," he wrote, "in the presence of Perenelle only, which I transmuted truly into almost as much pure gold."

Flamel created gold, he said, only three times. But it was far more than he ever needed. He and Perenelle lived modestly and they used their wealth to benefit others. During the remaining years of their lives they founded and supported fourteen hospitals, commissioned religious monuments, built chapels, paid for the upkeep of churches and church graveyards, and gave generously to poor widows and orphans. Perenelle died in 1397 and Flamel spent his last years writing about alchemy. He died on March 22, 1417, and was buried in the church of Saint-Jacques la Boucherie, near his home.

What are we to make of Flamel's story? Did he really make gold? Or did he make up everything—the ancient book, the journey to Spain, the Sorcerer's Stone? Our only source of information is Flamel himself. But some of the facts are beyond doubt. Nicholas Flamel was a real person; his gifts and good deeds were real (some of the monuments he built lasted for centuries), and the story of his alchemical quest helped keep alive the belief that alchemy was a real science and that the Sorcerer's Stone could be made.

180

By the seventeenth century Flamel's story had become the stuff of legend. It was widely reported that soon after his death looters broke into Flamel's home and ripped it apart looking for gold. Failing to find any, they pried opened the great alchemist's coffin, hoping to find a piece of the Stone. Instead they found the coffin empty—no Stone and no Flamel! The truth, some said, was that Flamel and Perenelle had never really died at all. They had used the Stone to become immortal. A rash of Flamel sightings were reported. One account issued by an emissary of King Louis XIV had them residing in India. In 1761, they were reportedly seen attending a performance at the Paris Opera. And most recently, according to a rumor spread by none other than Albus Dumbledore, the couple was said to be contemplating giving up immortality in favor of a nice long rest.

Owl

As far as we know, the **wizards** and **witches** of Harry Potter's England are the first to be lucky enough to have reliable, door-to-door mail service provided by owls. However, the close association of owls with **sorcerers** does have a long history. The owls of the fabled wizards of medieval Europe may not have carried letters for their masters, but they are said to have been loyal companions, relied upon for their keen powers of observation and their ability to memorize complicated formulas and **spells.** According to legend, many an absentminded wizard like Neville Longbottom sought the aid of a feathered friend when caught in a sticky situation.

Hedwig's ability to communicate with Harry and understand his commands can be traced to the beliefs of the ancient Greeks, who were convinced that owls were highly intelligent. Athena, the Greek goddess of wisdom, was often portrayed with an owl on her shoulder. Some said she could even transform herself into an owl, using this disguise to patrol her realm and learn her subjects' secrets and concerns. Wealthy citizens of Athens often walked the streets with owls on their shoulders or carried them about in cages. Many believed that the birds understood human speech and could converse with people if they wished.

In other cultures, however, owls have been associated with death and the forces of evil, perhaps because they are creatures of the night and efficient birds of prey. In China, owls were once associated with Lei Kung, the god of thunder, while in Japan they were believed to bring famine and pestilence. In ancient Egypt owls were a symbol of death and night, and in ancient Rome seeing an owl during the daytime was believed to be a terrible omen. Many superstitious Romans were certain that the only way to prevent disaster after an owl sighting was to catch and kill the owl, then scatter its ashes in the Tiber River. According to legend, the hooting of owls predicted the murder of the Roman emperor Julius Caesar.

Although Harry and his friends would cringe to hear it, many cultures have supported the belief that owning or carrying a piece of an owl (feet, feathers, eyes, hearts, bones, or even whole owl bodies) can provide a person with special protections and powers. Possession of owl parts might protect the owner from rabies or epilepsy, or might bring him energy, wisdom, and courage. The professional healers of medieval Europe stocked owl parts to meet the demands of a wide variety of customers, from the warrior seeking strength in battle to the lover wishing to learn the secrets of the beloved. No doubt a **potions** master like Severus Snape would have them on hand as well.

 SS 8/135

Palmistry

$\mathcal{I}$f Harry's left palm is any indication, he may have very little time left on this Earth. At least that's what it sounds like when Professor Trelawney begins her lesson in palmistry by announcing that Harry has the shortest life line she's ever seen. So much for tact!

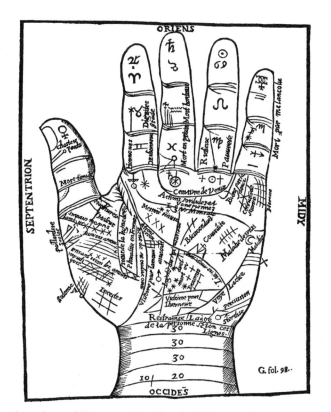

Palm reading could be very complicated. A detailed map of the human hand from 1640 shows the relationship between the signs of the zodiac and the lines on the palm.

Palmistry, also known as *chiromancy* (from the Greek *cheiro*, meaning "hand" and *mancy*, meaning "prophecy"), is a complex method of fortune-telling and character analysis based on the lines on a person's palms and the shape, size, and texture of their hands. This system of divination probably originated in India and is at least five thousand years old. It was practiced in ancient China, Tibet, Persia, Mesopotamia, and Egypt. Legend holds that the Greek philosopher Aristotle, who described the hand as the "principle organ" of the body, taught palmistry to his most famous pupil, Alexander the Great. Julius Caesar is said to have thought himself so skilled at deciphering palms that he judged his men by the appearance of their hands.

Although the ancients praised the merits of palmistry, systematic guides to the art were not developed until the Renaissance. The first

complete manual on the subject, *The Chiromantic Art,* appeared in Germany in 1475, not long after the invention of the printing press. In this and many works that followed, readers could find detailed maps of the hand that gave names and specific meanings to each line, pad (or "mount"), and valley on the palm. Analysis of these details was said to provide clues not only to a person's character and destiny but also to his or her risk for heart trouble, liver disease, and other illnesses. In the seventeenth century, courses on palmistry were on the curriculum of several major universities.

Palm reading reached its heyday at the end of the nineteenth century with the rise of its most famous practitioner, Count Louis Hamon. Working in London under the professional name of Cheiro, Hamon conducted thousands of readings each year, using a system he had learned from his Irish mother. He developed a reputation for remarkable accuracy and attracted many notable clients, including kings Edward VII and Edward VIII of England, King Leopold of Belgium, Czar Nicholas II of Russia, Grover Cleveland, Thomas Edison, Mark Twain, and Oscar Wilde. The excitement stirred by Hamon's successes has never quite faded, and professional palm readers still thrive throughout much of Europe and the United States.

Palm-Reading Basics

Most palm readers examine both hands. The left is said to reveal an individual's inherited characteristics, while the right indicates choices to be made and the victories and defeats that lie ahead. Each line and mount on the palm is examined separately, but a complete reading takes into account the collective meaning of all features of the hand.

A glance at your own hands will reveal dozens of lines, long and short, bold and subtle. Many elaborate systems of palmistry attribute significance to each line, as well as to the distance between lines and the ways in which lines cross one another. But every system begins with these principle lines:

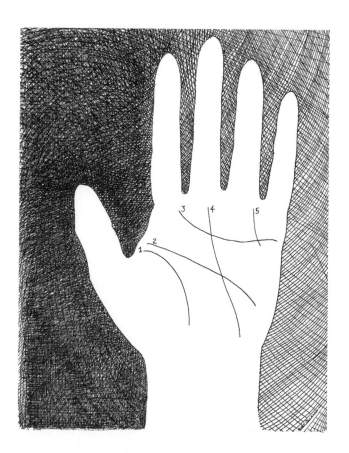

1. THE LIFE LINE: Contrary to popular belief (and Professor Trelawney's implication), this line does not indicate how long a person will live, but provides a general picture of the subject's quality of life and vitality. A strong downward curve, even in a short line, indicates physical strength; a relatively straight line suggests limited endurance.

2. THE HEAD LINE: This reflects a person's intellectual capacities. It reveals creative potential, powers of concentration, and problem-solving skills. A long line indicates the ability to focus.

3. THE HEART LINE: This line provides the key to understanding emotions. It reveals the subject's style of interacting with others and his or her expectations regarding love and relationships.

4. FATE LINE: This line indicates the degree of control one exercises over one's life and circumstances. It also reveals how well a person handles responsibility and makes use of innate talents.

5. THE APOLLO LINE: Sometimes known as the Line of the Sun, this line measures inner contentment. Not everyone has an Apollo line, but when it appears it's a sign of a capacity to enjoy life and derive satisfaction from work. In some systems, a long Apollo line indicates good luck.

 PA 12/235

Petrification

In some sense, we all know what it's like to be petrified—possessed by fear so complete it renders us unable to move. But fortunately none of us have shared Hermione's unpleasant experience of *literal* petrification—being turned to stone.

In the mythology of ancient Greece, many unfortunate souls knew what it was like to have their limbs stiffen into permanent immobility. Some were the victims of the monster Medusa, whose hideous face and hair of hissing **snakes** made her so terrifying that anyone who looked upon her was instantly turned to stone. The cave in which she lived was filled with the statue-like figures of all who had dared approach her. Medusa was eventually killed by the young hero Perseus,

who cut off her head while looking at her reflection in his shield, thus avoiding a direct (and fatal) glance at her face. Medusa's head retained its power to petrify even after her death, and Perseus took his trophy with him on many adventures, pulling it out of his bag and holding it aloft to stop his enemies in their tracks.

Turning people to stone was by no means a pleasure reserved for monsters like Medusa. Petrification was also a punishment favored by the gods of Olympus, especially for mortals they considered arrogant or disobedient. Most famous among these was Niobe, the Queen of Thebes, who angered the gods by boasting that she had twelve children, while the goddess Leto had only two. Bristling at this insult to their mother, Leto's children, Apollo and Artemis, quickly descended from the heavens and shot all of Niobe's offspring with deadly arrows. The devastated Niobe began to weep uncontrollably. Sinking to the ground in motionless grief, she was transformed into a stone that would remain perpetually wet with tears.

Petrification has also been a prominent theme in folklore, especially wherever unusual rock formations spark the imagination to see humans or animals in their shapes. In a town in Germany where the cliffs resemble men (at least to the open-minded), locals have long told the story of a group of mountain **dwarfs** who were out celebrating a wedding when they were turned to stone by an evil **ghost.** In Scandinavia, strangely shaped rocks are often said to be the petrified bodies of **trolls,** who were turned to stone when they failed to return to their underground homes before daylight.

In British folklore, the petrification of living people is said to account for the presence of hundreds of stone circles, mysterious monuments actually constructed by the prehistoric peoples of western Europe between 3000 and 1200 B.C. In local legend, "Long Meg and Her Daughters," a stone circle in Cumbria, England, is said to be a gathering of witches who were turned to stone by a wizard who discovered them. One of the Stanton Drew circles in Avon, England, is said to contain the bride, groom, dancers, and fiddlers of a wedding party, all turned to stone by the Devil, who joined their celebration in disguise.

The United States is not dotted with mysterious stone monuments, but that hasn't stopped its citizens from being interested in tales about petrification. During the nineteenth century, American newspapers published dozens of reports about petrified human bodies found buried in the ground, sitting on boulders, or mummified in tree trunks. There were even reports of men who had seen other men turn to stone before their very eyes! All were hoaxes invented by enterprising journalists who needed to fill space and entertain the gullible public. *Huckleberry Finn* author Mark Twain wrote one of the more exaggerated of these stories in an attempt to ridicule this trend, but much to his dismay, his readers were simply eager to hear more.

 CS 9/142

Phoenix

The most remarkable thing about the phoenix, as Harry learns firsthand while waiting in Albus Dumbledore's office, is that periodically—every five hundred years or so—this legendary bird bursts into flame, is reduced to ashes, and rises from those ashes newborn. In ancient Greek and Egyptian mythology this cycle of fiery death and rebirth was associated with the cycle of the sun, which "died" every night, plunging the world into darkness, and was born again the following day. During the Middle Ages the phoenix became part of Christian symbolism, representing death, resurrection, and eternal life, while today it is a common metaphor for triumph over adversity. Anyone who has overcome defeat or recovered from a terrible calamity is

said to have "risen from the ashes." In a somewhat different form, the phoenix is also part of Chinese mythology, where for centuries it has been a symbol of power, integrity, loyalty, honesty, and justice.

Classical Greek and Roman writers tell us that there was but a single phoenix in the world, and he lived in Arabia, near a cool well where each morning he bathed and sang a sweet song. "Part of his plumage is gold-colored, and part crimson, and he is for the most part very much like an eagle in outline and bulk," reported the Greek historian Herodotus, who also cautioned his readers, "I have not seen it myself, except in a picture." The phoenix dined on frankincense, cinnamon, and myrrh, and when he sensed the end of his days were near, he gathered the woods and bark of these aromatic plants and built a final nest—some called it a funeral pyre—on the top of a palm or oak tree. There he flapped his wings rapidly until he burst into flame and was reduced to a smoldering heap of ashes, out of which a new, fledgling phoenix arose. After it gained its strength and tested its wings, the new phoenix gathered up the ashes of its former self, sealed them inside an egg made of myrrh, and flew them to the Temple of the Sun in Heliopolis, Egypt, where it placed the egg on the alter of the sun god Ra. The phoenix was then free to return to Arabia and begin another five centuries of life.

While Dumbledore's phoenix, Fawkes, most resembles the legendary bird of classical mythology, he has some of the Chinese phoenix in him as well. For it is the Chinese bird—talons bared and wings spread wide—that is traditionally depicted attacking **snakes** such as the **basilisk**. And while we know of no precedent for Fawkes' ability to heal wounds with his tears or empower wands with his tail feathers, we also suspect there is a great deal more about this remarkable bird we have yet to discover.

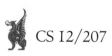

Pixie

When Gilderoy Lockhart unleashes a cageful of Cornish pixies into his classroom, utter pandemonium erupts, with ink, books, and broken glass flying every which way. The fact that pixies cause such chaos under Lockhart's watch may tell us something about the good professor's character, for these tiny redheaded **fairies** of western England have a reputation for picking on people they consider lazy. In the folklore of Somerset, Devon, and Cornwall, pixies are known to help out people in need, but those who fail to do their share or forget to reward their wee helpers with a bowl of cream to drink and a clean-swept hearth to dance upon are advised not to leave their prized possessions within reach.

Although similar to many other fairies in behavior, pixies are quite distinctive in appearance. In addition to their fiery red hair, they can be identified by their pointed ears, turned up noses, and distinctive squint. They are usually about seven or eight inches tall, although some stories suggest they can be any size they choose. Pixies almost always dress in green and often wear a pointed cap. They live underground, or in caves, meadows, or groves of trees, but can also be enticed to move indoors. A homeowner eager to enlist the aid of these fairies—to lend a hand with the spinning or give a quick pinch to a lazy housemaid—might try leaving the last harvest of apples under the trees, a practice known as "pixyworting." It is a mistake to reward your pixies with new clothes, however; like **elves** and other household helpers, pixies are compelled to leave if offered such a present.

Pixies have a number of tricks up their little sleeves, some of them quite malevolent. A favorite is to lead travelers astray. Many of us have had the experience of walking in a familiar place only to suddenly find ourselves hopelessly lost, unable to find a recognizable landmark. In western England, this disconcerting experience is known as being "pixy led" or "pixilated." Pixies are also notorious horse thieves, said to steal the animals during the night and ride them around in circles, twisting their manes and tails into impossible knots. Another form of nightly entertainment is dancing in a forest fairy ring (see **Fairy**) to the music of chirping crickets and frogs. If a human happens to step into a fairy ring, he or she is likely to be compelled to dance all night. The best way to counteract this effect, as well as to avoid being pixy led, is to wear your coat or clothing inside out. Finally, many stories tell of pixies stealing human babies and leaving fairy changelings in their place. As recently as the nineteenth century, women in Somerset and Devon still tied their babies into their cribs to keep pixies from stealing them.

 CS 6/101

Poltergeist

Plagued by things that go bump in the night? You may well have inherited a poltergeist. These so-called "noisy **ghosts**" (their name literally means "racketing spirit" in German) are some of the peskiest specters around. Unlike phantoms, apparitions, and most other varieties of ghosts, poltergeists don't haunt a particular building or house; instead, they attach themselves to a specific person, whom they

follow from place to place. Their victims are often young people, especially adolescents who are said to possess a strong psychic ability that
attracts supernatural forces to them.

Although Hogwarts' resident racketing spirit, Peeves the Poltergeist, can be seen by those he pesters, most poltergeists are invisible.
They announce their presence by making loud crashing sounds or rap-

ping on walls—hence their reputation for noisiness. Some especially violent and ill-tempered poltergeists have also been known to overturn furniture, start fires, and send people flying across the room. (Peeves appears to be unique, however, in his love of water balloons.)

Strange disembodied noises, flying tables and chairs, and other poltergeist-like phenomena have been reported for over 2,400 years. The fifth-century B.C. Greek politician Andocides described an acquaintance who "keeps an evil spirit in his house who upsets his table." Some five hundred years later, the Roman historian Suetonius wrote of an unfortunate nobleman who was "thrown out of his bed by a sudden unknown force," only to be found the next morning "semiconscious in front of the doors along with the bedclothes." Still, it was not until the nineteenth century that the specific term "poltergeist" was introduced.

Opinion on the true nature of poltergeists is divided. Some investigators claim that poltergeists are really "psychic disturbances" caused by youngsters with extraordinary abilities. Skeptics claim that these disturbances are actually hoaxes staged by imaginative teenagers. True believers insist that the hauntings are the genuine manifestations of a uniquely petty and childish breed of ghost. Just how juvenile some poltergeists can be is apparent from a popular nineteenth-century English story called "The Case of the Stockwell Ghost," in which the spirit in question likes to knock over beer kegs and hurl rotten eggs at cats. It is best, however, never to underestimate the potential malice of a poltergeist. More than one of them has been known to burn down houses with the unfortunate occupants still inside.

In recent years, poltergeists have received a great deal of exposure on television and in the movies, and alleged poltergeist sightings remain common throughout Europe and North America. Fortunately, most poltergeist hauntings last only a few days before the troublesome spirits vanish on their own.

SS 7/129

Potion

Potions, remarkable brews with remarkable ingredients, have always been an essential part of the magician's toolkit. The **witches** of classical mythology cooked up potions to restore youth, turn men into animals, and make themselves invisible. Medieval legends and fairy tales tell of sleeping potions, love potions, potions of forgetfulness, and potions to cause jealousy and strife. Alice, in her journey through Wonderland, drinks one potion that makes her small and another that makes her tall. And it's a potion that transforms Harry and Ron, at least outwardly, into two of their least favorite people: Crabbe and Goyle.

Legends about the magical powers of potions (from the Latin *potio,* meaning "drink") no doubt evolved from the very real effects that many substances can have on the body and mind. Tonics that bring on sleep, induce hallucinations, cause paralysis, speed up or slow down the heart, and intoxicate or cloud the brain, have long been known and used both to heal and to harm. It is not hard to imagine that with the right combination of ingredients, a potion might cause the body to change shape or turn the emotions of the drinker from hate to love.

A striking thing about many potions, including those in the Hogwarts recipe book, is the revolting ingredients they often contain. This venerable tradition is traceable to ancient Greece and Rome, where real potions, used as medicines as well as for their supposed magical effects, typically called for bats' blood, crushed beetles, **toads,** feathers, pulverized lizards, bird and animal claws, **snake** skeletons, and animal entrails, as well as many kinds of dried and fresh herbs. Other popular ingredients, as immortalized by the witches of Shakespeare's *Macbeth,* include eye of newt, toe of frog, wool of bat, and tongue of dog.

Aristocratic ladies were not above purchasing love potions, either for their own use or to win the right spouse for a son or daughter.

Why beetles? Why toads? There seems to be no explaining many potion ingredients in a way that makes sense to our modern minds. It's clear, however, that the common use of certain animal parts reflected the ancient belief that the desirable qualities of an animal could be gained by eating that animal. For example, since bats were believed to be able to see in the dark, drinking a potion containing bats or bats' eyes (or rubbing your own eyes with bats' blood) was thought to improve vision. Similarly, the legs of a hare would convey speed and the flesh or shell of a tortoise (which lives to an old age) would increase longevity. Ron and Harry exploit a similar principle by adding hairs from the heads of Crabbe and Goyle to Polyjuice Potion in order to transfer their foes' physical features to themselves. (An ancient superstition warns of leaving your clipped hair or nails around where an evil

witch or **wizard** might find them and use them against you.) The frequent use of toads in potions may have come about because of the very real effects of a nasty substance that toads secrete when frightened—as they must have been on the way to the **cauldron**. This toxic chemical, sometimes known as "toad's milk," can cause hallucinations and has an effect on the heart similar to that of the drug digitalis, which strengthens the contractions of the heart muscle while lowering the heart rate.

Affecting the heart, in quite a different way, is the purpose of love potions. Also known as philters, these brews (which are banned at Hogwarts) have been part of magical lore and actual practice since antiquity, when they were as common as chewing gum is today. Manufactured and sold by local wise women and fortune-tellers, love potions were reputed to make the drinker fall instantly in love with the giver. They were used primarily although not exclusively by women (men preferred using **spells**) and were usually slipped into the beloved's favorite beverage. As usual, ingredients were bizarre; one authentic recipe calls for the pulverized bones from the left side of a toad that had been eaten by ants. In ancient Rome so many people became sick from drinking love potions that early emperors decreed the sale of philters illegal. This apparently did little to deter their use, which continued for centuries.

By the Middle Ages, love potions had become more palatable, and most were made of herbal rather than animal ingredients. A typical formula might include oranges, **mandrake** root, vervain, and fern seed, mixed in water, tea, or wine. Love potions began to go out of fashion during the seventeenth and eighteenth centuries, when spells and **charms** became the preferred method of wooing by magic. Today's most favored love potions work in a different way, and are known as perfumes.

196

Red Cap

Many an American train traveler has eagerly sought the services of a redcap—a helpful porter who will carry your luggage through the station. Riders of the Hogwarts Express, however, know well enough to keep their distance from red caps—at least the terrifying kind studied in Defense Against the Dark Arts. Also called a "bloody cap" or "red comb," a red cap is an evil **goblin** of English folklore that haunts the ruins of castles where bloody battles have oc-

curred. With his long gray hair, fiery red eyes, and protruding teeth, the red cap might be mistaken for a very ugly old man, were it not for his distinctive red hat, which gains its color by being soaked in blood. He carries a walking stick tipped with a metal spike, and will happily use it against anyone foolish enough to wander into a ruined castle. After all, the blood of a fresh victim is just what's needed to brighten the color of his crimson cap.

For those who can't resist visiting old ruins, tradition holds there is one sure way to protect yourself against a red cap. Read the Bible aloud and he will utter a shriek and vanish, leaving behind one of his hideous teeth as a souvenir.

Runes

If you're interested in learning the ABCs of magic, you might try signing up for a Hogwarts class on ancient runes. A series of characters and symbols drawn from the earliest known Germanic alphabet, runes have always been associated with **magic** and mystery. In fact, the word rune or *roun* means "mystery" or "secret" in Danish.

According to ancient German legend, the first runes were discovered by the Norse god Odin, who bravely underwent a painful ritual of self-sacrifice in the pursuit of knowledge. After piercing his side with a spear, Odin hung for nine days from the branches of the Scandinavian tree of life. As his body moved in the wind, some twigs were dislodged, and they fell to the ground in a pattern that formed the runic alphabet.

Of course, the historical evidence paints a slightly different picture, suggesting that runes were invented by mortals in Denmark or Sweden, sometime around 200 A.D. The earliest Germanic runes (known as *futhark* runes) were extremely primitive, often consisting of nothing more than a series of straight lines arranged in different combinations. They were used for a variety of non-magical purposes, including writing letters, setting down instructions, and identifying the owners of property. One of the best known runic inscriptions, from the Sigurd runestone in Sweden, commemorates the construction of a bridge.

From the beginning, however, runes were also invested with magical significance. The Vikings and other Germanic peoples used runes as tools of **divination;** carved runes into their swords to make themselves invincible in battle; inscribed them on stone **amulets** to ward off disease and sorcery; and chiseled them into burial markers to discourage grave robbers. Starting around 450 A.D., runes also became popular

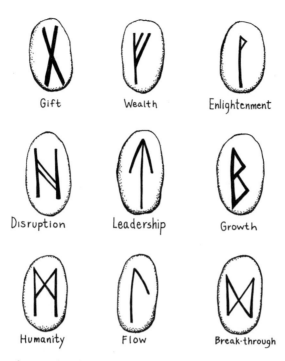

Gift	Wealth	Enlightenment
Disruption	Leadership	Growth
Humanity	Flow	Break-through

A selection of Nordic rune stones and their traditional interpretations.

in England, where Anglo-Saxon **magicians** used them to make **amulets** and predict the future.

To date, more than four thousand runic inscriptions have been found throughout Sweden, Norway, Denmark, and England, most of them dating from the height of the Viking period around 800 A.D. Runes have been located not just on weapons, amulets, and gravestones, but also on coins, jewelry, and mysterious slabs of wood. There are even some runes inscribed on the rim of Professor Dumbledore's magical pensieve.

Unfortunately, the widespread popularity of the Latin alphabet has led to a dramatic decline in runic literacy rates over the last millennium. Today, despite the best efforts of institutions like Hogwarts, only a handful of wizards and muggles can still read these mysterious characters that once cost poor Odin so much.

Rune Casting

The ancient practice of using runes to foretell the future, known as rune casting, has experienced a remarkable revival of popularity in the past century. When the Vikings and Anglo-Saxons used runes for divination, they began by carving runic symbols into thin strips of wood cut from the branches of fruit-bearing trees. These strips were tossed or "cast" at random onto a clean white cloth, and then a seer or rune master would select three (while gazing at the sky for divine inspiration) and interpret their meaning. Today, an aspiring fortune-teller can purchase a set of sixteen to thirty-three "rune stones"—round or oblong tiles made of stone or clay and inscribed with runic characters. In a simple modern rune-casting system, the stones are mixed in a bag and then scattered onto a flat surface. Some rune casters "read" all stones that come out face up. Others close their eyes and select just three, representing past, present, and future. While some rune casters base their readings only on what scholars know about the ancient meanings of the symbols, many have invented their own systems of interpretation.

Salamander

Most of us know the salamander as a cute, colorful little amphibian we might encounter during a walk in the woods. If you've seen one, you probably stopped for a moment to examine it and

then resumed your journey without a second thought. In centuries past, however, these tiny, lizard-like creatures were likely to attract exclamations of amazement and delight. Like those Hagrid brings to Care of Magical Creatures class, the salamanders of ancient times were reputed to frolic among the hottest flames without getting burned. Not only could they emerge from the fire unscathed, legend held, but their icy skin could even extinguish flames on contact.

The fireproof qualities of the marvelous salamander were discussed with enthusiasm in ancient Greece and Rome. In his *Natural History*, the Latin writer Pliny reported that the brave salamander was so inspired by the sight of fire that he would charge headlong toward the flames as if to vanquish an enemy. More fanciful folk suggested that salamanders might be brought to the rescue when a house was burning down! Other ancient thinkers, however, cast a skeptical eye on these notions, and decided to do a little experimentation. The Roman physician

Galen and others told of seizing unsuspecting salamanders, throwing them into the flames, and watching them burn to a crisp.

Despite reports of several such experiments, belief in the salamander's immunity to fire persisted well into the Renaissance, when cloth labeled as "salamander wool," said to be incombustible, was sold at a hefty price. Such cloth was used to make clothes for people whose occupations brought them near open flames, and for making envelopes to mail precious (and flammable) items. While there is no such thing as salamander wool (salamanders don't even have fur), buyers of this cloth were not completely out of luck. The material *was* actually flame resistant. Apparently, merchants discovered that their fabric could command a higher price if it was said to come from the legendary "lizard" rather than its true source—the mineral asbestos.

Although there's no truth to the notion that salamanders can survive fire, the source of this belief is clear enough. People do actually see salamanders scampering around in the ashes. That's because the tiny creatures like to hibernate in old logs. When those logs get thrown into the fireplace, along go the salamanders who call them home. Awakened in such an unpleasant fashion, salamanders may occasionally be able to escape from the flames, protected for a second or two by the natural secretions of their skin. Although such a feat is hardly miraculous, it has earned the salamander a place in the popular imagination, as well as in the dictionary—in addition to being a little amphibian, a salamander is "an object, such as a poker, used in a fire or capable of withstanding heat."

 PA 12/235

Sibyl

$\mathfrak{J}$t's fitting that Professor Trelawney, the Hogwarts **divination** teacher, is named Sibyll. In the mythology of Greece and Rome, sibyls were women known for their ability to prophesy the future while in a trance. In fact, Professor Trelawney herself was in a trance on the one occasion we can recall her making a reliable prediction.

According to legend, there were ten sibyls in the ancient world, scattered across Egypt, Babylonia, Persia, Libya, and Greece. All had different names, but all were called sibyls in honor of the original prophetess of Greek legend whose name was Sibylla, and who was said to be a daughter of Zeus. While most diviners provided their services upon request, sibyls issued prophecies whenever they were inspired, often writing their predictions on leaves. Sibyls foretold wars, perilous storms, and the rise and fall of rulers and empires.

The most famous sibyl was Amalthaea, known as the Sibyl of Cumae, who was a priestess of the Greek god Apollo. In a legend told by the Roman writer Ovid, Apollo fell in love with her and promised her anything she wished. The sibyl pointed to a pile of sand and asked for a year of life for each grain. Apollo granted her request. However, she neglected to ask for perpetual youth—a mistake made by several other characters in Greek mythology—and was consequently fated to grow exceedingly old and frail. She eventually took up residence in an underground cave in the town of Cumae, near Naples, Italy, where she lived for a thousand years.

Another legend describes what happened when the Sibyl of Cumae approached Tarquin, the last king of Rome, and offered to sell him nine volumes of her prophecies, which concerned the future of

SIBILLA FRIGIA·

ANVNCIABITVR VIRGO· 9

Fortune telling.

*Although sibyls were originally described as wild women who lived in caves,
many artists preferred to depict them as graceful classical figures.*

204

Rome and the destiny of the empire. He thought her asking price was
too high and refused to pay, perhaps expecting her to bargain. Instead,
she burned three of the books. A year later, she returned and offered
the remaining six books at the same price. Again being refused, she
burned three more, and a year later, offered the final three books, still
at the original price. Defeated, Tarquin bought the books and Amalthaea
was never seen again.

The story of the Sibyl of Cumae is mythical, but the prophecies
attributed to her actually existed. Written in the form of riddles, they
were inscribed on palm leaves—by whom no one knows—and bound
in books. Those collections, which included both predictions and sug-

gestions for ways to appease the gods during hard times, were consulted by the Roman senate for centuries, until they were destroyed in a fire in 83 B.C. Afterwards, the Roman senate sent emissaries to collect prophecies from oracles in Sicily and Asia Minor. Those prophecies were kept in the Temple of Apollo in Rome until 408 A.D., when the temple was destroyed in battle.

Long after the prophetic books disappeared, the Sibyl of Cumae continued to fascinate people. During the Middle Ages, Christian writers reinterpreted and added to the prophecies attributed to her so that she appeared to have predicted the coming of Jesus Christ. Her status grew until it equaled that of the Old Testament prophets—a fact that is beautifully documented by her inclusion, along with four other sibyls, on the ceiling of Michelangelo's Sistine Chapel in Rome.

 PA 6/101

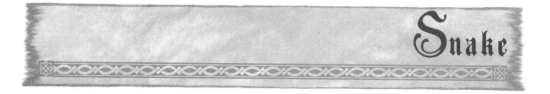

Snake

When Harry's classmates discover he can talk with snakes, most are horrified and suspect the worst—that Harry is really a dark **wizard.** After all, in the wizarding community, snakes are virtually synonymous with evil. The Dark Mark, sign of the Death Eaters, features a snake tongue jutting from the mouth of a human skull; Slytherin House, apparent home to many enthusiasts of the **Dark Arts,** is represented by the sign of the serpent; and Lord Voldemort is nourished by the venom of his serpentine companion Nagini. Yet chances are we've only heard half the story about snakes, and why it is that Harry can chat so easily with a boa constrictor or command an attacking serpent to behave itself. In cultures all over the world, serpents have been held in the highest regard and have been associated not only with evil but with wisdom, insight, and healing.

The human fascination with snakes dates back far earlier than written language, to the earliest paintings and carvings that have survived on rocks and in caves. More cults have been dedicated to the worship of snakes than any other animal. At one time or another, they were sacred to the Norse of northern Europe, the Aztecs of Central America, and tribal kingdoms of West Africa, as well as peoples of the Middle East, the Mediterranean basin, China, and India. In India, *Nagini* are a group of snake beings portrayed as lovely women with the heads of serpents or surrounded by coiled serpents. Voldemort's snake shares her name with these auspicious beings, who are believed to provide protection from all kinds of hazards, including snakebite.

Even where snakes were worshipped, however, they were also feared. Wicked, deceitful serpents rear their heads in many Egyptian myths. In the ancient Egyptian *Book of the Dead,* the monstrous serpent Apophis appears frequently as an aggressive and treacherous instrument of evil. Known as the "demon of darkness," Apophis wages constant battle with the sun god, Ra, and each day's sunrise and sunset indicates another successful defeat of Ra's serpentine enemy. In Norse mythology, the serpent Nidhogg, also known as the Dread Biter, lives at the foot of the Tree of Life, continually gnawing at it and representing the evil powers of the universe. The most villainous snake in Western culture is the one responsible for the expulsion of Adam and Eve from the Garden of Eden, as recounted in the Old Testament book of Genesis. Elsewhere in the Bible, serpents appear frequently as objects of danger and dread, and in Jewish and Christian culture, the snake has remained a symbol of evil. Muslims also shun the snake as a symbol of the fall of man.

But despite such powerful associations with evil, noble qualities have very often been attributed to the snake in myth, folklore, and religion. The snake-fearing Egyptians revered the cobra as the repository of supreme wisdom. The Cretan Mother Goddess, a protector of households, is shown on coins caressing a snake. In many agricultural societies, serpents were regarded as symbols of fertility and the key to good crops. (For good reason: They ate the rodents that would have otherwise helped themselves to grain.) The serpent was a symbol of healing to the ancient Greeks, twisting itself around the staff of Asclepius, the god of medicine (see **magic wand**). In Rome, snakes were often kept as house pets, and carved snake **amulets** were quite popular. Because it sheds its skin, the snake is almost universally linked with rebirth and renewal.

It may be because most of us have little contact with snakes that even the most basic facts about them are not well known. For example, when Harry speaks to snakes he's engaging in a pretty unusual pursuit, since snakes have no outer ears and can't hear in the way that humans and most other animals do, though they are very sensitive to the vibrations made by sound. The vast majority of snakes are harmless. Of the 2,700 kinds of snakes in the world, only four hundred species are poisonous, and fewer than fifty species pose any serious danger to humans. Yet many people are so terrified of these mostly gentle reptiles that they feel faint at the very mention of them.

Snakes' swift, silent movements and unchanging expressions support their reputation for mystery and inscrutability. Slithery and sinuous (but not actually slimy), snakes appear and disappear silently, without warning. Many can make loud hissing sounds, puff themselves up, and give off bad smells. And of course the ability of some types of snakes to kill with deadly venom or a fatally tight squeeze give people good reason to avoid them.

Since so many people are terrified by snakes, it's not unusual for serpents to guard important places,

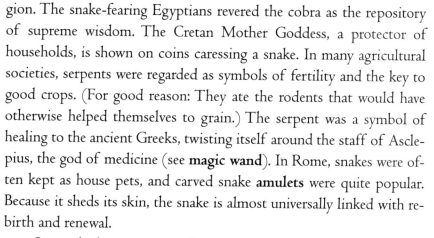

The familiar circular shape of the snake with its tail in its mouth, called an ouroboros, *symbolizes the positive qualities associated with the serpent in most primitive cultures. It is said to represent the eternal cycle of life, death, and rebirth.*

like caves filled with treasure, life-giving springs, and the Hogwarts Chamber of Secrets. This may also explain why thousands of ordinary people all over the world keep all kinds of snakes, both harmless and deadly, as pets. We can't say if there's any truth to the English legend that a snakeskin in the house will keep reptiles from slithering in. But a live snake in the parlor is certainly an excellent way to deter unwelcome guests.

 SS 2/27

Sorcerer

Of the many words for **magician,** perhaps none conveys the image of power and mastery over the world as well as "sorcerer." More than just a mixer of potions, a sorcerer commands the powers of nature. He summons storms, moves mountains, hurls lightening, and turns worthless trinkets into priceless jewels. Or at least some sorcerers do. By other accounts, a sorcerer is a practitioner of the **Dark Arts,** an evil wizard (like You-Know-Who) with an unquenchable lust for power and the desire to harm mankind. So, which is it?

Actually, it's both. Historically, the word "sorcerer" has been applied to agents of both good and evil, and the idea of what a sorcerer is and does has changed over the centuries. One of the earliest and best-known images of a sorcerer was drawn on the walls of a cave in southern France more than 10,000 years ago. Known as the *Sorcerer of*

Trois Frères Caves, the drawing depicts a man in animal costume, wearing antlers, and performing a ritual dance. Anthropologists believe this figure represents the most ancient form of tribal **magician**—the shaman—who was responsible for protecting the community, ensuring a good hunt, and controlling the weather. This type of sorcerer was vital to the health of society and was usually held in the highest esteem.

In the ancient civilizations of Babylonia, however, the most feared and reviled agents of evil magic were also known as sorcerers. They specialized in curses, poked wax images with pins, called upon malevolent **demons,** and tried to raise the spirits of the dead. In pre-Christian Greece and Rome, sorcerers may have practiced **divination** (the word "sorcery" comes from the Latin *sors,* meaning "casting of lots," "prophecy," or "fate"), but most were professional **spell** casters and **potion** makers who could be hired to inflict harm on an enemy.

During the Middle Ages, whether someone was considered to be a sorcerer often depended on the outcome of the magic, rather than on the intentions of the magician. If the results were beneficial, the practitioner was a **wizard;** if harmful, he was a sorcerer. But things were not always clear cut. What if the type of magic involved was a **charm** or potion intended to heal a sick person, but instead of getting better, the patient got worse? Was the magician then a sorcerer? Questions like this often arose when people accused of "sorcery" were put on trial.

Charges of sorcery might be brought by a disgruntled farmer against a neighbor, accusing him or her of harming animals or children, or causing a storm or a drought. Often these charges originated in village squabbles and had economic or vindictive motivations, but if evidence of traditional sorcery (such as a **curse** tablet or a wax doll) could be produced, a guilty verdict was likely.

Although sorcery continued to have some negative connotations, during the Renaissance a positive and even flattering use of the term developed in some circles. Scholars and physicians believed to possess the secrets of "white," or beneficial, magic were called sorcerers. So were alchemists like **Nicholas Flamel,** who struggled in their laboratories to create the Philosopher's Stone (or **Sorcerer's Stone**), a substance that would turn common metals such as lead, tin, or mercury into gold. Even Albus Dumbledore includes "Grand Sorcerer" among his many titles on Hogwarts letterhead. In common usage, a sorcerer became anyone with magical knowledge.

The image of a sorcerer as a super-wizard who can do anything was popularized worldwide by the 1940 animated film *Fantasia,* which featured a telling of "The Sorcerer's Apprentice." Based on a story by the second-century Roman author Lucian (later retold by the German writer Goethe), the tale centers around a would-be magician who, in his master's absence, brings a broom to life and orders it to fetch water from a stream. Although the apprentice is mistaken in thinking he can control the powers he summons (the broom won't stop fetching water and the house floods), sorcery itself is portrayed as something marvelous, if obtainable only by a master magician.

SS 4/51

Sorcerer's Stone

For centuries, the legendary magical substance known as the Sorcerer's Stone (or, more commonly, the Philosopher's Stone) has embodied two of mankind's most enduring dreams: eternal life and limitless wealth. Lord Voldemort hoped to steal the Stone from Hogwarts so he could use it to regain his strength and rise again to spread dark **magic** throughout the world. Countless others, both fictional and

Alchemy was an extremely difficult pursuit with many opportunities for things to go wrong. These sixteenth-century alchemists seem more dazed and confused than enlightened.

real, have sought the Stone to help them make gold or to create the Elixir of Life, a **potion** that would bestow immortality on whoever drank it.

The legend of the Sorcerer's Stone evolved out of alchemy, an ancient art founded in Alexandria, Egypt, around the first century and dedicated to transforming common metals into silver or gold. As imagined by its originators, alchemy (from the Greek *kemeia*, meaning "transmutation") was a scientific process, utilizing furnaces, chemicals, and laboratory apparatus. In went iron, lead, tin, mercury, and other metals and, after a series of secret operations, out came gold. That this could not possibly have happened (the laws of physics being no different then than now) did not stop the early alchemists from believing they had succeeded. They were, in fact, experts in coloring metals and producing alloys that looked like gold, contained some gold, and apparently passed for pure gold.

In the centuries that followed, alchemical knowledge was preserved and developed in the Arab world, and eventually entered medieval Europe around 1200 when the works of the Arab alchemists were translated into Latin. These manuscripts—filled with complex formulas and depicting sophisticated laboratory apparatus previously undreamed of—came as a revelation to the scholars and churchmen who read them.

Apparently, a way of producing fabulous wealth had existed for more than a thousand years, and yet the best minds of Europe had known nothing about it. Now, seemingly, the method was at hand.

The lure of alchemy was irresistible. By the end of the fourteenth century alchemy was flourishing throughout all of Western Europe; most people had heard of it and there were hundreds if not thousands of practitioners. And a new idea had emerged. Instead of trying to turn lesser metals directly into gold, as the early alchemists had apparently done, medieval alchemists like **Nicholas Flamel** now spoke of producing a new substance—an extraordinarily potent catalyst that when added to common metals would trigger their transmutation, Midas-like, into gold. This new substance became known as the Philosopher's Stone. As the lore about it grew, so did its imagined power to cure disease and prolong life indefinitely.

Although the Stone was by some definitions a magical substance, it was believed to have purely natural origins and therefore, in theory, could be made by anyone. But that did not mean it was easy to make. Manuscripts of alchemical instruction were difficult to locate and even more difficult to understand. Not only were they written in

Latin (which only the clergy and the well educated could read), but also in order to protect the secrets of transmutation from falling into the wrong hands, alchemical writers deliberately obscured their meaning and wrote in what amounted to a secret code. For example, instead of using the common term *"aqua regia"* for the mixture of nitric and hydrochloric acids, alchemists called it "The Green Dragon." Lead was known as "The Black Crow." Once you got through the process of deciphering these documents, if you ever could, you then needed the furnaces, metals, chemicals, and glassware required to set up an alchemical laboratory, and the patience to spend months or even years in pursuit of the elusive Stone. Nonetheless, many alchemists were willing to devote much of their lives to the task. Alchemy was thought to be a spiritual pursuit as well as a material one, and many alchemists believed that as long as they remained dedicated to their work, they too would eventually become "golden," and evolve into a "higher self."

With belief in the Stone so widespread, it was not surprising that enterprising swindlers developed a number of get-rich-quick schemes to separate would-be alchemists from their savings. Tricksters used sleight-of-hand techniques as well as mechanical devices to give the illusion of turning mercury into gold. Then they sold the stones that had supposedly caused the transformation (and sometimes the laboratory equipment and chemicals as well) to the gullible buyer. At the same time, both swindlers and sincere alchemists might put themselves in real danger by claiming to have the stone, for they could easily become the victims of thieves. For this reason, most alchemists operated in secret.

Alchemy remained a serious endeavor until the late seventeenth century, when its underlying theories were replaced by the more valid theories of modern chemistry. Although the alchemists never realized their impossible goals, they did discover many important chemicals useful in science and medicine; they also invented basic laboratory techniques and designed almost all of the chemical apparatus in use until the middle of the seventeenth century.

The Making of the Stone—
The Theory Behind Alchemy

While the goals of alchemy may seem far-fetched to modern minds, to its ancient and medieval practitioners alchemy made perfect sense. According to the theories of the early Greek philosophers, which were widely believed until the dawn of modern science, everything in the physical world was composed of one underlying substance called "first matter." First matter could exhibit different qualities and characteristics, but essentially there was only one basic "stuff." Moreover, all matter was thought to be alive. Metals and minerals as well as plants and animals were said to contain a "universal spirit," or life-force, which the ancient philosophers called *pneuma* (from the Greek word meaning "breath" or "wind").

Given this understanding of the physical world, alchemists saw no reason why they could not begin with base metals such as iron or tin, reduce the metals to the condition of first matter (by heating them in furnaces and treating them with acids and reagents), and then cause the first matter to reform as gold. The alchemists of ancient Greece and Egypt believed they could trigger the transformation by adding a small amount of real gold to the alchemical brew where it would act as a seed and, being alive, grow into a larger quantity of gold, using the first matter as a nutrient. The medieval alchemists, on the other hand, believed that as they heated their mixtures, the *pneuma* contained in them would be released in the form of a gas which, along with other vapors, could be captured in distilling apparatus and converted to liquid form. By continually refining and distilling this liquid many hundreds of times—perhaps even for years—the alchemists believed they would eventually end up with an extraordinarily potent, purified, concentrated essence of *pneuma*. This was the fabled Philosopher's Stone. When added to first matter it would, in theory at least, cause the matter to transmute into its most perfect form, gold. Taken as an elixir, being the essence of life-force, it would cure all disease and lead to eternal life.

The Faking of the Stone—Alchemical Frauds

A clear demonstration of gold making was the best way for a fraudulent alchemist to prove he had a genuine piece of the Sorcerer's Stone. Many clever swindles were devised for this purpose, but the most convincing method allowed the prospective buyer to actually *see* the transmutation taking place. This was not as difficult as it might seem. A very impressive demonstration, no doubt staged in some out-of-the-way, makeshift laboratory, looked like this:

The trickster alchemist poured a small amount of mercury into a crucible (a porcelain bowl used for melting metals) and heated it in a furnace. With a dramatic flourish, he next produced a small tube of red powder, said to be the potent Sorcerer's Stone. Adding a tiny pinch to the mercury—no more than would fit on the head of a pin—he stirred the mixture, continuing to apply heat. While many alchemical processes took weeks or months, this one took only minutes. Soon the mercury could be seen mysteriously changing color, from silver to gold.

When removed from the heat and allowed to cool, it solidified into a gleaming nugget. Amazingly, anyone with expertise could verify that the new substance did not just look like gold—it *was* gold!

The secret of this apparent transmutation involved a clever combination of chemistry and trickery. The chemistry lay in the fact that mercury has a much lower boiling point than gold. The trickery lay in the innocent-looking rod used to stir the ingredients. Although it appeared to be a solid piece of black metal, it was actually a hollow tube into which the swindler had previously placed a small quantity of powdered gold. A plug of blackened wax sealed the end of the rod and kept the gold in place. As the mercury was heated and stirred, the wax melted and allowed the gold to trickle into the crucible where it mixed with the mercury. As the heat intensified, the mercury evaporated into the interior of the furnace, leaving behind the gold, and perhaps a trace of "the Stone," which might have been nothing more than a bit of colored chalk. The Stone was then sold at an appropriately high price, and the bogus alchemist skipped town.

Spell

Potions take a while to brew and herbs take time to grow, but a spell can be cast in an instant. Ron uses a levitating spell to knock out a mountain **troll** with its own club. Harry finds his way through a maze with the aid of a pointing spell. An unlocking spell enables Hermione to enter a forbidden corridor. Spells are powerful tools that affect people, animals, objects, and even places. Indeed, all of Hogwarts is under a spell that makes it look like a crumbling old ruin to the non-wizarding world.

Naturally, the magical spells of literature produce the most dramatic results. But real people in almost every culture have also believed in the power of spells to influence human behavior and alter the course of events. In the ancient world, professional **wizards** made a good living casting spells to help their clients find love, harm enemies (a negative spell is called a **"curse"**), gain wealth, cure illness, excel at sports, chase rats from the house, or cancel out the effect of incoming spells cast by rival wizards. "Do-it-yourself" spells were also performed by amateurs. Spells were everywhere, and even one of the most skeptical writers of first-century Rome admitted that "there is no one who is not afraid of spells and incantations."

A spell is a spoken or written word or phrase meant to have a magical effect. Most spells consist of incantations in which the desired outcome (such as money, health, or fame) is clearly stated, repeated many times, and accompanied by a ritual, such as lighting a candle, burning incense, and pointing or gesturing. Some ancient Egyptians copied spells onto papyrus, dissolved them in beer, and drank them. Ancient Greek and Roman wizards created spells while spinning a wheel known as a "rhombus." Depending upon the culture, a spell might include the use of **magic words** or a plea for assistance from a deity. Some spells were sung or chanted. The entire magical procedure, from start to finish, is often known as "casting" or "weaving" a spell.

Spells intended to influence the behavior of another person—such as love spells, healing spells, and curses—were thought to be most effective if a snippet of the target's hair, a fingernail clipping, or a piece of clothing or some other personal item could be incorporated into the ceremony. This reflects an ancient belief that things that were once physically connected—a woman and her fingernails, for example—retain a "magical" connection even when separated by miles. In the absence of such an item, words could be used to make the link between the ritual and the target. "As I melt this wax," says a love spell from the first century, "so may his heart melt for me. As I burn these herbs, so may his passions burn for me. As I knot this thread, so may he be tied to me." Spell casting also sometimes involved the use of wax or clay figurines or stuffed dolls made to represent the recipient of the spell. In a love spell, the figure might be wrapped with thread so as to "bind" the love of the target to the enchanter. In the case of a healing spell, the doll might be stuffed with medicinal herbs. If the spell was intended to harm (see **Dark Arts**), the figure would be damaged.

Of course, the spells of fairy tales and literature required no such devices. A simple flick of a wizard's wand could turn a timid poet into a brave knight or make a horse-drawn carriage take to the air and fly. At Hogwarts, professors can keep students honest simply by subjecting their quills to an anti-cheating spell at exam time. Today, we still use the word "spellbound" to indicate the sense of delighted fascination that such tales evoke.

 SS 10/176

218

Sphinx

It's hard to find a monster with a longer history than the sphinx. A majestic creature with the body of a lion and the head and bust of a human, the sphinx has been the stuff of legends for over five thousand years. In ancient Egypt, where it was first introduced, the sphinx was a symbol of royalty, fertility, and life after death. Its image was often associated with the annual flooding of the Nile, which brought life to the parched Egyptian desert, and statues of sphinxes were placed outside most Egyptian tombs and temples.

The most celebrated of the Egyptian sphinx statues is the 240-foot-long, 66-foot-high Great Sphinx, which lies on a strip of desert known as the Giza Plateau. More than 4,500 years old, this colossal limestone carving joins the rippling, powerful body of a lion with the regal head of an Egyptian pharaoh, or king. Most historians believe it is a tribute to the ancient Egyptian ruler Khafre, whose pyramid sits nearby.

From ancient Egypt, the myth of the sphinx made its way across the Mediterranean Sea to the lands of Mesopotamia (modern-day Syria and Iraq) and ancient Greece. In these countries, the half-man, half-lion took on a more sinister meaning, often representing not just the underworld, but also senseless violence and destruction. The throne of the Greek god Zeus at Olympia, the holy mountain on which the gods resided, was supposedly engraved with a ring of sphinxes, shown carrying off small children. Other Greek and Roman sphinxes were depicted as tearing apart their victims or slavering over their mangled remains. The basic anatomy of the sphinx also changed as it moved northeast: In Mesopotamia the mythical beast was often shown with

the head of a ram or an eagle; in Greece it was given wings, and the face and breasts of a woman.

Although she lacks wings, the sphinx that Harry Potter encounters during the Triwizard Tournament is probably Greek in character. Not only does she have a woman's face, she uses her wits to defend a dark secret, much like the sphinx in the ancient Greek myth of Oedipus. In that story, a menacing sphinx stalks the countryside around the city of Thebes, posing impossible questions to travelers and eating them if they fail her test. She finally meets her match in the young wanderer Oedipus, who solves the riddle "What animal walks on four legs in the morning, two in the afternoon, and three at night?" (The answer, of course, is man, who crawls as an infant, walks as an adult, and leans on a cane in his final years.) Having successfully defeated the sphinx, Oedipus, like Harry, is allowed to proceed to his final destination, where a fate even darker than Lord Voldemort's wrath awaits him.

Over time, the Greek image of the sphinx as a dark and enigmatic creature has become the most prominent. The word itself comes from the Greek *sphingein,* meaning to "squeeze," "strangle," or "bind." Despite the claims of some medieval writers, there is no evidence to suggest that the ancient Egyptians, Mesopotamians, or Greeks believed the sphinx was a real animal. Their legends, artwork, and literature consistently present it as a mythical creature, symbolizing power and forbidden knowledge. This did not stop later writers, such as the seventeenth-century zoologist Edward Topsell, from claiming that the sphinx was descended from a bizarre Ethiopian ape. In honor of such misguided scientific observations, there is now a species of ape called the Sphinx, or Sphinga, baboon.

 GF 31/628

Talisman

Although Hogwarts students eagerly purchase talismans to protect themselves against a mysterious epidemic of **petrification,** these powerful objects are more commonly used to perform magic than to ward it off. Unlike **amulets,** which are specifically designed to keep the wearer safe from harm, talismans are valued for their ability to produce supernatural transformations—making their owners invisible, inhumanly strong, immune to disease, or able to remember every word a teacher says. A talisman can be any kind of object—a statue, a book, a ring, an item of clothing, a strip of metal, or a piece of parchment. Even the rotting newt's tail purchased by a panicked Neville Longbottom can be a talisman if it has magic powers. Some objects, such as

A medieval talisman said to provide its owner with good luck and the ability to make wise decisions when gambling.

gemstones, have traditionally been viewed as magical by nature. But throughout history most talismans have been purposefully endowed with their potency through rituals intended to harness the forces of nature or the power of gods. Many were inscribed with magic words, the names or images of deities, or brief **charms.**

Talismans were very much in demand in the ancient world. Archaeologists have discovered papyrus talismans from ancient Egypt, as well as hundreds of stone and metal talismans throughout the Mediterranean region. Especially popular for curing illness, they also were used to attract love, improve memory, and ensure success in politics, sports, or gambling.

In medieval times, there was a talisman for just about any purpose you could think of. Tying a hare's foot to the left arm was said to enable a person to venture into dangerous territory without risk of harm. Carrying mistletoe would prevent a guilty verdict for those on trial. Possessing a sprig of the herb heliotrope bundled with a wolf's tooth and wrapped in laurel leaves would stop people from gossiping about you. So great was the belief in the power of talismans in fourteenth-century England that rules for dueling were revised to require that each participant swear that he was not carrying a magic ring, stone, or other talisman that would give him an unfair advantage.

Because the heavenly bodies were thought to hold sway over earthly life (see **astrology**), many talismans were designed to capture the influence of a particular planet. Someone who wanted to succeed in combat, for example, might make a talisman to harness the influence of the planet Mars, which was said to govern bodily strength. The talisman would be fashioned from iron (the metal traditionally associated with Mars) at a time when Mars was believed to radiate its power most intensely. It might also be engraved with the planet's special number, five, or painted Mars' color, red.

Such astrological talismans were especially popular among Renaissance alchemists, who followed elaborate rituals to make objects they hoped would help them to transform base metals into gold. After waiting for the right celestial moment to arrive, they would recite incantations to summon spirits or **demons** whom they hoped would endow their talismans with the necessary power. The **Sorcerer's Stone,** which was believed to offer eternal life as well as endless wealth, was the most desirable talisman of all.

Talismans remained popular into the nineteenth century, when one all-purpose talisman engraved on silver during the proper phase of the moon was said to be able to make the owner healthy, wealthy, pleasant, cheerful, honored by others, and able to make all journeys safely. Although people today are not likely to engrave magic words on metal, those who carry a rabbit's foot or insist on wearing their "lucky socks" to every playoff game keep the use of talismans alive.

 CS 11/185

Tea-Leaf Reading

Where Ron sees an innocent bowler hat, Professor Trelawney sees a menacing club. Where he sees a sheep, she sees a terrible black dog known as a **grim.** Both are staring into the bottom of Harry's teacup, practicing a popular form of **divination** called *tasseomancy,* or tea-leaf reading.

The custom of telling fortunes by examining tea leaves began in China, probably during the sixth century. Tea was unknown in the West until 1609, when Dutch traders began importing it from the Orient. Although the new beverage was initially regarded with suspicion, people were drinking it in France by 1636, and in 1650 it arrived at the shops in England, where it would eventually become a much-loved staple of daily life. By the middle of the seventeenth century, tea consumption was widespread, and tea leaves were being read by fortune-tellers across much of Europe.

The concepts behind tea-leaf reading were not entirely new to Europeans, since the ancient Romans had told fortunes by *oinomancy*— the interpretation of sediment left in the bottom of a wine cup—and medieval diviners had studied the patterns made by melting wax, molten lead, and other substances. But the new art did require knowledge of how to prepare a teacup for a reading, as well as mastery of the meanings of dozens, if not hundreds, of images that might appear in the cup. During the eighteenth and nineteenth centuries, easily accessible booklets provided the curious with instruction in all aspects of tasseomancy (from the Arabic *tass,* meaning "cup" and the Greek *mancy,* meaning "prophecy"). As a result, the practice became common not only in the back rooms of fortune-tellers, but also in the parlors of the well-to-do.

Methods for reading tea leaves vary somewhat in their details, but the procedure described here is representative of most approaches. Tea (ideally a dark-colored Chinese or Indian variety) is brewed from loose leaves and poured into a light-colored cup without the use of a strainer. The person whose fortune is being told drinks the tea, leaving a small amount of liquid and all of the leaves at the bottom. After swirling the remains around three times, he or she turns the cup upside down on a saucer and taps the bottom three times so that most of the leaves fall out. The reader then picks up the cup and examines the pattern of leaves that remain stuck to the base and sides.

What can be learned from the dregs of a cup of tea? Well, tea-leaf readers claim to see the shape of things to come. Patterns of lines, dots, and geometric shapes, as well as images that suggest plants, animals,

and objects, are all said to have specific meanings. A single straight line, for example, indicates careful planning and peace of mind; two parallel lines mean a rewarding journey is in store. A circle with a cross on top is usually a bad sign, suggesting enforced confinement, as in a prison or hospital, while a tree indicates success and an acorn predicts good health. The closer the image is to the rim of the cup, the sooner it will occur. An event indicated by an image at the bottom of the cup is said to lie in the distant future.

Like Professor Trelawney, many diviners insist only someone with well-honed psychic abilities can read tea leaves properly. According to this theory, the tea leaves stimulate the intuitive powers of the reader, who will be able to foretell the future and perceive truths that would otherwise remain hidden. However, this doesn't stop thousands of nonpsychic people from trying a little tasseomancy just for fun. If you want to try it and you don't have a copy of *Unfogging the Future* on hand, you might use some of these traditional interpretations:

Acorn	Good health
Anchor	Voyage
Arrow	Bad news in a letter
Balloon	Troubles lifting
Banana	A business trip
Bat	Disappointment
Bee	Meeting friends
Bells	Good news
Bird	Good luck
Boat	Visit from a friend
Book	Awareness, learning
Branch	New friendship
Butterfly	Happiness
Cat	Treachery
Chair	Unexpected guest
Circle	Love
Clock	Recovery from illness
Clouds	Doubt

Coin	Payment of debt
Crab	An enemy nearby
Cross	Trouble on the way
Cup	Great success
Dagger	Danger from foes
Diamond	An expensive gift
Dog	Faithful friends
Donkey	Patience needed
Dove	Good luck
Dragon	Changes
Drum	Gossip
Egg	Fertility, increase
Envelope	News
Eye	Exercise caution
Face	New friends
Feather	Requires more effort
Fish	News from abroad
Flag	Danger
Flowers	Love, honor, esteem
Fork	Diversion from a goal
Frog	Business upswing
Giraffe	A misunderstanding
Glove	Luck and honor
Goat	Misfortune
Goose	An invitation
Grapes	Good times with friends
Guitar	Romance on the horizon
Gun	Danger, strife, catastrophe
Hammer	Triumph over adversity, hard work
Hand	Friendship
Hat	A new work situation
Horn	Abundance
Horseshoe	Good luck
House	Stability
Kangaroo	Unexpected travel

Kettle	A friendly home
Key	Unveiling of mystery
Keyhole	Unwanted news
Lace	Fragile matters
Ladder	Advancement, movement, success
Lamp	Monetary gain
Leaf	Good luck
Lion	Helpful friends
Lizard	Hidden enemies
Man	An unexpected visitor
Mermaid	Temptation
Moon	Love
Mountain	Journey or hindrance
Mouse	Financial insecurity
Mushroom	Expect delays
Musical instruments	Good company
Needle	Respect from others
Nest	Shelter
Noose	Danger ahead
Oar	Temporary problem
Owl	Scandal, bad health
Ox	Arguments with associates
Parrot	A disturbance
Pendulum	Indecision
Pig	Difficulty in relationship
Pipe	New ideas
Pumpkin	A warm relationship
Question mark	Uncertainty, change
Rabbit	Success
Rainbow	Good luck
Rat	Danger, lost possession
Ring	Marriage
Saw	Trouble with a stranger
Scales	Justice, success at law
Scepter	More responsibilities

Scissors	Angry words, family misunderstandings
Scythe	Good harvest, or a death warning
Scorpion	An enemy's plot
Sheep	Good luck
Shoe	A career change
Skeleton	Illness
Snake	Falsehood, temptation
Spade	Good fortune through industry
Spider	Good luck, money
Squirrel	Future wealth
Stairs	Improvement coming
Star	Good luck
Sun	Continued happiness
Sword	Argument with close friend
Table	A pleasant get-together
Thistle	High ambitions
Tortoise	Criticism
Tree	Success
Triangle	Unexpected event
Umbrella	Annoyances
Vase	A friend in need of help
Violin	Loneliness
Walking stick	Need for support
Waterfall	Affluence
Web	Intrigue, complications
Window	Help from a friend
Wine glass	New acquaintances
Wings	News

229

 PA 6/104

Three-Headed Dog

Fluffy, the room-size, three-headed dog who guards the Sorcerer's Stone at Hogwarts, has a mythological heritage dating back almost three thousand years. His most venerable ancestor is Cerberus, the savage hound of Greek and Roman legend who guards the entrance to the underworld. In the eighth century B.C., the poet Hesiod described Cerberus as having fifty heads and a voice of brass. Just two centuries later, however, fifty heads apparently seemed excessive even for a vicious guard dog. In what became the standard image of the beast, artists depicted Cerberus with a mere three heads, a dragon's tail, and a backbone that bristled with serpents.

The ancient Greeks believed that when someone died, his or her spirit went to the world below. Ruled by the god Hades and his wife Persephone, this "underworld" was the destination of all souls, good or bad, but the quality of their lives there depended on how they had behaved on Earth. As the watchdog of the underworld, Cerberus' job was to make sure no one escaped the kingdom of Hades after passing through the gates. Born of two terrible monsters (his father was a fire-breathing **giant** covered in **snakes** and his mother a half-woman, half-serpent who ate men raw), Cerberus had little trouble frightening people. If the sheer sight of him was not enough, the sharp teeth of three wild dogs' heads and the spikes in his tail could be used quite effectively.

Only a few mythological characters managed to elude Cerberus and make the journey back to the land of the living. The nymph Psyche managed to sneak past by feeding the dog a drugged honey cake, and the Trojan war hero Aeneas followed her example. The musician

Orpheus, who ventured into the underworld in search of his dead wife, Eurydice, played his lyre so beautifully that Cerberus closed his eyes in ecstasy and allowed him to pass. (Fluffy reacts to music in much the same way.) And Hercules, completing the last of his twelve labors, wrestled Cerberus with his bare hands, managing to drag the beast back up to Earth for a brief time.

Legend holds that during his days in the world of the living, Cerberus drooled, as dogs will. A few drops of his saliva fell on the earth, from which sprang a poisonous plant called aconite. Also known as wolfsbane, aconite is a real plant that was commonly used in the **potions** and ointments of both fictional and real **witches.**

 SS 9/160

Toad

arry has Hedwig, Hermione's got Crookshanks, and Neville keeps company with his beloved toad, Trevor. Like **owls** and **cats,** toads have long been associated with **witches** and **sorcerers** in popular legend and lore. Although there's little doubt that Trevor is a very nice fellow, most toads have a rather unsavory reputation.

During the years of **witch persecution** in seventeenth-century England and Scotland, witches were said to keep toads as "familiars"— minor **demons** disguised as animals who could be sent out to perform all manner of mischief for their mistresses. After all, how much easier for a toad than a witch to creep into a neighbor's well and poison the water or secretly place an evil **charm** under a victim's pillow? Toads were also rumored to play an important role in the initiation ceremonies of new witches, who might be required to nurture or kiss toads as part of the process of pledging their allegiance to the Devil. Occasionally, witches were said to transform into toads themselves.

In testimony given at witch trials, some witnesses claimed to have seen witches baptize and name their toads, dressing them up in black or scarlet velvet outfits and tying little bells to their feet. Such care suggested that witches were quite attached to their pets, and many people believed it risky to harm a toad, lest it be a witch's warty pal. One tale from Somerset, England, recounts how an old woman went out for a walk carrying her three pet toads, Duke, Dick, and Merryboy, in a basket. When she stopped to watch three farmers at work cutting wheat, one toad escaped and jumped into the path of a farmer's scythe. Laughing, the farmer let the blade fall upon the toad, killing it. "I'll show you!" cried the woman. "None of you will finish

According to popular belief, witches dressed their pet toads in tiny cloaks and fastened bells around their ankles. Apparently, these toads enjoyed their party clothes.

today's work!" Within moments, the first farmer had sliced his hand with his scythe. Soon the second man cut across the toe of his boot with his blade, and then the third sliced his own boot open from one side to the other. Frightened, the farmers fled the field, leaving day's work left undone.

According to some popular lore, however, the relationship between witches and toads wasn't always so loving. Any toad not lucky enough to be kept as a pampered pet was believed to be raw material for brewing **potions** and casting **spells.** To do away with an enemy, a witch might baptize a toad with the enemy's name and then kill the toad in a particularly unpleasant manner. Wherever the human victim was, he would supposedly suffer the same fate. To make themselves invisible, witches were rumored to apply a skin lotion made of toad saliva mixed with the sap of the sowthistle plant.

Toadstones

Can't afford a diamond? How about a toadstone? These gray or light brown stones may not sparkle in the sunlight, but legend holds that these magical objects change color or temperature in the presence of poison. Generally worn set in rings or other jewelry, toadstones were popular during the Middle Ages, when they were said to come from inside the heads of very old toads.

According to tradition, a toadstone could be extracted from a toad's head if necessary, but the toad might obligingly vomit up his treasure if asked. If someone gave you a toadstone ring, you could find out whether the stone was real by placing it in front of a toad. If he leaped forward, it was genuine; if he turned away in disdain, it was a fraud. (In reality, all toadstones were simply ordinary stones of a color and shape that vaguely resembled a toad.)

In addition to serving as poison detectors, toadstones were valued as **talismans** to attain perfect happiness and bring victory in battle. They were also used as **amulets** to protect houses and boats from harm and were believed to have curative value when laid against bites and stings.

The widespread idea that toads were standard ingredients in noxious potions probably stems from the fact that the creatures do secrete a mild poison when alarmed. The effects of this natural defense mechanism were often exaggerated, as evidenced by the claim of the third-century Roman writer Aelian that a drink of wine mixed with toad's blood would cause instant death. In 1591, a group of confessed witches admitted to plotting to poison King James VI of Scotland by soaking a

piece of his clothing in the venom of a black toad. The plot failed, they said, because they had been unable to obtain an appropriate garment. But they insisted that if they succeeded the king would have died in great agony. (Instead, he lived to become King of England and write his *Demonology,* a book endorsing the continued persecution of witches.)

As a result of the toad's long-standing link with witchcraft, close association with toads has generally been considered risky. Even the mere gaze of these little amphibians was thought dangerous by some as recently as the eighteenth century, when it was said to cause sudden fainting spells, palpitations, and convulsions. Toads were also said to bite cattle and other livestock, causing disease. Yet getting rid of these pests was no simple matter. Even if there were no witches around one might hesitate to kill a toad, since doing so was thought to bring on thunderstorms. And if you had thoughts about simply relocating the creatures, well, handling them was never advised. After all, you might get warts.

 SS 6/104

Transfiguration

Professor McGonagall wastes no time showing her first-year students what transfiguration is all about. In the blink of an eye, she changes her desk into a pig. She could just as easily have turned herself into a **cat,** or transformed one of her students into a tortoise or a block of wood. Transfiguration—the magical changing of a person, an-

imal, or object into the form of another—is a complex and dangerous subject requiring years of study. But novices must begin with much less challenging assignments, like turning buttons into beetles.

Tales of transfiguration (from the Latin *trans*, meaning "across," and *figura*, meaning "shape") are found in myths, fairy tales, and folklore from around the world. Cinderella's fairy godmother transfigures a pumpkin into a coach and mice into horses. In classic tales such as "The Frog Prince" and "Beauty and the Beast," handsome young men become croaking reptiles or repulsive ogres. The Greek witch **Circe** turns her front lawn into a virtual petting zoo by changing her visitors into tame lions, bears, and wolves (her less fortunate guests end up in the pigsty).

Perhaps the most famous stories are found in *Metamorphoses*, by the Roman poet Ovid. Written in the first century, the book tells the history of the world, beginning with the transformation of chaos into order and ending in Ovid's own time with the transfiguration of the emperor Julius Caesar into a star. In between are some 250 stories of gods, heroes, and mortals featuring amazing and sometimes shocking transfigurations. The hunter Acteon is transformed from a man to a stag as a punishment for catching a peek of the goddess Diana bathing, and is ripped to pieces by his own dogs. Arachne, a master weaver, is transfigured into a spider for having the audacity to challenge the goddess Minerva to a weaving contest. And the nymph Daphne is transfigured, mid-stride, into a laurel tree as she flees from the god Apollo. As Ovid describes it, "... a deep languor took hold on her limbs, her soft breast was enclosed in thick bark, her hair grew into leaves, her arms into branches, and her feet that were

The nymph Daphne is transfigured into a laurel tree.

lately so swift were held fast by sluggish roots, while her face became the treetop. Nothing of her was left, except her shining loveliness."

While most of Ovid's transfigurations are triggered by the anger or kindness of a god, many creatures of mythology and folklore can change form at will, an ability known as shape-shifting. The Norse gods Odin and Loki specialized in assuming animal forms, as did the Greek god Zeus, who often transformed himself into a bull, a ram, an eagle, a dove, or a swan. Many fairies and most demons, including **veela, ghouls,** and **trolls,** are master shape-shifters and can appear as anything at all—an alluring woman, a puff of smoke, a bowl of water, a rock, a sandstorm, or even as your best friend. Folktales world wide recount the lightning-fast transfigurations that occur when shape-shifters flee their enemies or do battle with each other. In a medieval Welsh fable, the character Gwion Bach steals the gift of prophecy from the **cauldron** of the witch Ceridwen. He races off in the form of a hare, but the witch pursues him in the shape of a greyhound. He dives into a river and becomes a fish; she follows him as an otter. He takes flight as a small bird and she gives chase as a hawk. Spying a heap of freshly cut wheat on the floor of a barn, Gwion descends and transfigures into what seems like the perfect disguise—a single grain of wheat among thousands. Ceridwen, however, has the last word. She lands in the barn, changes into a black hen, scratches about until she finds the right grain of wheat—and eats it.

The most notorious shape-shifters, at least by reputation, have been witches. As early as the second century A.D. the Roman writer Apuleius described witches who could take the form of birds, dogs, weasels, mice, and—like a certain reporter for the *Daily Prophet*—bugs, so as to gain entry to people's homes and go about their wicked business unobserved. Apuleius was writing fiction (much of it reflecting the beliefs of his time), but centuries later during the era of **witch persecution** (1450–1700), the belief that witches could transfigure into animals, especially cats, was commonplace. Trials from the period are filled with "evidence" of such transfigurations, mainly in the form of stories about injuries done to animals which later appeared on the bodies of the accused. At a sixteenth-century trial in Ferrara, Italy, for example, a man testified that he had beaten a cat with a stick after seeing it attack his infant son. The next day, a neighborhood woman was seen covered by bruises—proof that it was she, in feline form, who had attacked the infant. At a Scottish witch trial in 1718, a man testified that he had been so annoyed by cats who were chatting in human voices near his house that he killed two and wounded several others. Soon afterward, two local women were found dead in their beds, and another had a mysterious gash in her leg, again proving that the cats had really been shape-shifting witches in disguise.

World folklore is also filled with tales of men and women who, like Sirius Black, James Potter, and Peter Pettigrew, can assume just one animal form. In Europe, the best-known legends concerned **werewolves**—men who turned into bloodthirsty wolves for short periods of time. But in parts of the world where wolves were uncommon, other *were*-creatures prowled the night (*wer* means "man" in Old English). In the Amazon there were tales of jaguar-men, in India tiger-men, in Africa hyena-men, and in other parts of the world, men were fabled to transform into coyotes, bears, jackals, crocodiles, and snakes. Many of these legends probably grew out of the rituals of tribal **magicians** and shamans who, on ceremonial occasions, dressed in animal skins and imitated animal behavior (snorting, howling, and pawing the ground) and perhaps, in their own minds and the minds of their audiences, temporarily *became* a stag, a bear, or a jaguar.

No doubt many of us have imagined what it might be like to actually be another creature—to experience the power or grace of a leopard or see the world from an eagle's point of view. But few would want to experience the taste of rodent life that Mad-Eye Moody gives Draco Malfoy by transfiguring him into a bouncing ferret. Sometimes it seems better to just be yourself.

 SS 8/134

Troll

Although the word "troll" has been used to describe many a monster, very specific traits distinguish actual trolls from other beings that go bump in the night. Trolls are extremely ugly supernatural creatures that make their homes in the cold, northern European countries of Scandinavia. They are fierce, evil beings with a taste for human flesh and an eye for stolen treasure; they are also gigantic, tremendously strong, and notoriously dumb. But perhaps all of these off-putting traits can be forgiven, at least momentarily, when we recall that it was due to a twelve-foot mountain troll that Harry, Ron, and Hermione became fast friends.

Trolls have reportedly lived in the woods and mountains of Scandinavia since man first inhabited that region of the world at the end of the Ice Age. They appear in the earliest myths and folktales of Norway and Sweden. In addition to their gigantic size, trolls' most prominent features are their long, crooked noses, bushy tails, huge flat feet, shortage of fingers and toes (they only have three or four), and the shaggy, mossy growth that covers their heads and noses. There have also been reports of trolls that have only a single eye in the middle of their wrinkled foreheads, trolls with two or three heads, and still others that have trees growing out of their noses. In later folktales trolls were described as being either very small or human size and more intelligent than their ancient predecessors.

Trolls live in communities deep inside caves, mountains, or hills. Some also live underground, or under rocks or uprooted trees. Their preference for subterranean living makes perfect sense given that they hate noise and exposure to daylight turns them into stone, or can even

make them burst. Bizarre shaped rocks that enliven the Scandinavian countryside are said to be trolls who ignored their crucial curfew.

Troll dwellings are described as gorgeous, glowing palaces filled with stolen treasure. Exceedingly greedy, trolls pilfer all the gold and silver they can find. Their avarice is not only for human treasure but for treasured humans. They abduct human children, replacing them with their own infants, in the hope of having them raised as human. Legend has it that if a human mother suspects her baby is a troll changeling, she should threaten to burn the child in a fire. Supposedly, the easily fooled troll mother will rush to her baby's rescue, at which point a human mother can recover her own child. However, this nuisance can be avoided completely if the child is baptized, as trolls despise Christianity (the sound of church bells is enough to send them fleeing in the opposite direction).

Unfortunately, brainpower and church bells aren't always enough to protect people from trolls, who possess many invincible magical powers. They are adept shape-shifters and can make themselves invisible. These talents help them both to steal treasure and to hide it, which they often do by making their ill-gotten gold resemble something completely different, like a pile of rocks and stones. Anyone who encounters a troll and is unable to escape usually suffers a horrible fate, such as being imprisoned, enslaved, or worst of all, eaten. Trolls have a strong appetite for human flesh and blood, and all that remains of their unfortunate victims are bare, gnawed skeletons.

There have been rare reports of benevolent trolls who reward families they like with riches and good luck. These trolls are masterful craftsmen and talented metalworkers who create distinctive swords, knives, and bracelets. They use their knowledge of magic and herbs to cure sickness and they are very fond of music and dancing. However, given the higher likelihood of encountering the flesh-eating variety of troll, if you find yourself in a forest that is particularly *trolsk* (Norwegian for "spooky"), we recommend that you *flykte* (Norwegian for "get out quick!").

 SS 10/174

Unicorn

Few animals, real or imaginary, have captured the imagination as consistently as the unicorn. Ever since the single-horned creature was first described more than two thousand years ago by the Greek physician Ctesias, people have written about, painted, sculpted, and hunted unicorns—all the while arguing about whether they really exist.

The unicorns described in antiquity bear only slight resemblance to the noble, innocent, and pure creatures that inhabit the **Forbidden Forest** at Hogwarts. According to Ctesias, the unicorn was native to India. It was about the size of a donkey, had a dark red head, a white body, blue eyes, and a single horn, about eighteen inches long, extending from its forehead. White at the base, black in the middle, and flaming red at the top, the horn had a remarkable quality. When separated from its owner and made into a drinking cup, it protected all who drank from it from poisons, convulsions, and epilepsy. Such vessels were not easy to come by, however, since

During the fifteenth and sixteenth centuries, European travelers returned from Asia, Africa, and the Americas with new reports of unicorn sightings. Since descriptions differed, unicorns were assumed to come in several varieties.

the speed, strength, and vicious temperament of the unicorn made it almost impossible to capture.

Over the next several centuries, belief in the elusive creature grew, though evidence of its existence was still wanting. Aristotle and Julius Caesar both described one-horned animals and were cited as authorities. The Roman naturalist Pliny added new details to the unicorn's appearance, giving it a deer's head, elephant's feet, a boar's tail, and a three-foot-long black horn. (Later writers suggest that early unicorn reports were based on misleading descriptions of the Indian rhinoceros, or on sightings of two-horned animals such as goats or ibex that were either viewed in profile or had lost a horn). Pliny also confirmed the unicorn's ferocious nature and said the beast had a deep, bellowing voice.

By the Middle Ages, the popular image of the unicorn had evolved from the collage of animal parts described by the ancients to the graceful creature we recognize today. Paintings and tapestries of the period portray a beautiful, white, horse-like animal with a spiraling, pure white horn and the cloven hoofs of a deer. In literature, the unicorn came to represent strength, power, and purity. It was incorporated into Christian symbolism and became part of the royal coat of arms of England and Scotland. Unicorns appeared in Arthurian legend, fairy tales, and romanticized accounts of the exploits of Genghis Khan and Alexander the Great.

A typical medieval story emphasizing the purity of the unicorn tells of a group of forest animals that came to a pool to drink but found the water poisoned. The thirsty animals were saved when a unicorn appeared and dipped his horn into the water, causing it to become fresh and untainted. So great is the unicorn's love of all things innocent and pure, according to another tale, that when a unicorn comes upon an innocent maiden sitting beneath a tree, he will lay his head in her lap and fall asleep. This idea greatly appealed to those interested in capturing unicorns to relieve them of their valuable horns. Unicorn hunting was a fearsome business, since the animals were rumored to be able to use their horns as swords and, if pursued, would jump off cliffs, landing on their horns and walking away unscathed. A safer and less strenuous approach, it seemed, would be to use a virtuous maiden as bait. Once the unicorn was asleep in her lap, the waiting hunters could move in and capture him.

Interest in catching unicorns finally died out in the eighteenth century, as numerous skeptics pointed out that it was impossible to find anyone who had actually *seen* one of the creatures with his own eyes. A few writers persisted in including unicorns in their books of natural history, repeating ancient and medieval accounts, but most became convinced that it was time to retire the animal to the realm of fable. This hardly dampened popular enthusiasm for the unicorn, which lived on in art, literature, and imagination, as it does to this day.

 GF 24/436

Hornswoggled

hornswoggle (hôrn′swog′əl) *tr.v.* **-gled, -gling, gles.** To bamboozle; deceive. [Origin unknown.]

Impossible as it was in the sixteenth century to find anyone who had seen a unicorn, locating a unicorn horn was another story altogether. That's because unicorn horn was for sale in every apothecary shop (the equivalent of today's pharmacy) as a cure for most diseases and a protection against poisons. Demand was great and prices were sky high. Ground into a powder the horn—also known as "alicorn"—could be taken in pure form or combined with other medicinal agents. Those unable to afford the precious product could instead purchase a vial of water into which a unicorn's horn had allegedly been dipped.

Of course, the product sold in apothecary shops did not really come from unicorns. Instead, it was the tusk of the narwhal, a species of arctic whale that has a single, twisted horn that can grow up to nine feet long. As the number of whaling expeditions grew in the sixteenth and seventeenth centuries, so, too, did the supply of supposed unicorn horn. Tests to verify the authenticity of alicorn—most of which involved placing spiders near the horn and observing their reactions—were numerous, but apparently few detected bogus horn, for narwhal tusks, masquerading as unicorn horn, made their way into shops across Europe.

Not all alicorn was consumed in medicine. The legendary property of unicorn horn cups to neutralize poisons, first reported by Ctesias more than one thousand years earlier, continued to make them a highly valued possession, especially among royalty, for whom fear of poisoning was a daily fact of life. Alicorn cups were so valuable that in 1565 King Frederick II of Denmark was able to use just one as security for a loan to finance a war against Sweden.

Seventeenth-century drawing of a narwhal, the arctic whale whose spiraled tusk was sold at a hefty price as unicorn horn. The present-day narwhal population is estimated at 25,000 to 45,000.

Vampire

Solitary and friendless, they walk the night in an eternal search for fresh blood. They while away the daylight hours asleep in musty crypts and mountaintop castles. They never age, and they don't fear death, for they are already dead. And if you should see one in the street, you might have no idea that you're staring a monster in the face.

Of all the **ghosts, ghouls,** and **demons** studied in Defense Against the Dark Arts, none is as universally recognized as the bloodthirsty vampire. Physical descriptions vary from culture to culture, ranging from a red-eyed beast with green or pink hair (China), to a snakelike creature with a woman's head (the Greek *Lamia*), to the tall, sophisticated gentleman in a high-collared cloak derived from Eastern European legend. In most tales, a vampire is a human being who, once dead, rises again with a compulsion to drink the blood of the living.

Vampires have been part of folklore for hundreds of years, but did not achieve real notoriety until the 1897 publication of Bram Stoker's classic novel, *Dracula.* The canine teeth of Stoker's title vampire were slightly elongated and pointed, he had hair on his palms, and he was unusually pale, but he was otherwise relatively human in his physical appearance. In all likelihood, Count Dracula was based upon Vlad Tepes, the notoriously bloody and violent ruler of Walachia (part of present-day Romania) in the fifteenth century. Vlad was known for impaling his enemies through the heart with wooden stakes, as well as bathing in the blood of the slain after particularly grueling battles. With time, these habits evolved into important elements of the vampire legend. Vlad, apparently a dramatic sort of fellow, signed his let-

ters "Vlad Dracula," which can be loosely translated as "Vlad, son of the Devil."

The powers of the vampire have been elaborated over the centuries. In the sixteenth century, Spanish conquistadors in Central and South America encountered a species of bat with eating habits not unlike those of Count Dracula and his kin. Ever since, it has been said that vampires can turn into bats at will. They are also believed to be capable of transforming into wolves, rats, or mice. Some are thought to control and communicate with these creatures as well. Vampires are blessed with strength and dexterity far beyond that of a human being, and some have the power of flight. Finally, some of the more powerful vampires have the ability to hypnotize human beings with a gaze, controlling that person's actions and even seeing through his or her eyes.

For all its powers, however, the vampire also has many weaknesses. It is common knowledge that vampires cannot abide sunlight. The sun has long been considered a symbol of truth and goodness, concepts that go against the nature of vampires. Consequently, exposure to direct sunlight will destroy the vampire, usually reducing it to a harmless pile of dust. Other well-known ways to destroy a vampire include beheading, cremation, and driving a wooden stake through its heart. Contrary to popular belief, most legends hold that vampires are not vulnerable to weapons fashioned from silver; rather, iron is the metal of choice if you plan to fight one of these creatures. In Slavic folklore, a vampire can be destroyed by dousing it with holy water, conducting an exorcism, or by stealing its left sock, filling the sock with stones, and then throwing it in a river.

As Professor Quirrell knows, vampires cannot stand the smell of fresh garlic. Garlands of the potent herb may be placed in bedrooms (or classrooms) in order to protect their occupants. Superstitious folk will stuff the eyes, ears, and nostrils of the newly dead with cloves of garlic to keep them from becoming vampires. Vampires are also believed to have a powerful fascination with counting; if a vampire should come across scattered seeds, it will begin counting them, not stopping until it has finished—even if it means a dusty death in the early rays of dawn. Finally, a vampire must sleep each night in earth from its homeland. Thus, when Stoker's Dracula comes to England from Transylvania (a town located just south of Vlad's Walachia), he brings with him several crates of Romanian earth and installs them in his new London residence.

Different legends provide varying accounts of the vampire's personality. Some stories depict the creature as a mindless, soulless killer. Bram Stoker's Count Dracula, however, was intelligent and charming, with impeccable manners and good breeding. Other tales imagine vampires as essentially decent beings, eternally tortured by the terrible things they must do in order to survive. This versatility is probably one reason that the vampire continues to inspire new legends to this day.

 SS 8/134

Veela

Sports fans have often fallen under the spell of cheerleaders, but rarely have they tumbled out of the stands as Harry and Ron nearly do at the sight of the veela, those beguiling mascots of the Bulgarian Quidditch team.

Female spirits of Eastern European folklore, veela are shape-shifting creatures believed to dwell in forests, lakes, mountains, and clouds. In their animal forms they can appear as swans, horses, falcons, **snakes,** or wolves, but they are at their most alluring and dan-

gerous in human form, as beautiful young girls with long flowing hair who dress in misty robes and dance under the midsummer moon. Young men who fall under their sway lose all reason: They become dazed and forget to eat, drink, or sleep, often for days. Anyone unlucky enough to come upon veela dancing must join them and dance, dance, dance until they die of exhaustion. And woe to anyone who steps on a **fairy** ring—the tamped down circle of grass where the veela have danced—for bad luck or illness is sure to follow. Although veela can be benevolent toward humans and share their gifts of healing and prophecy, they are quite temperamental. They will not tolerate being lied to or deceived and can inflict terrible punishments, especially on anyone who breaks a promise.

In some traditions, veela have been known to marry humans, settle down, and raise families, apparently without ill effect for either species. Fleur Delacour, Beauxbatons' Triwizard champion, had a veela grandmother, and she seems nice enough, but we wouldn't want to get her angry.

250

 GF 8/103

Werewolf

In folklore from around the world, a werewolf is a human with the capacity to transform into an unusually ferocious wolf. Active only at night and often (but not always) under a full moon, he devours men, women, children, and livestock, ripping out their throats with his claws

and fangs. In some stories, a man who becomes a werewolf is the unwilling victim of bad genes, a **curse,** or a bite from another werewolf (as in the case of a certain Hogwarts professor). Much as he may loathe the harm he causes, he is unable to control his actions. In other tales, a **sorcerer** makes a conscious decision to become a werewolf—often by using an enchanted belt or special ointment—so that he can carry out his terrible deeds, usually in league with the Devil. Although werewolves are almost always men, tales of female and child werewolves also exist.

Tales of man-wolves have been around since antiquity. Greek mythology tells of a bloodthirsty tyrant named Lycaon who greatly angered Zeus by serving him the flesh of a human child. As punishment, Zeus turned Lycaon into a wolf, although some of his human features remained. This story is the source of the word "lycanthrope," another term for werewolf. Greek writers of the fourth century B.C. described folk beliefs in werewolves, and by the first century A.D., the Roman natural historian Pliny was writing of the creatures' existence as fact.

Werewolf legends and beliefs were fully entrenched in Europe by the early Middle Ages. Surprisingly, the image of the werewolf during this time was not all bad. While in some stories wicked stepmothers and villains turn out to be werewolves, in others the werewolf might be a hero, a saint, or a comic figure. In a famous French tale, when a nobleman confesses to his wife that he is a werewolf, she and her lover steal his clothing the next time he transforms. Unable to return to human form without his clothes, the nobleman is trapped as a wolf. He becomes a tame pet to the king until the truth is finally revealed. His clothes are returned, the evil wife and her lover are banished, and the noble werewolf is triumphant. In another legend, the people of a small village are startled to see a wolf dash down the main street and leap at a piece of meat left hanging up high to dry. Missing its target, the wolf falls into a well. When the townspeople look into the well, all they see is a very embarrassed naked woman!

By the sixteenth century, however, werewolves were no longer portrayed as heroes or figures of fun. Instead, they were regarded as a very real threat. As **witch persecution** gained momentum across Europe, dozens of people in France, Germany, Switzerland, and Italy were arrested, tried, and executed for being werewolves. Witch-hunters claimed that werewolves were actually **witches** or **wizards** who had made pacts with the Devil that enabled them to become wolves. Accused of horrific acts of mass murder and cannibalism, many of these alleged werewolves confessed under torture.

More than a dozen books on werewolves were published during this period. Many described how a wizard prepared for the transformation by shedding his clothes and rubbing his body with magic ointments made out of belladonna root, deadly nightshade, bat's blood, cinquefoil, henbane, soot, and an assortment of other, equally unpleasant ingredients. Next, the wizard donned a wolf's skin or an enchanted belt and uttered incantations to the Devil, who granted him the supernatural strength and speed with which to satisfy his appetite for human flesh and blood.

It is no coincidence that werewolf trials occurred in places where the problem of real wolves was quite serious. Wolf populations had surged in continental Europe after the great plague of the fourteenth century led to the abandonment of land formerly used for farming. Although wolves were much more likely to attack livestock than humans, they did occasionally claim a human victim, and such incidents were often attributed to werewolves. In England, where wolves had become extinct by the sixteenth century, tales of werewolves were quite rare.

"Real" Werewolves

Why have so many people been convinced that men really can turn into wolves? A medical explanation suggests that at least some supposed werewolves were brought to trial because they actually *looked* like werewolves—owing to a rare genetic condition known as hypertrichosis. Victims of this disease develop dense facial hair that can cover the cheeks, forehead, nose, and eyelids. In some cases, every part of the body but the palms of the hands and the soles of the feet appears furry, making sufferers look as if they've just emerged from a Hollywood makeup studio. Doctors have dubbed the gene responsible for this condition "the werewolf gene."

An equally rare genetic condition called porphyria may explain other apparent signs of being a werewolf. This disease causes extreme sensitivity to light, so that, like werewolves, those affected by it usually venture out only at night. As the condition progresses, it causes sores or marks on the skin, which could easily have been interpreted as the wounds a werewolf was said to receive while running through the forest and hunting prey. Finally, porphyria can cause the teeth and fingernails to become red, making it appear as if a bloody meal has just been consumed.

Witch

Thinking of Hermione as a witch can take some getting used to. Most of us imagine witches as cackling old women with long warty noses and pointy black hats. Yet, in many ways Hermione and the other witches of Hogwarts aren't so different from the witches of yore; they cast **spells** and brew **potions,** turn everyday objects into live animals, ride on **broomsticks,** and keep company with **cats, owls,** and **toads.** These activities have been associated with witches—both fictional and historical—for hundreds of years.

Witches of one kind or another have existed in every civilization, from ancient Assyria and Babylonia to the villages of medieval Europe to the present-day tribes of central and southern Africa. By definition, a witch is simply an individual believed to have supernatural powers. While the exact nature of these powers differs from culture to culture, it's commonly believed that witches have the ability to harm or heal with magic herbs, kill from a distance with a glance or a spell, control the weather, fly, or transform into an animal. Although a witch may use these magical techniques with the best of intentions, in most societies witches are regarded as agents of evil and misfortune. Western culture has come to define witches as female, but the term may also be applied to a man. (Sometimes, a male witch is called a warlock).

The literature of ancient Greece and Rome abounds with tales of witches, who spent much of their time mixing magical potions from herbs and gruesome animal parts. Described as having long disheveled hair and going about barefoot, they were popularly believed to frequent graveyards, where they might be found at midnight digging up bones and poisonous plants or worshipping Diana, goddess of the moon and

Many people believed that witches could change the weather. In this fifteenth-century woodcut, a snake and a rooster are tossed into a cauldron to cause a hailstorm.

hunting, or Hecate, goddess of fertility and queen of the night. Some were said to raise up the spirits of the dead, others to kill with a mere glance. The witches of Thessaly, in northern Greece, were believed to be so skilled that they could draw the moon down to earth to use its powers for their own purposes. The second-century Roman poet Apuleius described witches as "capable of bringing down the sky, making springs dry up, [and] sweeping away mountains."

During the Middle Ages, the word "witch" was sometimes used to refer to the local wise women who used herbs to treat illness, made **amulets** to ward off evil spirits, and practiced **divination** to find lost

property or identify criminals. Many people also believed these "white witches" could perform such impressive feats as conjuring rain, foretelling the future, and guaranteeing fair winds for sailing. Like **wizards,** they were both respected and feared by their neighbors, who trusted them for aid and advice but believed they could cause misfortune if angered.

These local wise women were among the first to be accused during the witchcraft panic that spread through western Europe during the sixteenth and seventeenth centuries. Soon, however, accusations of witchcraft began to include women and men from all walks of life. Defined as heretics (enemies of the Christian church) and Devil worshippers, accused witches were blamed for everything from crop failures to sudden infant death to the spread of disease among livestock. Witches were said to associate with **demons** and to participate regularly in horrific acts of ritual murder, vampirism, and cannibalism. According to popular lore, they held frequent *Sabbats*—wild nighttime gatherings in secluded fields or woods—where they praised the Devil with feasting and dancing. Air travel was allegedly the most common mode of transportation to these parties, either by broomstick or on the back of a demon or animal companion known as a familiar.

Such wild imaginings sparked a wealth of literature on witches, and by the end of the **witch persecution** era in the early eighteenth century, the stereotypical witch was fairly well defined. Weather-beaten and wrinkled, she usually had a hooked nose and pointed chin, scraggly hair, and fleshy, drooping lips. She was poor, had a reputation for eccentric behavior, and a fondness for cats. Like the witch of the Grimm's fairy tale "Hansel and Gretel," she was likely to live in a small cottage in some out-of-the-way

The stereotypical witch of European folklore.

place. In many cases this image was mirrored in reality, since witch hunters sought out easy targets and were quick to accuse old women who lived alone and were already partially cast out of the community. Although charges of witchcraft were not limited to the old and ugly (many accused witches were young, attractive, and prosperous), the stereotypical image of the witch has remained largely unchanged since the eighteenth century.

 SS 4/55

The Witch's Familiar

Witches may have been social outcasts, but according to popular belief they were not without companionship. Each witch was said to possess at least one "familiar"—a **demon** in the shape of a small animal who would offer her advice and carry out malicious errands, including murder, at her command. **Cats,** dogs, **toads,** rabbits, blackbirds, and crows were the most common familiars, but an occasional witch was accused of keeping a hedgehog, weasel, ferret, mole, mouse, rat, bee, or grasshopper as her demonic pet.

Having supposedly received their familiars directly from the Devil, witches were said to bestow tender care upon them, baptizing and naming them (Pyewackit, Gibbe, Rutterkin, Greedigut, or Elemauzer, for example) and offering them the best tidbits of food. A job well done was traditionally rewarded with a few drops of the mistress's blood.

Familiars became a standard part of witch lore during the English and Scottish witch trials of the sixteenth century and eventually made their way to the American colonies as well. It was widely believed that familiars served as witches' spies and did much of their dirty work, even casting **spells** and working **curses.** Thus, when someone saw a cat or dog they didn't recognize, especially if it seemed to look at them in an odd way, they had cause to worry that it was a witch's trusty servant out to cause them harm.

When the time came for an accused witch's trial, her supposedly loyal familiar nearly always managed to be missing. This was fortunate for the hapless pet, since those few demons in disguise who were caught were immediately executed.

Witches were said to treat their familiars with great tenderness.

Witch Persecution

It would be nice to think that Bathilda Bagshot's *History of Magic* told the whole story of witch persecution in early modern Europe. There Harry reads that **witches** and **wizards** who were burned at the stake suffered no pain—instead, a simple **charm** made the flames feel like a pleasant tickle. But the good Ms. Bagshot is silent on the fate of the thousands of ordinary women and men who were falsely accused of witchcraft and had no magic powers to protect them. Sadly, such people were the true casualties of the witch hunting hysteria that gripped much of Europe from the middle of the fifteenth century until the end of the seventeenth century.

For roughly 250 years, people at all levels of society were convinced that a vast conspiracy of witches threatened their lives. Malicious individuals devoted to the overthrow of Christianity were believed to be doing the Devil's work everywhere, from the dairy barn to the royal chambers. Traditional legal and ethical standards were set aside as zealous judges and religious leaders strove to root out the evildoers and exterminate all witches from the face of the earth. Modern scholars estimate that during this period anywhere from 30,000 to as many as several hundred thousand people were viciously tortured and executed as witches, on the basis of evidence that was flimsy at best, and often nonexistent.

Why did these horrific events take place? No one can say for sure. But certainly religious conflict, including the division of the Christian church into opposing Catholic and Protestant camps, played a large role in creating an atmosphere of mistrust among neighbors, and even within families. Also important was the invention of the printing press

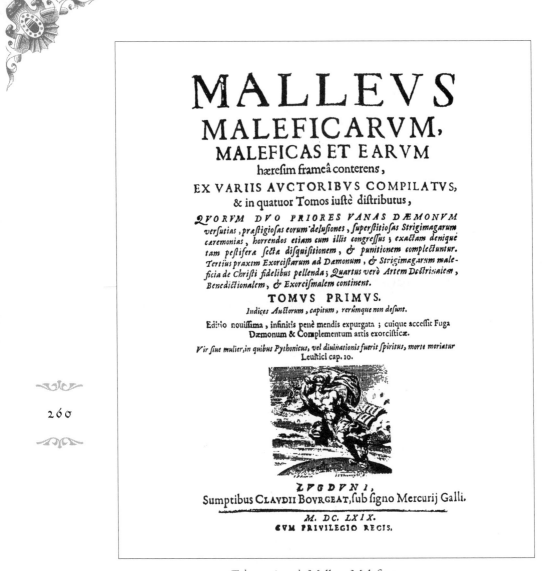

MALLEVS
MALEFICARVM,
MALEFICAS ET EARVM
hæresim frameâ conterens,
EX VARIIS AVCTORIBVS COMPILATVS,
& in quatuor Tomos iustè distributus,

*QVORVM DVO PRIORES VANAS DÆMONVM
versutias, præstigiosas eorum delusiones, superstitiosas Strigimagarum
cæremonias, horrendos etiam cum illis congressus; exactam deniquè
tam pestiferæ sectæ disquisitionem, & punitionem complectuntur.
Tertius praxim Exorcistarum ad Dæmonum, & Strigimagarum male-
ficia de Christi fidelibus pellenda; Quartus verò Artem Doctrinalem,
Benedictionalem, & Exorcismalem continent.*

TOMVS PRIMVS.
Indices Auctorum, capitum, rerùmque non desunt.

Editio nouissima, infinitis penè mendis expurgata; cuique accessit Fuga
Dæmonum & Complementum artis exorcisticæ.

*Vir siue mulier, in quibus Pythonicus, vel diuinationis fuerit spiritus, morte moriatur
Leuitici cap. 10.*

LVGDVNI,
Sumptibus CLAVDII BOVRGEAT, sub signo Mercurij Galli.

M. DC. LXIX.
CVM PRIVILEGIO REGIS.

Title page from the Malleus Maleficarum.

in the mid-1400s, which allowed for the rapid spread of ideas and fears about witchcraft among people in positions of power.

Many of these ideas could be found in the *Malleus Maleficarum,* or *Hammer of Witches,* a comprehensive guide to identifying, prosecuting, and punishing witches written by two German witch hunters in 1486. The book was an immediate success, read by churchmen, lawmakers, and just about anyone who could read. It was so popular that, for nearly two hundred years, it was second only to the Bible in sales. Although

the book did not create the phenomenon of witch persecution, by popularizing and supporting the beliefs that lay behind the witch trials, the *Malleus* helped perpetuate the stereotypes and misinformation that condemned thousands of innocent people to death.

The authors of the *Malleus*, Heinrich Kramer and James Sprenger, provided terrifying details of how witches made pacts with the Devil, transformed themselves into wild beasts, and sacrificed infants. With an endorsement by Pope Innocent VIII, their claims were widely regarded as irrefutable truth. Hundreds of witchcraft trials were modeled on the procedures they set forth, which denied accused witches the right to have lawyers or call witnesses and recommended torture. Referring to the Biblical pronouncement "Thou shall not suffer a witch to live" (Exodus 22:18), the authors assured the public that the only way to react to the threat of Satan was to root out and destroy his servants on earth.

Much of the responsibility for this weighty task initially fell to the Inquisition—the office of the Catholic Church dedicated to identifying and exterminating heresy (beliefs and practices contrary to those of the Church). Professional inquisitors were given broad powers to seek out and punish evildoers, and individuals known to practice magic were an obvious target of their campaign. Although the Church had never approved of the village wise women and wizards who made love **potions** and healing charms, these people were an integral part of their communities, and authorities had never seriously tried to shut them down. Now, however, the Church insisted that anyone reputed to have supernatural abilities must have received their powers from the Devil, and was therefore guilty of heresy—a crime punishable by death. This rule applied to village healers and diviners as well as those suspected of clearly malevolent forms of magic such as casting spells to harm people or destroy crops.

Accusations of witchcraft weren't limited to those with reputations for magical practices. As the hysteria spread and the witch-hunting cause was taken up by secular as well as Catholic and Protestant authorities, all God-fearing citizens were urged to come forward and identify as many suspects as possible. An old woman might be accused simply on the basis of her appearance, or because she went

The guilt or innocence of accused witches was often determined by throwing them into the water. Floating was a sign of guilt, while sinking—and occasionally drowning—was a sign of innocence. Witch hunters could control the outcome of the ordeal by manipulating the ropes that bound the suspect.

about the village muttering to herself or kept a broomstick in her house. A petty dispute might end with a charge of witchcraft if the injured party suggested to authorities that his neighbor had put a curse on him. In areas where the property of convicted witches was seized, the wealthiest people in town were the most likely targets. But men and women of all ages, both rich and poor, were accused, tried, tortured, and burned at the stake. Anonymous accusations could be made against anyone, and the accuser never had to worry about facing the person they'd charged with witchcraft.

Why Were Witches Women?

During the era of intense witch persecution, three women were accused of witchcraft for every man charged. This may strike us as a sign of prejudice, but to the witch-hunters it made perfect sense. From their perspective, the biblical story of Adam and Eve demonstrated that women were responsible for all sin in the world. It was obvious that women were physically, morally, and intellectually weaker than men, and therefore much more susceptible to temptation by the Devil. Moreover, witch hunters noted, women were clearly more vindictive than men, more spiteful, and more likely to tell lies.

Modern scholars suggest that, in addition to these clear signs of misogyny (hatred of women) in the culture that supported witch hunts, certain social conditions made women more vulnerable to accusations of witchcraft. For example, women were the midwives who helped deliver babies, and when newborns died (as they often did), parents might blame the midwife. It was a short step in the public's mind from midwife to witch, since sudden deaths were considered evidence of witchcraft. But probably the largest group of accused witches were older women—either spinsters or widows—who lived alone. In a male-dominated society in which women generally had neither rights nor property, a woman who was not under the immediate control of a father or husband was often shunned as a threat to society, or, at best, regarded with mistrust. The witch trials may have served as a convenient way to get rid of such distasteful members of a community.

It's also quite possible that more women than men actually practiced some form of sorcery. Since they had little power to redress grievances, resolve disagreements, or indeed exert any control over their own destinies by legal means, women might instead turn to illegal magical practices— spells, potions, or curses—in an effort to exert some influence on their lives and the world around them. Although such activities were usually harmless, they could have grave consequences if they led to a charge of witchcraft.

Once arrested, accused witches were put on trial and were considered guilty until proven otherwise. After all, the *Malleus Maleficarum* said that judges need not exercise undue caution in reaching their verdicts, as God would never permit an innocent person to be convicted of witchcraft. In Germany, France, and Switzerland, suspects were routinely tortured to elicit detailed confessions. Under these excruciating circumstances, the accused almost always confessed to whatever the inquisitors demanded of them—worshipping Satan, summoning and consorting with **demons,** flying on **broomsticks** to midnight gatherings, casting spells to harm their neighbors, and a variety of other crimes. Each new confession confirmed the accusers' belief that the diabolical conspiracy was of monumental proportions and fueled their passion to search more diligently and punish ever more harshly. In England and Scandinavia, where torture was illegal, judges relied on the unsupported testimony of witnesses, as well as the presence of a so-called "witch's mark" (any mole or birthmark would do) or assertions that the accused had a demonic animal companion, or familiar (see **Witch**). Each "witch" was also forced to supply the names of accomplices so that new trials could be set in motion. This procedure sometimes set off a chain reaction resulting in the destruction of an entire village. In 1589, 133 residents of the town of Quedlinburg, Germany, were executed as witches in a single day.

Certainly, not everyone believed in witchcraft. Not everyone suspected their neighbors of making pacts with the Devil. So why didn't sensible people speak out against witch persecution and put an end to it? Well, some tried, but the witch trials were supported by powerful authorities, and anyone who openly doubted the reality of witchcraft, or even the guilt of a harmless old lady, risked ending up on trial themselves. Only those with protection in high places could take such a risk, but for the most part their protests had little effect.

Ultimately, however, the witchcraft panic died out on its own, as the scientific revolution brought a new skepticism to Europe and magical beliefs became unfashionable among the upper classes. One of the last major outbreaks of witchcraft hysteria occurred in the American colony of Salem, Massachusetts, in 1692. The last English witch trial

was held in 1712, the last French trial in 1745, and the last German trial in 1775. The laws prohibiting witchcraft were repealed in England and Scotland in 1736. Those who still believed in the Devil's interference in earthly affairs tended to keep it to themselves. No longer a heresy, witchcraft once again entered the realm of simple folk magic. Nonetheless, the popular association of witches with evil never completely disappeared. Outbreaks of violence against suspected witches were recorded in Europe and the United States into the early twentieth century.

 PA 1/2

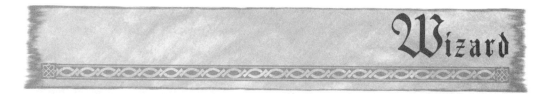

Wizard

In many ways, Albus Dumbledore is the quintessential wizard. At its root, "wizard" means "wise," and the Hogwarts headmaster is certainly adept at dispensing sage advice and handling sticky situations. His magical powers are unparalleled, and his flowing purple robes, silver beard, and pointy hat complete the picture of wizardry we have all come to expect.

This image of the wizard is the product of both fiction and history. From **Merlin** to Dumbledore himself, the delightful products of literary invention include wizards who can turn into **cats** or **owls**, produce lavish banquets with a wave of the wand, disappear into thin air, or cast **spells** to make castles look like cabbages. Their historical ancestors included thousands of very real men and women of medieval and

Renaissance Europe who were widely believed to have both special wisdom and magical abilities. The women were known as wise women, cunning women, or white **witches;** the men were called wise men, cunning men, or wizards.

Most villages in medieval Europe had at least one professional wizard, who offered his clients an assortment of magical services, including finding lost objects, hidden treasure, or missing persons; detecting criminals; curing illnesses; telling fortunes; casting and breaking spells; making **amulets** and **charms** to ward off both natural and supernatural harm; and concocting **potions.** Belief in **magic** was widespread, and the wizard was generally both respected and feared by the community he served. As late as the seventeenth century, a wizard's identification of a thief (usually made by asking the victim about potential suspects and then practicing some form of **divination**) was taken seriously, sometimes providing the basis for legal arrests.

A villager might seek out a wizard's magical assistance for almost any purpose—to win at cards or dice, protect a house from rodents, make children sleep through the night, or avoid arrest for unpaid debts. As the local wise man, a wizard might also be asked to offer advice on matters of the heart or help decide between two courses of action. In response to a request, he—or his female counterpart—might read the future in a **crystal ball,** fashion a protective amulet, brew a potion, or instruct the client to gather a certain herb while uttering an incantation. In return, he would receive a small fee or donation.

Most patrons were poor, and so were most wizards and wise women. But members of the upper classes did not hesitate to consult them when the occasion warranted it, and a wizard who developed a reputation among aristocrats could make an excellent living. Many wealthy women sought out love potions to win the husband they desired or regain the affections of a wayward spouse. Men engaged in politics were sometimes said to turn to a wizard for help, whether to gain the favor of a king, carry out a rebellious plot, or ensure success in a delicate diplomatic mission.

Because the services they provided were in such demand, village wizards were relatively safe from the legal prosecution that was applied to all forms of magical practice at one time or another. In England, three Witchcraft Acts passed between 1542 and 1604 made it a felony to tell fortunes, make healing charms or love potions, or divine for treasure or stolen property. However, the number of people prosecuted for such crimes was quite small compared to the number who stood trial for engaging in malevolent forms of magic such as consorting with the Devil or conjuring evil spirits. For the most part, village wizards were protected by their customers. Nonetheless, they were vulnerable to the whims of dissatisfied patrons, who might report them to the authorities or accuse them of witchcraft.

During the sixteenth century, the word "wizard" began to take on new meanings. The term was applied not only to village wise men, but to **magicians** who practiced alchemy and summoned **demons,** court astrologers, and conjurers who performed magic tricks as entertainment. Eventually, it came to refer to practitioners of any kind of magic and became the favorite term of storytellers, who endowed their characters with magical powers more spectacular than any historical wizard had even imagined.

 SS 4/50

Yeti

In Nepal, it is called a *rakshasa*, the Sanskrit word for "**demon.**" If you live in Canada, you might call it a *sasquatch* (Native American for "hairy man"), while in the United States it's known simply as *Bigfoot.* Its proper name, however, is "yeti," and it has allegedly stalked the Earth for millennia. Accounts of its existence date from as early as the fourth century B.C. and persist to this day. Many people claim to have seen one, yet there's little evidence to suggest that the creature is real. But if there's one expert to consult, it's probably Rubeus Hagrid, for in the language of Tibet *yeti* means "magical creature."

According to most lore, the typical yeti is seven to ten feet tall, with long arms, an ape-like face, and a flat nose. Young members of the species are covered with a thick layer of red hair, which turns black as they grow into adulthood. Tremendously strong, yetis are said to be able to toss around boulders like softballs. They are also remarkably quick on their big feet—twice as fast as the most accomplished human sprinters. They communicate with loud roars and whistling noises. Unfortunately, the yeti isn't terribly fond of personal hygiene; virtually every legend emphasizes the creature's overwhelming odor, which is said to be bad enough to curl your hair and make your eyes water.

With such a distinctive appearance, you might expect that it would be easy to find a yeti. But even Professor Gilderoy Lockhart, who claimed to have spent *A Year with the Yeti*, probably faired no better than most yeti seekers. First of all, the yeti is notoriously shy, and hundreds of expeditions aimed at locating the creature have produced only blurred photographs and footprints, most of them regarded as hoaxes. Sir Edmund Hillary, the English explorer who was the first person to reach the summit of Mount Everest, conducted an extensive search of the Himalayas for the elusive creature (dubbed the "Abominable Snowman" by newspaper reporters). All he could find was an enormous skull and some footprints of a size not carried at your local shoe store.

Furthermore, the locations frequented by the yeti are not exactly hospitable. The creatures have reportedly been spotted in pleasant parts of Australia (where locals call them *Yowies*), Canada's Queen Charlotte Islands (where they are called *Gogete* and are believed to predate humanity), the Middle East, and most recently Spalding, Idaho. But the places the yeti most often makes its home—the Rocky Mountains, the Himalayas, and the Australian outback—are marked by harsh conditions not welcoming to human travelers.

The final obstacle is the fact that the creatures are not known to be the most gracious hosts. Some accounts suggest that the yeti is quite gentle unless threatened, but others describe aggressive behavior in response to people. Former United States President Teddy Roosevelt told of the experience of a trapper friend who ventured into yeti territory with his partner. The creature, frightened of the campfire, loitered in the nearby forest but did not approach the trappers for a few days. Eventually, however, it overcame its apprehension and set upon them; one died a rather unpleasant death, and the other was fortunate to escape to tell the tale.

So if you should be wandering in the Himalayas some snowy afternoon, and you see a flash of red fur and smell a sweet scent that reminds you of rotting garbage, take a moment to wave politely; you *are* in the presence of a celebrity, after all. Then pack your bags and be on your way. The yeti may be nothing but a gentle "magical creature," but you can never be too careful.

CS 6/100

Zombie

When Professor Quirrell boasts that he got his turban as a thank-you gift for driving off a bothersome zombie, many of his students have their doubts. For one thing, his unusual headgear reeks of garlic, a sign that it may really be designed to protect its owner from **vampires.** For another, the good professor quickly changes the subject when asked just how he fought the zombie. It's a question any qualified Defense Against the Dark Arts instructor should be able to answer, since the zombie is the creation of one of the most malicious of black magicians, the voodoo **sorcerer.**

A zombie is essentially a walking corpse—a being that looks human but has no mind, soul, or will and acts at the command of its creator. Incapable of feeling pain, fear, or remorse, the zombie is a dangerous weapon for any practitioner of the **Dark Arts.** Although there's no evidence that zombies really exist, zombie legends abound wherever the voodoo religion is practiced.

Voodoo, also known as *vodoun,* is a system of religious beliefs developed by slaves brought from Africa to Haiti during the seventeenth and eighteenth centuries. Magical rites are an integral part of voodoo, often for purposes of worship or healing, but also for harming enemies or gaining power. People who work harmful magic, known as *bokors,* are said to create zombies to be their slaves. Some zombies are allegedly put to work as menial laborers and farm workers, while others have reportedly held office jobs. The most wicked bokors, however, may turn their zombies to darker purposes, using them to destroy the property of enemies or even to commit murder.

According to tradition, a bokor may make a zombie from either a living human or a corpse. In some accounts, the bokor gives the victim a po-

tion to induce a deep coma. Believed dead, the victim is buried by his family, only to be dug up soon afterward by the bokor. A second potion makes the victim walk, talk, and breathe again, but leaves him under the bokor's complete control. In other accounts, the bokor actually murders the victim or steals the body of someone who has recently died. After capturing the person's soul, which in voodoo is believed to remain with the body at least for a short period of time, the bokor is said to use **spells** to magically restore the body to life as a zombie. Whatever the method, attempting to create a zombie is still viewed today as an evil act throughout the Caribbean islands. In fact, current Haitian law defines zombie making as murder, subject to the same penalties as any other killing.

Fear of being made into a zombie was widespread in Haiti for centuries and may still exist today. Relatives often buried their deceased with a knife to be used to stab an intruding bokor. Some folklore advised filling an occupied coffin with seeds which, according to tradition, a bokor must count before removing the body. If there are enough seeds, the bokor will fail to complete his count before the sun comes up and will be unable to perform his ritual, since dark magic cannot be done during the daylight.

Getting rid of a zombie is a challenge. Although some are said to be slow of speech, moving listlessly and generally behaving like dullards (from which we get the phrase, "acting like a zombie"), a well-made zombie is said to be indistinguishable from an ordinary human and may respond quickly to its bokor's demands. As Professor Quirrell may or may not know, some traditions hold that sprinkling salt on a zombie will cause it to return to its grave (and presumably also free a live zombie from its mindless stupor). Alternately, one can appeal for divine intervention. Ghede, the Haitian god of the dead, is said to abhor zombies and may be persuaded to restore them to life by returning their souls. Failing that, however, the best chance of vanquishing a zombie is probably to defeat the bokor that created it. Like many evil beings, a zombie is only as dangerous as the commands it receives from its master.

Acknowledgments

No doubt much of the information contained in this book could have been found in the Hogwarts library. But since Hogwarts has yet to join the interlibrary loan system, we had to rely on our own libraries and the generous help of friends in bringing together the facts, folklore, ideas, and illustrations that make up *The Sorcerer's Companion.*

We are deeply grateful to Joyce Seltzer for her assistance in getting this project started in the right direction and for providing valuable advice and encouragement along the way. We are also grateful to our agent, Neeti Madan, for finding the perfect editor in Ann Campbell, whose enthusiasm for the project has been an inspiration.

We thank Nancy Hathaway for her contributions to individual entries and for patiently answering our many questions. Frank Ferrara assisted greatly with research on several scary monsters, Bob Fisher advised us on matters of astronomy, and Rebecca Sokolovsky served as our expert on the European witch craze. Our admiration and gratitude also go to Ruby Jackson for creating all of the original illustrations that enliven these pages.

Our very special thanks go to three people: Jessica Meyerson for her significant contributions to several entries and her boundless enthusiasm for all things Harry Potter; Bibi Wein for her careful readings,

excellent advice, and inexhaustible support; and Sheri Wilner, who not only conducted research for individual entries but spent countless hours in the archives tracking down the historical illustrations that form such an important part of this book.

Finally, and most of all, we thank our spouses, Ruby and Vaughn, for their love, support, patience, and encouragement throughout the writing of this book. We couldn't have done it without them.

Bibliography

Ariosto, Lodovico. *Orlando Furioso*, trans. Barbara Reynolds. New York: Viking Penguin, 1975.

Arrowsmith, Nancy. *A Field Guide to the Little People.* New York: Hill & Wang, 1977.

Barber, Richard, and Anne Riches. *A Dictionary of Fabulous Beasts.* Woodbridge, Suffolk, UK: Boydell Press, 1971.

Besterman, Theodore. *Crystal-Gazing.* New Hyde Park, NY: University Books, 1965.

Biederman, Hans. *Dictionary of Symbolism.* New York: Facts on File, 1992.

Briggs, Katherine M. *An Anatomy of Puck.* London: Routledge & Keegan Paul, 1959.

———. *An Encyclopedia of Fairies (Hobgoblins, Brownies, Bogies & Other Supernatural Creatures).* New York: Pantheon, 1976.

———. *Nine Lives. The Folklore of Cats.* New York: Random House, 1980.

Borges, Jorge Luis. *The Book of Imaginary Beings.* New York: Dutton, 1969.

Brewer, Ebenezer Cobham. *Brewer's Dictionary of Phrase and Fable.* Philadelphia: Henry Altemus, 1898.

Budge, E. A. Wallis. *Egyptian Magic.* 1899. Reprint, New York: Bell Publishing, 1991.

Bulfinch, Thomas. *Bulfinch's Mythology.* New York: Avenel Books, 1984.

Burger, Eugene, and Robert E. Neal. *Magic and Meaning.* Seattle: Hermetic Press, 1995.

Burton, Richard, trans. *The Arabian Nights Entertainments, or The Book of a Thousand Nights and a Night.* New York: The Modern Library, 1932.

Butler, E. M. *The Myth of the Magus.* 1948. Reprint, New York: Canto, 1993.

———. *Ritual Magic.* 1949. Reprint, Pennsylvania State University Press, 1998.

Caflin, Edward and Jeff Sheridan. *Street Magic.* New York: Doubleday, 1977.

Carrington, Richard. *Mermaids and Mastodons.* New York: Rinhart & Company, Inc, 1957.

Cavendish, Richard. *A History of Magic.* 1987. Reprint, New York: Viking Penguin, 1987.

———. *The Black Arts.* 1967. Reprint, New York, The Berkeley Publishing Group, 1983.

———. *The Tarot,* 1975. Reprint, New York: Crescent Books, 1986.

———. *Man, Myth & Magic: An Illustrated Encyclopedia of the Supernatural.* New York: The Marshall Cavendish Company, 1970.

———. *The World of Ghosts and the Supernatural.* New York: Facts on File, 1994.

Cenzato, Elena, and Fabio Santopietro. *Owls. Art, Legend, History.* Boston: Little, Brown, 1991.

Christopher, Milbourne. *Magic, A Picture History.* New York: Dover Publications, 1962.

Christopher, Milbourne, and Maurine Christopher. *The Illustrated History of Magic.* Portsmouth, NH: Heinmann, 1996.

Clark, Ann. *Beasts and Bawdy. A Book of Fabulous and Fantastical Beasts.* New York: Taplinger, 1975.

Cohen, Daniel. *Magicians, Wizards, & Sorcerers.* New York: J. B. Lippincott Company, 1973.

Comte, Fernand. *Mythology.* New York: Champers, Ltd., 1991.

Dale-Green, Patricia. *The Cult of the Cat.* Boston: Houghton Mifflin, 1963.

Dawood, N. J., trans. *The Koran.* Harmondsworth, England: Penguin, 1956.

Dodson, Aidan, and Salima Ikram. *The Mummy in Ancient Egypt: Equipping the Dead for Eternity.* London: Thames and Hudson, 1998.

Evans, E. P. *The Criminal Prosecution and Capital Punishment of Animals.* New York: E. P. Dutton, 1906.

Felton, D. *Haunted Greece and Rome: Ghost Stories from Classical Antiquity.* Austin: University of Texas Press, 1999.

Fraud, Brian, and Alan Lee. *Faeries.* New York: Harry N. Abrams, 1978.

Frazer, Sir James George. *The New Golden Bough.* New York: Doubleday, 1961.

Gordon, Lesley. *Green Magic. Flowers, Plants, and Herbs in Lore and Legend.* Exeter, UK: Webb and Bower, 1977.

Gibson, Walter B., and Litzka R. Gibson. *The Complete Illustrated Book of Divination & Prophecy.* New York: Doubleday, 1973.

Graves, Robert. *The Greek Myths.* 2 Vols. Harmondsworth, England: Penguin, 1960.

Grimal, Pierre, ed. *Larousse World Mythology.* London: Paul Hamlyn, Ltd., 1965.

Grimm, Jacob, and Wilhelm Grimm. *The Complete Grimms Fairy Tales,* ed. James Stern. New York: Random House, 1976.

Guiley, Rosemary Ellen. *The Encyclopedia of Witches and Witchcraft.* Second Edition. New York: Facts on File, 1999.

Halliday, William Reginald. *Greek and Roman Folklore.* New York: Cooper Square Publishers, 1963.

Hamilton, Edith. *Mythology: Timeless Tales of Gods and Heroes.* New York: Mentor, 1969.

Hatto, A. T., trans. *The Niebelunglied.* Harmondsworth, England: Penguin, 1969.

Holmgren, Virginia C. *Owls in Folklore and Natural History.* Santa Barbara, CA: Capra Press, 1988.

Holmyard, E. J. *Alchemy.* 1957. Reprint, New York: Dover Publications, 1990.

Homer. *The Odyssey.* Translated by E. V. Rieu, revised by D.C.H. Rieu. New York: Penguin Books, 1991.

Ingersoll, Ernest. *Birds in Legend, Fable, and Folklore.* New York: Longmans, Green, and Co., 1923.

Jordan, Paul. *Riddles of the Sphinx.* New York: NYU Press, 1998.

Keightley, Thomas. *The Fairy Mythology.* London: Whitacker-Treacher, 1833.

Kieckhefer, Richard. *Magic in the Middle Ages.* 1989. Reprint, Cambridge: Cambridge University Press, 1997.

King, Francis X. *Magic, The Western Tradition.* New York: Thames and Hudson Inc., 1975.

———. *Witchcraft and Demonology.* New York: Exeter Books, 1987.

Lantiere, Joe. *The Magician's Wand.* Oakville, CT: Joe Lantiere Books, 1990.

Luck, Georg. *Arcana Mundi, Magic and the Occult in the Greek and Roman Worlds.* Baltimore: The John Hopkins University Press, 1985.

MacGregor-Mathers, S. L. *The Book of the Sacred Mage of the Abra-Merlin the Mage.* Wellingborough: The Aquarian Press, 1976.

Mack, Carol K., and Dinah Mack. *A Field Guide to Demons, Fairies, Fallen Angels, and Other Subversive Spirits.* New York: Henry Holt and Company, 1998.

McNamee, Gregory, ed. *The Serpent's Tale. Snakes in Folklore and Literature.* Athens, GA: The University of Georgia Press, 2000.

Malory, Thomas. *Le Morte d'Arthur.* 2 Vols. London: J. M. Dent and Sons, 1906. Reprint, 1967.

Masello, Robert. *Raising Hell. A Concise History of the Black Arts and Those Who Dared to Practice Them.* New York: Perigee, 1996.

Maven, Max. *Max Maven's Book of Fortunetelling.* New York: Prentice Hall, 1992.

Melchior-Bonnet, Sabine. *The Mirror: A History.* New York: Routledge, 2001.

Nigg, Joseph, ed. *The Book of Fabulous Beasts: A Treasury of Writings from Ancient Times to the Present.* New York: Oxford University Press, 1999.

———. *Wonder Beasts. Tales and Lore of the Phoenix, the Griffin, the Unicorn, and the Dragon.* Englewood, CO: Libraries Unlimited, 1995.

Nissenson, Marilyn, and Susan Jonas. *Snake Charm.* New York: Harry N. Abrams, 1995.

Ogden, Tom. *Wizards and Sorcerers.* New York: Facts on File, 1997.

Otten, Charlotte F., ed. *A Lycanthropy Reader. Werewolves in Western Culture.* Syracuse, NY: Syracuse University Press, 1986.

Ovid. *Metamorphoses.* Translated by Mary M. Innes. London: Penguin Books, 1955.

Peters, Edward. *The Magician the Witch & the Law.* Philadelphia: University of Pennsylvania Press, 1978.

Phillpotts, Beatrice. *The Faeryland Companion.* New York: Barnes and Noble Books, 1999.

Pickering, David. *Cassell Dictionary of Witchcraft.* London: Cassell, 1996.

Pinch, Geraldine. *Magic in Ancient Egypt.* Austin, TX: University of Texas Press, 1994.

Radford, E., and M. A. Radford. *Encyclopedia of Superstitions.* London: Hutchinson and Company, 1948.

Rauscher, William. *The Wand in Story and Symbol.* Woodbury, NY: William Rauscher, 1998.

Robbins, Russell Hope. *The Encyclopedia of Witchcraft and Demonology.* New York: Bonanza Books, 1981.

Rose, Carol. *Spirits, Fairies, Leprechauns, and Goblins. An Encyclopedia.* New York: Norton, 1996.

Rowling, J. K. *Harry Potter and the Sorcerer's Stone.* New York: Scholastic, 1998.

———. *Harry Potter and the Chamber of Secrets.* New York: Scholastic, 1999.

———. *Harry Potter and the Prisoner of Azkaban.* New York: Scholastic, 1999.

———. *Harry Potter and the Goblet of Fire.* New York: Scholastic, 2000.

Scott, Reginald. *The Discoverie of Witchcraft.* 1584. Reprint, New York: Dover, 1972.

Seligman, Kurt. *The History of Magic.* New York: Pantheon Books Inc., 1948.

Seymour, John, and Harry Neligan. *True Irish Ghost Stories.* London: Senate, 1994.

Sidky H. *Witchcraft, Lycanthropy, Drugs and Disease. An Anthropological Study of the European Witch-Hunts.* New York: Peter Lang, 1997.

Sitwell, Sacheverell. *Poltergeists.* New York: University Books, 1959.

Sweeney, Michelle. *Magic in Medieval Romance.* Dublin: Four Courts Press Ltd., 2000.

Taylor, F. Sherwood. *The Alchemists.* New York: Barnes and Noble Books, 1992.

Tester, Jim. *A History of Western Astrology.* New York: Ballantine Books, 1987.

Thomas, Keith. *Religion and the Decline of Magic.* New York: Charles Scribner's Sons, 1971.

———. *Man and the Natural World. A History of the Modern Sensibility.* New York: Pantheon, 1983.

Thorndike, Lynn A. *History of Magic and Experimental Science.* New York: Columbia University Press, 1923.

Tolstoy, Nikolai. *The Quest for Merlin.* New York: Little, Brown and Company, 1985.

Toulmin, Stephen, and June Goodfield. *The Fabric of the Heavens.* New York: Harper & Brothers, 1961.

Van De Castle, Robert L. *Our Dreaming Mind.* New York: Ballantine Books, 1994.

Walker, Charles. *The Encyclopedia of the Occult.* New York: Crescent Books, 1995.

White, T. H. *The Book of Beasts: Being a Translation from the Latin Bestiary of the Twelfth Century.* New York: Dover, 1984.

Yates, Frances A. *Giordano Bruno and the Hermetic Tradition.* Chicago: The University of Chicago Press, 1964.

On-Line Sources

The Archetype of the Magician. John Granrose, 1996.
www.granrose.com/thesis.htm.

The Encyclopedia Mythica. An Encyclopedia on Mythology Folklore and Legend. M. F. Lindemans, ed., 1995–2000.
www.pantheon.org/mythica/info/about.html.

Folklore and Mythology Electronic Texts. D. L. Ashliman, ed. University of Pittsburgh, 1996–2001. www.pitt.edu/~dash/folktexts.html.

Gareth Long's Encyclopedia of Monsters, Mythical Creatures and Fabulous Beasts. webhome.idirect.com/~donlong/monsters/monsters.htm.

Greek Mythology Link. Carlos Parada. www.hsa.brown.edu/~maicar.

Mything Links. An Annotated & Illustrated Collection of Worldwide Links to Mythologies, Fairy Tales & Folklore, Sacred Arts & Traditions. Kathleen Jenks, ed. www.mythinglinks.org.

Natural Magick. The Works and Life of John Baptist Porta.
members.tscnet.com/pages/omardl/jportat5.html.

The Perseus Digital Library. Gregory Crane, ed. Tufts University.
www.perseus.tufts.edu.

The Witching Hours. Medieval Through Enlightenment Period European Witch
History. Shantell Powell, 1995–1999.
shanmonster.bla-bla.com/witch/index.html.

𝕴llustration 𝕮redits

Every effort has been made to trace the copyright holders of all illustrations. We regret any unintentional omissions. We would be pleased to insert the appropriate acknowledgment in any subsequent edition of this publication.

281

Page 2. *Ankh,* from Ernst Lehner, *The Picture Book of Symbols.* New York: William Penn Publishing, 1956.

Page 3. Eye of Horus, from Ernst Lehner, *Symbols, Signs and Signets.* New York: Dover, 1950.

Page 11. Woodcut from a 1513 edition of Macrobius, *In Somnium Scipionis.*

Page 13. Portrait of Nostradamus. Engraving by Jean Charles Pellerin, c. 1800.

Page 17. From *The Random House College Dictionary.* Copyright © 1975 by Random House, Inc. Used by permission of Random House, Inc.

Page 20. From T. Crofton Crocker, *Fairy Legends and Traditions of the South of Ireland,* 1828.

Page 21. Basilisk, from Richard Huber, *Treasury of Fantastic and Mythological Creatures.* New York: Dover, 1981.

Page 23. From Trevor Smith, *Amazing Lizards.* London: Dorling Kindersley, 1990.

Page 27. Woodcut from Thomas Erastus, *Dialogues Touchant le Pouvoir Sorcières et de la Punition Qu'Elles Méritent,* 1579.

Page 33. Illustration by Zuber from M. Carron, *La Vie Exécrable de Guillemette Babin, Sorcière,* 1926. Fortean Picture Library.

Page 35. From Johannes Hevelius, *Firmamentum Sobiescianum sive Uranographia.* Gdansk, 1690. Courtesy of the Linda Hall Library of Science, Engineering, and Technology.

Page 40. Illustration by Walter Crane in *Echoes of Hellas.* London: Marcus Ward, 1887.

Page 42. "Alexander Crystal Ball" panel poster. Copyright © 1978 by Robert Lee Jacobs. Used by permission of the publisher, www.LeeJacobsProductions.com, P.O. Box 362, Pomeroy, OH 45769.

Page 49. Edward Kelley and Paul Waring raising the dead in Walton-le-Dale Churchyard. Seventeenth-century English engraving.

Page 52. Flying demon, from *The Temptation of St. Anthony,* by Martin Schongauer, 1480–90. Reproduced in Richard Huber, *Treasury of Fantastic and Mythological Creatures.* New York: Dover, 1981.

Page 53. Asmodeus, by L. Breton, from Collin De Plancy, *Dictionnaire Infernal,* 1863.

Page 54. Demon with owls, from *Orpheus in the Underworld,* by Pieter Breughel the Younger, c. 1600, reproduced in Richard Huber, *Treasury of Fantastic and Mythological Creatures.* New York: Dover, 1981.

Page 57. Title page of John Melton, *Astrologaster or the Figure-Caster,* 1620.

Page 58. Fifteenth-century engraving by Israhel von Mechenen.

Page 59. Nineteenth-century engraving. Reproduced in Jim Harter, *Animals: 1419 Copyright-Free Illustrations of Mammals, Birds, Fish, Insects, Etc.* New York: Dover, 1983.

Page 64. Swiss tarot cards based on the Marseilles pack, c. 1800.

Page 66. From a fifteenth-century German engraving. Reproduced in Richard Huber, *Treasury of Fantastic and Mythological Creatures.* New York: Dover, 1981.

Page 72. Original illustration by Ruby Jackson.

Page 74. Illustration by John D. Batton, from Joseph Jacobs, *English Fairy Tales.* New York: Dover, 1967.

Page 78. From Carol Belanger Grafton, *2001 Decorative Cuts and Ornaments.* New York: Dover, 1988.

Page 80. Frances Griffiths with fairies, photographed by Elsie Wright at Cottingley Glen, West Yorkshire, 1917. Fortean Picture Library.

Page 81. Drawing by T. H. Thomas in Wirt Sikes, *British Goblins: Welsh Folklore, Fairy Mythology, Legends and Traditions,* 1880. Fortean Picture Library.

Page 87. Nineteenth-century engraving.

Page 92. Illustration by John D. Batton, from Joseph Jacobs, *English Fairy Tales.* New York: Dover, 1967.

Page 97. Original illustration by Ruby Jackson.

Page 99. Original illustration by Ruby Jackson.

Page 101. Illustration by Yvonne Gilbert, from Katharine Briggs, *Abbey Lubbers, Banshees & Boggarts: An Illustrated Encyclopedia of Fairies.* New York: Pantheon, 1979. Reproduced by permission of Pantheon Books, a division of Random House, Inc.

Page 103. From Giambattista della Porta, *Phytognomonica,* 1588.

Page 106. From *Legendary Hex Signs.* Used with permission of Jacob Zook™ Hex Signs, P.O. Box 176, Paradise, PA 17562. www.hexsigns.com. All rights reserved.

Page 107. Illustration by T. H. Thomas in Wirt Sikes. *British Goblins: Welsh Folklore, Fairy Mythology, Legends and Traditions,* 1880.

Page 109. From a seventeenth-century Italian signet. Reproduced in Ernst and Johanna Lehner, *A Fantastic Bestiary.* New York: Tudor Publishing Company, 1969.

Page 112. Seventeenth-century English cartoon.

Page 114 Illustration by John D. Batton, from Joseph Jacobs, *English Fairy Tales.* New York: Dover, 1967.

Page 116. From Ernst and Johanna Lehner, *A Fantastic Bestiary.* New York: Tudor Publishing Company, 1969.

Page 118. Illustration by Bill Terry for *Other Worlds,* 1950. From Peter Haining, *The Leprechaun's Kingdom.* New York: Harmony Books, 1979.

Page 127. From Giambattista della Porta, *Physiognomonica,* 1588.

Page 129. Frontispiece of a seventeenth-century edition of *The Key of Solomon.*

Page 130. Title page of Christopher Marlowe's *The Tragicall Historie of the Life and Death of Doctor Faustus.* London, 1631.

Page 135. Eighteenth-century engraving of a Tungus shaman.

Page 137. Cunning man. From Larry Evans, *Illustrators' Resource File.* New York: Van Nostrand Reinhold, 1984.

Page 139. Portait of Agrippa von Nettesheim, from the title page of *De Occulta Philosophia,* 1533.

Page 141. 1404 drawing by Joseph of Ulm. Original manuscript preserved in Tübingen University Library, Germany. Reproduced in Milbourne Christopher, *Magic: A Picture History.* New York: Dover, 1991.

Page 142. *L'Escamoteur*, by Hieronymus Bosch, 1480. Reproduced in Milbourne Christopher, *Magic: A Picture History*. New York: Dover, 1991.

Page 144. Engraving from H. Decremps's *La Magie Blanche Dévoilée*, 1784. Reproduced in Milbourne Christopher, *Magic: A Picture History*. New York: Dover, 1991.

Page 150. The Magician card from the Rider-Waite Tarot Deck®. Copyright © 1971. Reproduced by permission of U.S. Games Systems, Inc. Stamford, CT 06902.

Page 150. The Magician card from the Tarot of Marseilles, © 1996, reproduced by permission of U.S. Games Systems, Inc. Stamford, CT 06902/Carta Mundi, Turnhout, Belgium.

Page 152. King with scepter, from Jacobus De Teramo, *Das Buch Belial*, 1473.

Page 153. Mercury with his caduceus, from title page of *The Merchant's Avizo*. London, 1616.

Page 160. From Johannes de Cuba, *Hortus Sanitatis*, 1485.

Page 161. Mandrake, from a twelfth-century manuscript ascribed to Dioscorides.

Page 163. Manticore, from Edward Topsell, *A History of Four-Footed Beasts*. London, 1658. Reproduced in Ernst and Johanna Lehner, *A Fantastic Bestiary*. New York: Tudor Publishing Company, 1969.

Page 166. Engraving by W. Ridgway after Gustave Doré.

Page 169. Mermaid, from Richard Huber, *Treasury of Fantastic and Mythological Creatures*. New York: Dover, 1981.

Page 170. Merman, from Ernst and Johanna Lehner, *A Fantastic Bestiary*. New York: Tudor Publishing, 1969.

Page 173. Painting of Morgan le Fay by Frederick Sandys, 1862–63. Fortean Picture Library.

Page 175. Original illustration by Ruby Jackson.

Page 177. Nineteenth-century drawing by Albert Poisson.

Page 179. From J. J. Manget, *Bibliotheca Chemica Curiosa*, 1702.

Page 181. From a sixteenth-century woodcut by Albrecht Dürer.

Page 183. Diagram of left hand, after Jean-Baptiste Belot, 1640.

Page 185. Original illustration by Ruby Jackson.

Page 189. From Ernst Lehner, *Symbols, Signs and Signets*. New York: Dover, 1950.

Page 192. Poltergeist. The New York Public Library Picture Collection.

Page 195. From Carol Belanger Grafton. *Medieval Life Illustrations*. New York: Dover, 1996.

Page 197. Original illustration by Ruby Jackson.

Page 199. Original illustration by Ruby Jackson.

Page 201. From Michael Majer, *Scrutinium Chymicum,* 1687.

Page 204. Sibyl. The New York Public Library Picture Collection.

Page 207. The oldest extant representation of Ouroboros, eleventh century. From Ernst and Johanna Lehner, *A Fantastic Bestiary.* New York: Tudor Publishing Company, 1969.

Page 211. *An Alchemist at Work,* by H. Weiditz, c. 1520.

Page 212. From Philippus Ulstadius, *Coelum Philosophorum.* Paris, 1544.

Page 220. Babylonian sphinx, based on an antique stone carving at the Nimrud Palace, Nineveh. From Ernst and Johanna Lehner, *A Fantastic Bestiary.* New York: Tudor Publishing Company, 1969.

Page 222. Jupiter talisman. Original illustration by Ruby Jackson.

Page 225. Nineteenth-century engraving of a gypsy fortuneteller. Mary Evans Picture Library.

Page 231. From Ernst Lehner, *The Picture Book of Symbols.* New York: William Penn Publishing, 1956.

Page 233. From Collin De Plancy, *Dictionnaire Infernal,* 1863.

Page 236. *Daphne and Apollo,* drawing by Erhard Schön. The New York Public Library Picture Collection.

Page 240. Troll, from *Norwegian Folktales* by Peter Christen Asbjørnsen and Jørgen Moe. Copyright © 1982. Illustrated by Erik Werenskiold and Theodor Kittelsen. Reproduced by permission of Pantheon Books, a division of Random House, Inc.

Page 242. Illustration by Erhard Renwick from *Perigrinationes ad Terram Sanctum,* 1486.

Page 245. From Peter Pomet, *Histoire des Drogues,* 1694.

Page 247. Original illustration by Ruby Jackson.

Page 249. Illustration by Ruby Jackson, after Ivan Bilibine.

Page 251. Werewolf. Detail of woodcut from Geiler von Kayersberg, *Die Emeis,* 1517.

Page 255. Woodcut from Ulrich Molitor, *De Ianijs et Phitonicius Mulieribus,* 1489.

Page 256. Witch from Carol Belanger Grafton. *Medieval Life Illustrations.* New York: Dover, 1996.

Page 258. Woodcut from John Ashton, *The Devil in Britain and America,* 1896.

Page 260. Title page from a seventeenth-century edition of the *Malleus Maleficarum.*

Page 262. From the title page of *Witches Apprehended, Examined and Executed for Notable Villainies Committed by Them Both by Land and Water.* London, 1613.

Page 266. From Milbourne Christopher, *Magic: A Picture History.* New York: Dover, 1962.

Page 268. Illustration by Harry Trumbore, from Loren Coleman and Patrick Huyghe, *The Field Guide to Bigfoot, Yeti, and Other Mystery Primates Worldwide.* New York: Avon Books, 1999. Reprinted by permission of HarperCollins Publishers, Inc.